dBASE III®
Tips & Traps

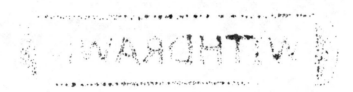

dBASE III® Tips & Traps

Dick Andersen
Cynthia Cooper
and
Bill Demsey

Osborne **McGraw-Hill**
Berkeley, California

Osborne **McGraw-Hill**
2600 Tenth Street
Berkeley, California 94710
U.S.A.

For information on translations and book distributors outside of the U.S.A., please write to Osborne **McGraw-Hill** at the above address.

A complete list of trademarks appears on page 263.

dBASE III® Tips & Traps

34567890 DODO 8987

ISBN 0-07-881195-3

Cynthia Hudson, Acquisitions Editor
Fran Haselsteiner, Project Editor
Yashi Okita, Cover Design

To Dr. James S.B. Mackie.

D.A. and C.C.

Contents

Acknowledgments

Thank you to Cindy Hudson, Jean Stein, Kevin Gleason, Les Squires, and Liz Fisher.

Introduction

This book differs from other books about dBASE III in a way that you will find very useful as you work with this exciting software product. Except for brief introductions to the chapters and sections, the information in this book is organized into *tips and traps:*

- A tip is a pointer on how to accomplish a particular task quickly and efficiently. Tips focus on the data-processing tasks that people face in real-world situations; you will learn precisely how to use dBASE III effectively for those tasks.

- A trap is a warning about problems that can occur if you are unaware of certain details in the way dBASE III operates, or if you are not careful. You will learn about ways to avoid each potential difficulty, either in the trap itself or in a tip immediately following the trap.

dBASE III has become one of the most popular software products because it offers the user a wealth of possibilities for organizing and processing data. But this breadth of range also makes dBASE III a challenge to master. We think the tips and traps approach is particularly helpful for learning to use such a complex program, since information is presented in small, goal-oriented units. You can focus on mastering the tools you need to accomplish one dBASE task, and then another, and another—until you are proficient in the entire range of features offered by the program.

How to Use This Book

One way to use this book is to find information on a particular topic as you need it. Each tip or trap entry consists of a descriptive heading followed by an explanation, and, when they help to clarify the text, examples and figures. The headings will tell you what topic is addressed by the tip or trap, so you can quickly locate information on a particular situation or task facing you. The index will also help you find tips and traps on particular topics.

Another way to use the book is to read through an entire chapter or section of a chapter to get an overview of a particular aspect of dBASE III. Each chapter and each chapter section are organized so that you can learn about a particular set of dBASE tools by reading through the tips and traps in the order in which they are presented.

This book is not intended to replace the dBASE III user's manual but to supplement it with precise, practical information on accomplishing particular tasks. It was not possible for us to cover every feature of dBASE III exhaustively in this one volume; we have tried to choose tips and traps that would be useful to a person who has some familiarity with dBASE III but is not an expert.

How the Book Is Organized

Here are brief descriptions of each chapter:

Chapter 1: The dBASE III Environment

This chapter explains different ways to interact with dBASE III, to get the program running efficiently on your computer, and to communicate with dBASE once it is running, as well as ways to customize the dBASE III working environment to suit your own needs and to make your work easier. Also included are tips and traps for managing your data disks and for using the dBASE III ASSIST and HELP modes as support while you learn to use the dBASE commands.

Chapter 2: Planning Applications
And Establishing Databases

If your dBASE III applications are going to work smoothly and effectively, you must carefully plan and design the application system as a whole, as well as each database file. This chapter presents tips and traps on designing an entire application system and describes in detail how dBASE III operates with a system of related database files. It also discusses the choices you will have to make as you decide how to store individual data items in the fields of a database file, how to incorporate part of one file in another, and how to change the structure of an existing file.

Chapter 3: Entering And Updating Data

This chapter focuses on the dBASE III data-entry and updating tools that help you correctly place data into your files, and keep your files up to date as you work with them. dBASE III provides a wide variety of approaches to these tasks and even allows you to write your own application programs to control data entry into your files. There are tips and traps on writing these programs, on protecting confidential data, and on validating data that is entered at the keyboard.

Chapter 4: Ordering And Retrieving Data

Once your data is entered into files, it must be organized and made readily available for processing. Most data-processing tasks involve locating a particular record or group of records to be processed in a certain way; ease of access to specific records is crucial. This chapter includes tips and traps on using dBASE III's powerful tools for organizing data precisely and retrieving it quickly.

Chapter 5: Working With More Than One Database File

When a wide range of data is stored in different database files, you must be able to access related data records in different files and to process these related records together. dBASE III allows you to work with as many as ten different database files at one time; this chapter focuses on the tools used in working with more than one file at a time.

Chapter 6: Customizing the Screen Display

The dBASE III screen displays data or the results of processing data, and prompts the user to enter data. The screen display becomes very important when you are designing an application that will be used by an inexpert dBASE III user (or one that you will use yourself for hours at a time). This chapter includes tips and traps on managing the screen display and data entered in response to screen prompts.

Chapter 7: The REPORT FORM Command

Printed reports are important in any data management system; they provide information in a permanent and useful form. This chapter discusses the various ways you can use dBASE III's many options for generating printed reports.

Chapter 8: Data Sharing and Conversion

Many business applications require data that has been processed by another program before it is entered into a dBASE file — for example, the results of calculations with a spreadsheet program or a document produced with a word processor. In other situations you may want one of these programs to access the data in a dBASE III file. This chapter includes tips and traps on sharing data between dBASE III and other types of business software products.

Chapter 9: Programming In dBASE III

One of dBASE III's most attractive features is that it allows you to write your own application programs. It is not possible for us to teach you everything about writing dBASE III programs in this one book, but the tips and traps in this chapter will help you. The chapter addresses the important issues of program design and documentation, of using memory variables and macro expansion, and of working with different program structures. Sample dBASE programs oriented to particular tasks are included throughout the book as well.

Introduction

The authors hope you will find *dBASE III Tips & Traps* to be useful and informative. If you discover tips and traps on your own as you work with dBASE III, we would like to help you share them with others. Please document them fully and send them to

Dick Andersen
Net 1
2525A Lucy Lane
Walnut Creek, CA 94595

We hope to include tips and traps from readers in subsequent editions of this book and will be happy to give you credit if we use one of yours.

D.A.
C.C.
B.D.

1

The dBASE III
Environment

dBASE III provides many powerful tools for storing, organizing, and processing data. To use these tools effectively, you need to be at home in the dBASE working environment: you must know how to interact with dBASE and how to use it to accomplish particular tasks. In this chapter you will learn to work efficiently within the dBASE working environment, and you will learn how to customize the environment to suit your needs.

An important part of working with dBASE is communication—telling dBASE what task you want done and how it should be done. Whenever you work with dBASE, you are in one of the three basic modes of communication: *interactive, built-in command,* or *program execution.*

The Interactive Mode

Figure 1-1 shows dBASE in interactive mode, awaiting instructions from the user. dBASE accepts a command typed in at the keyboard, executes the command, displays the results, and waits for another command to be entered. You enter this

```
. USE CHECKS INDEX CHK_CAT
.
. FIND FOOD
.
. LIST WHILE CATEGORY = "FOOD"
Record#   CHK_NO CHK_DATE PAY_TO              CHK_AMOUNT IS_CLEAR CATEGORY
        5   505   02/13/85 XYZ SUPERMARKET         71.65 .F.     FOOD
        9   509   02/15/85 CORNER STORE            22.12 .F.     FOOD
       15   516   02/18/85 XYZ SUPERMARKET         26.47 .F.     FOOD
       16   510   02/15/85 CORNER STORE            13.33 .F.     FOOD
.
. DELETE RECORD 15
        1   record deleted
.
. PACK
       15 records copied
Rebuilding index - A:CHK_CAT.ndx
       15 records indexed
.
```

Figure 1-1.   dBASE III in interactive mode

mode each time you load dBASE into your computer.

When dBASE is in interactive mode and is waiting for your command, it displays a period, called the *dot prompt*, at the left edge of a screen line, as shown in Figure 1-1. If the dot prompt is not visible, dBASE is still executing your last command and is not yet ready for another. Whenever the dot prompt appears, dBASE has finished executing the last command given and has returned to interactive mode. The cursor is positioned immediately to the right of the dot prompt. You type in your instructions (which are displayed on the same screen line as the prompt) and press RETURN when you have completed the command. dBASE executes your command if possible and displays the results.

If dBASE is unable to execute a command you entered at the keyboard, an error message is displayed. After some error messages, like the one in Figure 1-2,

```
. USE CHECKS INDEX CHK_CAT
.
. FIND FOOD
.
. LIST WHILE CATEGORY = "FOOD"
Record#   CHK_NO CHK_DATE PAY_TO              CHK_AMOUNT IS_CLEAR CATEGORY
        5   505   02/13/85 XYZ SUPERMARKET         71.65 .F.     FOOD
        9   509   02/15/85 CORNER STORE            22.12 .F.     FOOD
       15   510   02/15/85 CORNER STORE            13.33 .F.     FOOD
.
. DELETE REOCRD 9  ◄────────────────────────┤ Spelling error in command │
Unrecognized phrase/keyword in command
        ?
DELETE REOCRD 9
Do you want some help? (Y/N)
```

Figure 1-2.   "Unrecognized phrase/keyword in command" error message

you will be asked if you want some help with the command. If you enter the letter Y, a HELP screen will be displayed.

The error message helps you determine why your command was not accepted. For example, you get the message "Cannot erase open file" if you tell dBASE to erase a database file from the disk that is currently *open* (that is, being used by dBASE). Using the command USE, you can close the file and erase it from the disk.

dBASE error messages are specifically related to the structure of the command you have entered. Figure 1-2 shows the message "Unrecognized phrase/keyword in command", which means that dBASE was unable to interpret the words you entered. The most frequent reason for this error message is incorrect spelling, as in Figure 1-2, where the word RECORD is misspelled. To execute the command, just reenter it spelled correctly.

Each command entered at the dot prompt must begin with one of the dBASE command verbs, such as LIST, AVERAGE, or USE. If the first word of your entry is not one of the dBASE command verbs, dBASE responds "Unrecognized command verb". This is shown in Figure 1-3, where the entry begins with the word RECORD. You need to rephrase your entry so the first word is one of the dBASE command verbs.

Tips and traps on particular dBASE commands are placed in the appropriate chapters in this book; the index can help you find the pages that cover a certain command.

dBASE Built-in Command Modes

Many dBASE commands, such as CREATE and MODIFY STRUCTURE, require data entry from the keyboard to accomplish their tasks. When you enter one of these commands at the dot prompt, the screen display will change and you will be asked to enter the data that is needed. For instance, entering **CREATE** tells dBASE that you want to define the fields in a new database file. dBASE will present you with the screen display shown in Figure 1-4.

```
. USE CHECKS INDEX CHK_CAT
.
. LIST FOR CHK_AMOUNT > 24.99
Record#  CHK_NO CHK_DATE PAY_TO          CHK_AMOUNT IS_CLEAR CATEGORY
      2  502    02/12/85 MARCY'S             259.01 .F.      CLOTHES
      5  505    02/13/85 XYZ SUPERMARKET      71.65 .F.      FOOD
      6  506    02/14/85 KATHY REED           72.00 .F.      HOUSECLEAN
.
. RECORD 5 DELETE
*** Unrecognized command verb
.
```

Figure 1-3. "Unrecognized command verb" error message

```
A:NEWFILE.dbf                                        Bytes remaining:    4000
                                                     Fields defined:        0

      field name   type     width   dec       field name   type     width   dec
   1 [          ]  Char/text

   Names start with a letter; the remainder may be letters, digits, or underscore
```

Figure 1-4.   The dBASE III CREATE screen

dBASE provides prompt messages to help you enter the required data in these built-in command modes. In Figure 1-4, the prompt displayed at the bottom of the screen, "Names start with a letter; the remainder may be letters, digits, or underscore", tells you what type of data will be accepted for a field name. As you enter data into the CREATE screen, the prompt messages tell you what kind of input is needed at each step.

Some dBASE commands, such as EDIT and APPEND, give you access to an individual data record. Figure 1-5 shows the screen display when you enter EDIT; the current data record is displayed. dBASE allows you to move the cursor from field to field, making whatever changes are necessary in the data. When you have finished working with a record, you can press PGUP or PGDN to move to another record in the same database file; when you have finished using EDIT or APPEND on your records, pressing CTRL-END or CTRL-W returns you to the dot prompt.

```
   Record No.      11
   CHK_NO       [511]
   CHK_DATE     [02/15/85]
   PAY_TO       [P&T DRUGS        ]
   CHK_AMOUNT   [ 10.10]
   IS_CLEAR     [F]
   CATEGORY     [INCIDENTALS ]
```

Figure 1-5.   The dBASE III EDIT screen

You also have the option of executing any of these dBASE commands with the help of the ASSIST command; this command can be very helpful when you are learning how to use other dBASE commands. Each of these dBASE commands is discussed in detail in the appropriate chapter in this book. To find tips and traps on a particular dBASE command, consult the index.

Program Execution Mode

dBASE III lets you write your own programs. This programmability — one of the most powerful features of dBASE — effectively allows you to define new dBASE commands of your own. For example, if you had a database file named ORDERS containing a record for each customer order, you would want to print out various reports daily or weekly, summarizing orders by customer, by items sold, or by both. You could generate the report from the dot prompt each time you needed it, entering each command in order until the report had been printed. But a much more efficient approach would be to write a dBASE program named S_REPORT, which would list the commands needed to generate the report. The program would be stored in a file named S_REPORT.PRG, and you could tell dBASE to execute the entire sequence of commands by entering **DO S_REPORT** at the dot prompt.

There are many other examples of dBASE application programs throughout this book. Chapter 9 contains tips and traps on writing your own programs.

When you enter **DO PROGRAM** at the dot prompt, dBASE goes into program execution mode and executes each command in the file PROGRAM.PRG in order until the program is finished or an error condition exists. If there is an error, a message is displayed and you are returned to the dot prompt; otherwise, the dot prompt will reappear when the program commands have been completed.

Running dBASE III on Your Computer

 1.01 Trap: If you use DISKCOPY or FORMAT commands on the dBASE III master disk (System Disk #1), you will permanently destroy the master disk.

The dBASE III master disk, which is labeled System Disk #1, is copy-protected with a system called **PROLOK**. PROLOK uses a laser to burn a small hole in the disk; the hole is placed in a particular position on the disk, relative to the dBASE

III files. If you use the DISKCOPY or FORMAT commands on this disk, you will not be able to load dBASE III from the disk and will have to purchase a new copy from your dealer.

The master disk contains the dBASE III file DBASE.COM, which is the first file loaded into memory when you enter dBASE. Ashton-Tate provides you with two copies of the master disk; keep one in a safe place as a backup.

If you are working with a floppy disk system and DBASE.COM is accidentally damaged or erased on your working disk, use the following procedure to copy the file from the backup disk:

1. Load DOS into your computer so that the A> prompt is on the screen.

2. Place your working disk in drive B and the backup disk in drive A.

3. Enter the command

```
COPY DBASE.COM B:
```

Do not use the command DISKCOPY to attempt to copy the entire backup disk to your working disk; if you do, your working disk will be inoperable.

If you are working with a hard disk system and you accidentally erase DBASE.COM from the hard disk, you will have to "uninstall and reinstall" dBASE III from your hard disk. Follow the procedure described on pages 4 through 6 of the dBASE III manual, in the section called "Read Me First."

1.02 Tip: *If you are working with a floppy disk system, put DOS on System Disk #1 so you can load DOS and dBASE III without changing disks.*

To work with dBASE III on a floppy disk system, you must first load DOS into the computer and then begin loading dBASE III. If you add the DOS file to System Disk #1, you can load both programs from the same disk:

1. Load DOS into your computer so that the A> prompt is on the screen.

2. Keep the DOS disk in drive A and place your working copy of System Disk #1 in drive B.

3. Enter these commands:

```
SYS B:

COPY COMMAND.COM B:
```

1.03 Trap: *dBASE III will not run as efficiently as it is designed to run, unless a CONFIG.SYS file is on the disk used to load DOS.*

When you load DOS into your computer, it checks for a file that is named CON-FIG.SYS. If this file is present, it is executed automatically, and it tells DOS how to configure the computer's memory. dBASE III requires a CONFIG.SYS file containing these lines:

```
FILES=20

BUFFERS=15
```

If you don't have these lines in CONFIG.SYS, dBASE will operate much more slowly and you will have problems whenever you work with multiple files.
    See the following tip and trap.

1.04 Tip: *If you don't have a CONFIG.SYS file on the disk that you use to load DOS, add one with the DOS command COPY CON.*

Load DOS into your computer. When the A> prompt appears on the screen, enter

```
COPY CON: CONFIG.SYS
```

When you press RETURN, the cursor will move to the next line without showing a prompt. Enter

```
FILES=20

BUFFERS=15
```

After you press RETURN, enter CTRL-Z and press RETURN again. The file will be written to your disk, and DOS will respond "1 file copied."

When you load DOS from this disk, the computer will automatically be configured to run dBASE III properly.

 1.05 Trap: *If you already have a CONFIG.SYS file on your disk and you use COPY CON, you will destroy the old file.*

If you already have a **CONFIG.SYS** file on the disk used to load DOS into your computer, you want to add the lines **FILES=20** and **BUFFERS=15** to it, so that dBASE III can run properly. Do *not* follow the procedure in the preceding tip, or you will erase the existing CONFIG.SYS file. Instead, access the file from within your word processing program and add these two lines to it.

The Set Commands

1.06 Tip: *Use SET DEFAULT to specify the disk drive on which your data disk can be found.*

Unless you tell dBASE otherwise, it assumes that all files are located on the same drive as the dBASE system files. In a double-floppy system, the dBASE system disk is in drive A and your data disk is in drive B. dBASE needs to be told to find database files, program files, and the like on the B drive. There are two ways to instruct dBASE:

1. You can include the drive designator B: every time you enter the name of a file; for instance,

```
USE B:MAIL_LST
APPEND FROM B:CUSTOMER FOR STATE = "CA"
```

2. You can enter

```
SET DEFAULT TO B:
```

once, and dBASE will assume all files that you name thereafter are located in drive B. If you include this command in a **CONFIG.DB** file (see the following section of this chapter), the default drive will be set to B every time you load dBASE into your computer.

1.07 **Tip:** *You can turn off the bell that rings every time a field is filled with data.*

When you are entering data into a field or editing the existing contents of a field, dBASE rings a bell every time the full length of a field is filled with data. If you find this annoying, you can turn off the bell with

```
SET BELL OFF
```

If you want to turn the bell on again, just enter

```
SET BELL ON
```

Be sure to read the following trap.

1.08 **Trap:** *If you use the SET BELL OFF command, the bell will not ring when invalid data is entered into a field.*

If invalid data is entered into a field—for instance, if letters are entered into a numeric field—dBASE rings the bell to call attention to the error. It then displays an error message and keeps the cursor in the field for another entry. If you have entered SET BELL OFF, the bell will not ring, and the person entering data will have to watch the screen for error messages.

1.09 **Tip:** *Use the SET ALTERNATE command to create a disk file containing the results of dBASE operations.*

Suppose you want to include a report generated by **REPORT FORM** in a document that will be written using your word processing program (see Chapter 7 for tips and traps on using **REPORT FORM** to generate reports). You would like the results of REPORT FORM, which are usually output to the printer, stored in a text file on your disk.

You can use the SET ALTERNATE command to create a disk file containing the results of any dBASE processing operation except the full-screen data-entry and editing modes (such as EDIT and APPEND). All screen displays and keyboard entries will be included in the file.

To open the disk file for data entry, enter

```
SET ALTERNATE TO DISKFILE
```

The file will be given the extension .TXT unless you specify another extension in this command. Once the alternate file has been opened, tell dBASE to begin sending data to the disk file with the command

```
SET ALTERNATE ON
```

To stop the flow of data to the disk file, enter

```
SET ALTERNATE OFF
```

You can turn this disk output on and off as many times as needed; when you have finished and want to close the disk file, enter

```
SET ALTERNATE TO
```

 1.10 Trap: SET ALTERNATE TO diskfile merely opens the file on your disk; it does not send data to the alternate file.

Sending data to an alternate disk file requires two steps:

1. Opening the disk file with SET ALTERNATE TO *filename*
2. Telling dBASE to send data to the file with SET ALTERNATE ON.

Be sure to read the next trap and the preceding tip for detailed discussions of the SET ALTERNATE command.

 **1.11 Trap:** *SET ALTERNATE TO diskfile erases an existing file with the same name.*

Before choosing a name for an alternate disk file, be sure to check the disk directory. Otherwise, you might accidentally erase a file you want to keep by giving your new file a name already in use.

1.12 Tip: *Use the SET FILTER command to process only those records that meet a certain condition.*

If you want to work with a particular group of records in your database file, you can take either of two approaches:

- You can include a condition, such as FOR CITY = "BOSTON", with every command you enter. This will limit the action of the command to those records that meet the condition — in this case, only records with BOSTON in the field CITY.

- You can use SET FILTER to make dBASE ignore all records that do not meet a specified condition. Figure 1-6 shows how SET FILTER can be used. The database file contains records of people who live in several different cities, as shown in the first listing in the figure. To have dBASE

```
. LIST L_NAME, F_NAME, CITY FOR L_NAME < "E"
Record#   L_NAME              F_NAME              CITY
      1   ABRAMS              MICHAEL             BOSTON
      2   BENNETT             JAMES               CANTON
      3   BRICKLEY            SUSAN               MILTON
      4   CAMP                JEFFREY             BOSTON
      5   CAMPBELL            ALLEN               BOSTON
      6   DAVIS               JEROME              MILTON
      7   DAVISON             WILLIAM             CANTON
.
. SET FILTER TO CITY = "BOSTON"
.
. LIST L_NAME, F_NAME, CITY FOR L_NAME < "E"
Record#   L_NAME              F_NAME              CITY
      1   ABRAMS              MICHAEL             BOSTON
      4   CAMP                JEFFREY             BOSTON
      5   CAMPBELL            ALLEN               BOSTON
.
```

Figure 1-6. Using SET FILTER

ignore all records that do not have BOSTON in the field CITY, enter

```
SET FILTER TO CITY = "BOSTON"
```

The result is shown in the second listing in Figure 1-6: dBASE recognizes only those records with BOSTON in the field CITY and acts as if the other records were not in the file.

The SET FILTER command can be particularly helpful when you need to execute many commands on a group of records in a database file, since you can enter it once rather than having to include a condition with each command you enter.

To turn off the filter and once again access all records in the file, enter **SET FILTER TO** with no condition. If you are working with more than one database file, you can establish a separate filter in each open work area, since SET FILTER affects only the file in the currently selected workspace.

1.13 Tip: *Use the SET EXACT command to control the way dBASE compares character strings.*

The default mode of SET EXACT is OFF; in this mode dBASE considers two character strings equal if the right-hand string is identical to the beginning characters of the left-hand string. Thus, the expression "CATNAP" = "CAT" will evaluate as true. The most frequent application of this mode is a dBASE search for a particular record in your file. When dBASE executes FIND, SEEK, or LOCATE, each record is compared to the search criterion. If SET EXACT is OFF, a record is considered a match if the search string matches the beginning of the entry in the record. For example, in Figure 1-7, while SET EXACT is OFF, the command

```
FIND DAVI
```

moves the record pointer to the record containing DAVIS in the L __ NAME field.

This feature can be very useful. If you are working with a file that is indexed by last name, you can enter

```
FIND D
```

and the record pointer will be positioned at the first record in which L__NAME begins with the letter D; an exact search string is not required.

Many times, however, you want dBASE to accept only an exact match: if you search for the name "Smith" in your records, you don't want to be positioned at a record containing the name "Smithwick". Figure 1-7 illustrates the procedure for an exact match; enter

SET EXACT ON

Now, when dBASE is asked to move the record pointer to a record for the name "DAVI", the response is "No Find", since no record matches that name exactly.

1.14 Tip: *If you include the line SET ESCAPE OFF in your dBASE application programs, you will prevent an inexperienced dBASE user from using the ESC key to exit your program.*

When dBASE is loaded into your computer, SET ESCAPE is ON, which allows a user to interrupt execution of your application programs by pressing the ESC key. The program will stop executing immediately, and the user will be returned to the dot prompt. However, this can create problems. If, for example, your program

```
. LIST L_NAME, F_NAME, CITY FOR L_NAME < "E"
Record#   L_NAME              F_NAME              CITY
       1  ABRAMS              MICHAEL             BOSTON
       2  BENNETT             JAMES               CANTON
       3  BRICKLEY            SUSAN               MILTON
       4  CAMP                JEFFREY             BOSTON
       5  CAMPBELL            ALLEN               BOSTON
       6  DAVIS               JEROME              MILTON
       7  DAVISON             WILLIAM             CANTON
.
. FIND DAVI
.
. DISPLAY
Record#   L_NAME              F_NAME              CITY
       6  DAVIS               JEROME              MILTON
.
. SET EXACT ON
.
. FIND DAVI
No find
.
```

Figure 1-7. Using SET EXACT

is updating one file from another and the user exits the program by pressing the ESC key, some of the records will be updated, others will not be, and your files will not be properly closed. You could lose a lot of important data.

If you SET ESCAPE OFF in your application programs, you can prevent an inexperienced user from accidentally exiting the program by pressing ESC. This safety feature can be critical, since you don't want important processing to be interrupted.

1.15 Trap: *Don't include the line SET ESCAPE OFF in your application programs until they are completely debugged, or you may find that you can't return to the dot prompt when you test your program.*

To write, test, and debug dBASE application programs, you must run the program frequently, checking the results of the current version of your dBASE code lines. If you include SET ESCAPE OFF in your program code before it is tested, you deprive yourself of a valuable debugging tool: the ability to interrupt your program in order to see the results at any stage of processing.

SET ESCAPE OFF can present a major problem if you accidentally include an endless loop in your program lines (see the tips and traps on **DO WHILE** loops in Chapter 9). To exit from such a loop so that you can correct the program code, you will need the ESC key. If you have already SET ESCAPE OFF in your program, you must turn off your computer to exit the loop, thereby losing data from open files, or the most recent version of your program code if you haven't saved it yet. Insert SET ESCAPE OFF into the command file only when you are certain your program is working correctly.

Custom Configuration

1.16 Tip: *Use a CONFIG.DB file to establish certain working conditions automatically whenever dBASE is loaded into your computer.*

When dBASE is first loaded into your computer, it looks on the system disk for a file named CONFIG.DB. If such a file is found, its commands are executed automatically after dBASE has been loaded.

You can write a CONFIG.DB file with your word processing program or with the dBASE MODIFY COMMAND word processor. Either way, if the file is named CONFIG.DB and is located on your system disk, it will execute automatically when dBASE III is loaded. If you are working with a floppy disk system, place the CONFIG.DB file on System Disk #2, the disk that remains in drive A while you are working with dBASE III. If you have a hard disk, place CONFIG.DB in the same directory as DBASE.OVL.

A CONFIG.DB file can specify three kinds of dBASE parameters: SET commands, the programmable function keys, and some dBASE configuration commands. The following tips and traps discuss each of these parameters.

Each line of the CONFIG.DB file has the form *KEYWORD = VALUE*; for example,

DEFAULT=B:

has the same effect as entering SET DEFAULT TO B: from the dot prompt — it establishes drive B as the default disk drive. dBASE will expect to find database files, format files, program files, and the like on the B drive, unless another drive is specified when the filename is entered.

See the following tips and traps for more examples of CONFIG.DB command lines.

1.17 Tip: *You can include SET commands in a CONFIG.DB file, and they will be executed automatically whenever you load dBASE III.*

All ON/OFF SET commands can be included in a CONFIG.DB file. You omit the word SET and use an equal sign between the keyword and the setting desired; for example,

BELL=OFF

in a CONFIG.DB file has the same effect as entering SET BELL OFF from the dot prompt: the bell will not ring when a field is filled with data or when the incorrect type of data is entered into a field.

Some of the SET commands are discussed in the previous section of this chapter, and others, which have particular usefulness in certain data-processing tasks, are discussed in the relevant chapters throughout the book. See the index for the location of tips and traps for a particular SET command.

1.18 Tip: To save typing time, you can assign a particular string to one of the programmable function keys.

All of the function keys except F1 (which is reserved by dBASE for the HELP function) can be assigned a string, which will be inserted into the command line whenever the function key is pressed. For example, suppose your CONFIG.DB file includes the following lines:

```
F2=SET ALTERNATE ON;
F3=SET ALTERNATE OFF;
F4=SET ALTERNATE TO
```

Now you have easy control of an alternate output file (discussed in Tip 1.09 and Traps 1.10 and 1.11). To open the alternate disk file, press F4; the words "SET ALTERNATE TO" will appear on the command line. Complete the command by typing in the name of the disk file, and press RETURN to enter the command.

When you want to enter the command SET ALTERNATE ON, just press F2. The semicolon in the CONFIG.DB line is the equivalent of pressing RETURN, so one key press is all you need. Similarly, to turn off the disk output, just press F3.

Note that in the CONFIG.DB file, the strings are not delimited with quotes or with any other delimiter.

1.19 Tip: If your computer has enough available memory, you can configure dBASE to use an external word processor when you enter or edit data in a memo field or write files with *MODIFY COMMAND.*

dBASE III requires 256K of memory to run on your computer. If you have enough extra memory, you can tell dBASE to use an external word processor to write in memo fields and to write command files with MODIFY COMMAND.

For example, WordStar version 3.3 requires 128K of memory; if you have at least 384K of memory in your computer, you can use WordStar from within dBASE III. First, the WordStar files must be on the same disk as the dBASE.OVL file. Meeting this condition is not difficult with a hard disk system; if you are working with floppy disks, place the WordStar files WS.COM, WSMSGS.OVR, and WSOVLY1.OVR on System Disk #2, the disk that stays in drive A while you run dBASE III.

To use WordStar whenever you write in a memo field, include the line

```
WP=WS
```

in your CONFIG.DB file. To use WordStar when you enter MODIFY COMMAND, use the line

```
TEDIT=WS
```

You may use either or both of these assignments in your CONFIG.DB file.

When you have entered a memo field or entered MODIFY COMMAND using WordStar, you will find yourself editing a file called DBASEDIT.TMP. dBASE has created the file, opened WordStar, and opened the document for you. When you have finished working in WordStar, enter CTRL-KD. You will return to the dBASE dot prompt, and the file you worked on in WordStar will be saved either as the contents of the memo field or under the filename you specified when you entered MODIFY COMMAND.

Be sure to read the following trap.

■ *1.20 Trap: Using an external word processor will slow down your work in dBASE III.*

If you configure dBASE to load an external word processor to write in memo fields or when you enter MODIFY COMMAND, you will find that your work in dBASE is slowed down, since you must wait for the word processor to be loaded each time it is needed.

Sometimes it may be worth the extra delay — for example, if you are debugging or modifying a long program, or are writing in a file with many long memo fields, and you want to use the particular features of your word processor. But before you decide to use an external word processor from within dBASE III, you should consider that there is a definite trade-off between performance time and access to these features.

Getting Started in the dBASE III Environment

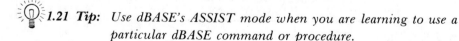 *1.21 Tip: Use dBASE's ASSIST mode when you are learning to use a particular dBASE command or procedure.*

```
                        The dBASE III
                          Assistant

          Assist uses menus to bring you the power of dBASE III


              KEY                        FUNCTION

       Esc                    Exit from current operation.
       Up arrow      (↑)      Move to previous menu.
       Down arrow    (↓)      Move to next menu.
       Left arrow    (←)      Move one item to the left.
       Right arrow   (→)      Move one item to the right.
       Home                   Go to first menu.
       End                    Go to right most item.
       Option Letter          Executes option (Unless otherwise noted
                              option letter is first letter of option.)


          PRESS ↓ (or ENTER) TO CONTINUE, ESC to EXIT ASSIST:
```

Figure 1-8.   dBASE III ASSIST mode

Entering ASSIST at the dot prompt puts you in the dBASE ASSIST mode, labeled "dBASE III Assistant" on your screen. It will lead you step by step through a particular dBASE command or operation. ASSIST mode works through menus that list available options; you select the dBASE task you wish to perform, and ASSIST describes the task and guides you through the steps necessary to accomplish it.

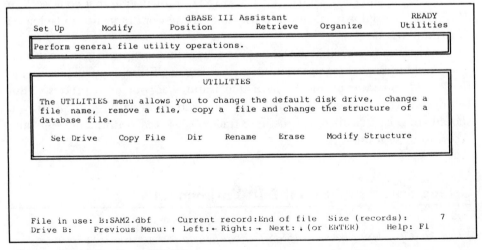

```
                              dBASE III Assistant              READY
     Set Up      Modify      Position      Retrieve   Organize  Utilities

    Perform general file utility operations.


                               UTILITIES

      The UTILITIES menu allows you to change the default disk drive,  change a
      file  name,  remove a file,  copy a  file and change the structure of  a
      database file.

        Set Drive    Copy File    Dir    Rename    Erase    Modify Structure




     File in use: B:SAM2.dbf    Current record:End of file  Size (records):    7
     Drive B:      Previous Menu: ↑ Left:← Right: →  Next: ↓ (or ENTER)    Help: F1
```

Figure 1-9.   The first ASSIST menu

The first ASSIST screen is shown in Figure 1-8; it tells you how to use the menus on all of the ASSIST screens. Press the down arrow or the RETURN key to move to the first menu, which is shown in Figure 1-9.

The six main ASSIST options are listed across the top of the screen. You use the left and right arrow keys to move the cursor. dBASE describes the functions you will be able to perform if you select each option. In Figure 1-9, the cursor is on Utilities, and the screen display identifies the different tasks that can be done if you choose the Utilities option.

Let's say you are using ASSIST mode to help you rename a file. Press RETURN with the cursor on the Utilities option, and you will move to the Utilities menu, as shown in Figure 1-10.

Again, the available options are listed across the top of the screen, and you select one by placing the cursor on that option. In Figure 1-10, the cursor is on Rename. The screen explains how the RENAME command is used and how ASSIST mode will help you rename a file. Press RETURN to select this option.

The first step in renaming a file is to choose the file that you will rename; ASSIST gives the names of all of the files on the default disk, as shown in Figure 1-11. The instruction line (in the box at the top of the screen) tells you to select a file by positioning the cursor on its name and pressing RETURN.

Notice the line "Command: Rename" near the bottom of the screen. This line shows you how ASSIST is building the dBASE command you need to accomplish your task — in this case, renaming a file. The first word of the command line will be RENAME. Once you select the file to be renamed, its name will

```
                             File Utilities                          READY
    Set Drive      Copy File      Dir      Rename      Erase     Modify Structure
   ┌─────────────────────────────────────────────────────────────────────────┐
   │ Rename an existing database.                                             │
   └─────────────────────────────────────────────────────────────────────────┘


   ┌─────────────────────────────────────────────────────────────────────────┐
   │                               RENAME                                     │
   │                                                                          │
   │   RENAME  is used to change the name of a file.   This is equivalent to the │
   │   DOS command, RENAME.  In ASSIST, the current file is selected from a list │
   │   of files and the new file name is entered from the keyboard.   File  name │
   │   extensions must be specified.                                          │
   │                                                                          │
   │        Command Format:  RENAME [old file name| TO [new file name|        │
   │                                                                          │
   └─────────────────────────────────────────────────────────────────────────┘



   Command: Rename
   File in use: B:SAM2.dbf    Current record:End of file  Size (records):     7
   Drive B:      Previous Menu: ↑ Left:← Right: → Next: ↓ (or ENTER)   Help: F1
```

Figure 1-10. The Utilities menu with RENAME selected

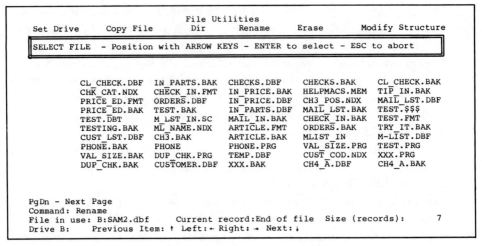

```
                                    File Utilities
     Set Drive      Copy File         Dir       Rename        Erase      Modify Structure

    ┌──────────────────────────────────────────────────────────────────────────────┐
    │ SELECT FILE - Position with ARROW KEYS - ENTER to select - ESC to abort        │
    └──────────────────────────────────────────────────────────────────────────────┘

           CL_CHECK.DBF   IN_PARTS.BAK   CHECKS.DBF    CHECKS.BAK    CL_CHECK.BAK
           CHK_CAT.NDX    CHECK_IN.FMT   IN_PRICE.BAK  HELPMACS.MEM  TIP_IN.BAK
           PRICE_ED.FMT   ORDERS.DBF     IN_PRICE.DBF  CH3_POS.NDX   MAIL_LST.DBF
           PRICE_ED.BAK   TEST.BAK       IN_PARTS.DBF  MAIL_LST.BAK  TEST.$$$
           TEST.DBT       M_LST_IN.SC    MAIL_IN.BAK   CHECK_IN.BAK  TEST.FMT
           TESTING.BAK    ML_NAME.NDX    ARTICLE.FMT   ORDERS.BAK    TRY_IT.BAK
           CUST_LST.DBF   CH3.BAK        ARTICLE.BAK   MLIST_IN      M-LIST.DBF
           PHONE.BAK      PHONE          PHONE.PRG     VAL_SIZE.PRG  TEST.PRG
           VAL_SIZE.BAK   DUP_CHK.PRG    TEMP.DBF      CUST_COD.NDX  XXX.PRG
           DUP_CHK.BAK    CUSTOMER.DBF   XXX.BAK       CH4_A.DBF     CH4_A.BAK


     PgDn - Next Page
     Command: Rename
     File in use: B:SAM2.dbf      Current record:End of file  Size (records):     7
     Drive B:     Previous Item: ↑ Left:← Right:→ Next:↓
```

Figure 1-11. Choosing the file to rename

be added to the command line, as shown in Figure 1-12.

The final part of a RENAME command is the new name to be assigned to the file. Figure 1-12 shows ASSIST mode asking you for this new name. Each ASSIST screen includes any relevant restrictions on the data that is entered, and the exact form of the filename is described for you. Enter the new name for the file and press RETURN; the complete RENAME command will be executed.

If you make an error while working in ASSIST mode, you will receive detailed instructions about the nature of your mistake and how to correct it.

```
                                    File Utilities
     Set Drive      Copy File         Dir       Rename        Erase      Modify Structure

    ┌──────────────────────────────────────────────────────────────────────────────┐
    │ Rename an existing database.                                                   │
    └──────────────────────────────────────────────────────────────────────────────┘





    ┌──────────────────────────────────────────────────────────────────────────────┐
    │  You must enter a file name (consisting of up to 8 letters or digits)          │
    │  followed by a period and a file name extension (consisting of up to 3         │
    │  letters or digits.)    Enter the name of the file:                            │
    └──────────────────────────────────────────────────────────────────────────────┘
     Command: Rename DUP_CHK.BAK TO
     File in use: B:SAM2.dbf      Current record:End of file  Size (records):     7
     Drive B:     Previous Item: ↑ Left:← Right:→ Next:↓
```

Figure 1-12. Entering the new name for the file

1.22 Trap: *ASSIST mode is a very slow and inefficient way to use dBASE III.*

ASSIST mode can be very helpful when you are first learning to use a dBASE command or to perform a particular task involving a sequence of several commands. But it is a very poor choice over the long term. ASSIST mode is very time-consuming; each command is constructed by progressing through a series of menus and selecting the appropriate option at each step.

Use ASSIST mode to help you learn to accomplish a particular dBASE task, but as soon as you feel confident, issue the commands yourself from the dot prompt.

See the following two tips for a way to get assistance from dBASE while you are in interactive mode, which is quicker than entering ASSIST mode.

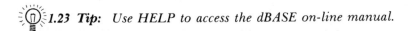 **1.23 Tip:** *Use HELP to access the dBASE on-line manual.*

If you enter HELP at the dot prompt, you will be presented with the screen shown in Figure 1-13. This is the main HELP menu. It shows you all of the types of information available in the dBASE on-line manual.

Unlike ASSIST mode (described in the preceding tip and trap), HELP will

```
                                                        MAIN MENU

     - maximum help -

                         dBASE III Main Menu
                         ===================

                         1 - Getting Started
                         2 - What Is a ...
                         3 - How Do I ...
                         4 - Creating a Database
                         5 - Using an Existing Database
                         6 - Commands and Functions




     ↑↓↵ =menu selection, PgUp=previous screen, Esc=exit HELP, or enter command.
                     ENTER >
```

Figure 1-13. The main HELP menu

```
                                                        WHAT IS A ...

  - maximum help -

                              What Is a ...
                              =============

                              1 - Command
                              2 - Expression
                              3 - Field List
                              4 - File
                              5 - Key Field
                              6 - Memory Variable (Memvar)
                              7 - Operator
                              8 - Record
                              9 - Scope
                              0 - Skeleton


  ↓↑↵ =menu selection, PgUp=previous screen, Esc=exit HELP, or enter command.
                    ENTER >
```

Figure 1-14.   Using HELP to learn about dBASE vocabulary

not take you step by step through the process of creating a particular dBASE
command. Instead, it gives you the information you need to write the command
line yourself, once you return to the dot prompt. For example, if you choose
option 2 (What Is a ...) from the main menu, you will see a list of different words
that are used in dBASE prompts and error messages, as shown in Figure 1-14.
Select the word you would like to read about by entering the corresponding
number and pressing RETURN.

```
                                                        MEMORY VARIABLE


                       Memory Variable (MEMVAR)
                       ========================


      Memory variables are named data items that are independently
      stored outside of the database structure.

      There are four memory variable data types:
      numeric, date, character, and logical.
      The type is determined by the kind of data stored.

      Memory variable names follow the same rules as field names.

      STORE 'CA' TO State      Stores CA to character memvar State.
      STORE 123.34 TO Price    Stores 123.34 to numeric memvar Price.
      STORE .T. TO Pass        Stores .T. to logical memvar Pass.

  PgUp=previous screen, Esc=exit HELP, ^Home=previous menu, or enter command.
                    ENTER >
```

Figure 1-15.   The HELP screen for memory variables

If you choose option 6, Memory Variable (Memvar), on the What Is a ... menu, you will see the screen display shown in Figure 1-15. This option defines a memory variable, explains the different types, and gives you examples to help clarify the definition. Use the HELP on-line manual in this manner to learn more about dBASE vocabulary and commands.

1.24 Tip: *You can access a specific HELP screen without going through the HELP menus.*

If you know exactly which dBASE command you need to learn about, you can access the relevant HELP screen directly from the dot prompt. For instance, if you enter

```
HELP RENAME
```

you will see the screen display shown in Figure 1-16, the HELP screen for the RENAME command.

This is a very practical way to use HELP; if you are not sure how to enter a particular command, you can call up the HELP screen on that command, read about how the command is used and how your entry should be structured, and then press ESC to return to the dot prompt and enter your command. This approach can be much faster than searching through the dBASE manual.

```
                                                      RENAME


                          RENAME
                          ======

   Syntax       :  RENAME <current file.extension> TO <new file.extension>

   Description  :  Changes the name of a file.  An open file cannot be
                   RENAMEd.  The default file extension is .dbf.




     PgUp=previous screen, Esc=exit HELP, ^Home=previous menu, or enter command.
                 ENTER >
```

Figure 1-16.   The HELP screen for RENAME

1.25 **Tip:** *You can abbreviate all dBASE commands to their first four letters.*

Entering the first four letters of any dBASE command will activate that command. For example, entering

```
CREA NEWFILE
```

has the same effect as entering

```
CREATE NEWFILE
```

This method is only effective with dBASE commands; it does not work with filenames or field names.

1.26 **Tip:** *Protect your data by making backup copies frequently.*

Whenever you are working with your files, they are vulnerable—to equipment failure, an interruption in the power supply, or human error. Disk drives can malfunction, and so can people; it's easy to enter an incorrect command without realizing it, to overwrite a file you need to keep, or to erase data that should be saved.

Protect your files (and the time and energy you've invested in them) by following three simple rules for protecting data:

- Never keep only one copy of any data worth saving.
- Keep backup copies on a separate disk, or on a tape or floppy disk backup if you have a hard disk system.
- Never make changes to the only current copy of a particular file.

The system used while this book was being written is easy to maintain and quite effective:

- All data is stored on three disks, a working disk and two backup disks labeled B/U I and B/U II.

- After a major task has been accomplished—say a file has been updated or an application program has been debugged—the working disk is copied onto a backup by using the **DOS DISKCOPY** command.

- The backup disks are used alternately. After the working disk has been copied onto a backup, the backup disk is placed behind the other backup disk in the disk file.

The first time you have an "Oh, no!" accident with your data, you'll be very glad you used a system like this or very sorry if you didn't.

 1.27 **Trap:** *Never exit from dBASE without entering QUIT.*

QUIT tells dBASE to close all open files, read in any data that is in the memory buffers, and update the file headers to reflect changes that have been made.

If you exit from dBASE without entering QUIT, you can lose data from your open files. You should therefore always end your work sessions with QUIT.

 1.28 **Trap:** *Never enter QUIT with the wrong data disk in the default drive.*

If you've been accessing files from different floppy disks during your dBASE session, then before you enter **QUIT** you must be sure that the disk in the default drive is the one that contains the files that are now open. If you enter **QUIT** when the disk in the default drive is *not* the source of the current data files, dBASE may overwrite the data on that disk.

See the following trap.

 1.29 **Trap:** *Don't change data disks without closing any open files first.*

When dBASE is working with data files, it does not write all data that is input directly to the files. Writing data to the disks takes time; some dBASE operations store data to the buffers in your computer's memory instead. When the file is closed, any data stored in a buffer is then written to the file.

If you need to access a file on another data disk, be sure to close all open files before you change disks. If you are working in one workspace only, you can enter USE with no filename; all database files and associated index and format files in the current workspace will be closed. If you have files open in more than one work area, enter CLOSE DATABASES to close all of the files.

2

Planning Applications
And Establishing
Databases

The structure of your application system—how many different databases you establish, and how they are related to one another—determines whether you will be able to take full advantage of the power of dBASE III. A poorly designed system is perpetually frustrating; data is not easy to find or update and may be lost accidentally. A well-planned system makes it easy for you to enter, retrieve, and manipulate the information stored in your databases, and to write programs that will accomplish routine tasks quickly and accurately.

This chapter contains tips and traps to help you design your overall database system and the individual files within it. The different data types are discussed so that you can store your information in a format that will make it easy to locate and process. There are also tips and traps concerning the use of the structure or data of another file and on how to modify the structure of an existing file.

Designing an Application System

 2.01 Trap: *Avoid thinking "the bigger, the better," or you'll end up with a database that is very hard to work with.*

Because dBASE is capable of handling very large database files—up to 128 fields—it's tempting to cram a lot of data into one file. Doing so can lead to many problems with entering, updating, and retrieving data.

In a noncomputerized record-keeping system—what we might call a manual data management system—moving back and forth between various documents to extract related information is frustrating and is a source of potential errors. It seems helpful to put as much related data as possible onto each record form, even if some data is repeated. For instance, in a manual system, the customer's address is entered on the order form every time an order is placed. This repetition assures that the data is available on the same document that contains the specific details of the order.

With dBASE, exactly the opposite approach is needed for two reasons: first, related data can be extracted from different database files very quickly and accurately; second, large files are difficult to update and process. The goals change—with dBASE, minimizing repetitions, saving data-entry time, and using memory storage space efficiently are most important.

 2.02 Trap: *If you have fields that repeat the same data for several records, you are wasting time and storage space.*

Let's say you are designing a system to process customer orders. In your manual system, the order form includes

- Order number and date.
- Customer name, street address, city, state, ZIP code, and phone number.
- For each item, part number, description, quantity, unit price, and total price.
- Total price for the order.

You could design a database file with one field for each of these pieces of information and then enter one record for each part ordered. However, this would result in some obvious problems. The order number, date, customer data, and total price would be repeated in every record, and the part descriptions and unit prices would have to be entered again each time a part was ordered.

The day-to-day effects of this repetition would make the whole system inefficient to use for the following reasons:

- There would be a lot of repetitive typing.

- Disk space would be used to store duplicated data. This could be a problem, particularly if you were working with floppy disks.

- Entering each order would take more time than entering the data just once.

- There would be more opportunities for input errors.

- Correcting data could be difficult. If you discovered that you had been entering the wrong address for one of your customers, you would have to change the address on all records involving that customer.

- dBASE takes more time to process a file with long records than to process a streamlined one.

2.03 Tip: *Analyze the repeating data in your system, and place each type of repeating field in its own database file.*

Let's continue with the example in the preceding trap. The proposed database file would have three types of repeating fields:

- The data relating to each customer — name, address, and the like — would be repeated for every record of an order and for every order by the same customer.

- The data relating to an order as a whole — order number, date, and total price — would be repeated for every record of the order.

- The data relating to each part — the part description and unit price — would be repeated each time that part appeared in different orders.

A more efficient system places each of these types of repeating fields in its own file. The result is four smaller files, related to one another by certain common fields:

CUSTOMER
   CUST _ CODE
   NAME
   STREET
   CITY
   STATE
   ZIP
   PHONE

The CUSTOMER file holds the address and phone number for each customer.

SUMMARY
   ORDER _ NO
   DATE
   CUST _ CODE
   TOTAL

The SUMMARY file holds date and total price data. It is related to CUSTOMER by the common field CUST _ CODE.

ORDER
   ORDER _ NO
   PART _ NO
   QUANTITY

The ORDER file holds the list of part numbers and quantities for each item ordered. It is related to SUMMARY by the common field ORDER _ NO.

PARTS
   PART _ NO
   DESCRIPT
   UNIT _ PRICE

The PARTS file holds the price and description of each part. It is related to ORDER by the common field PART _ NO.

See the following tip for a detailed discussion of how an application program works with these related files.

When you plan your database system, try to have a separate file for each category of information in the system. In the example just given, the system involves customers, parts, orders as a whole, and individual items within an order; each type of data is placed in its own file.

A system structured like this is easy to use: it's obvious that changes in the prices of parts should be entered into the PARTS file and that SUMMARY is the place to look for the total price of an order.

2.04 Tip: *Plan to use the dBASE tools that can relate data across files.*

Working with more than one database file is discussed in detail in Chapter 5. When you design your application system, remember that you will have access to as many as ten different database files at once, either directly from the dot prompt or from a dBASE program.

Let's use the customer order system developed in the preceding tip to illustrate how these files function together within an application system. The information in the system has been split into four smaller files, each with a special function:

- CUSTOMER works like a reference table and can be called on whenever data is needed on a particular customer.

- SUMMARY holds the data about an order as a whole, one record for each order.

- ORDER contains the details of an order and is the only database file with more than one record for each order placed. It's limited to three small fields to make data entry as efficient as possible.

- PARTS is a reference table for the data on individual parts.

The data is easy to keep updated, because changes can be made in one file to keep the whole system up to date.

Here's how an application program can use these files to process a customer order. First, data is entered into the system:

1. The customer name is entered.

The program searches the CUSTOMER file for this name. If the order is from an established customer, the customer code is noted. If this is a new customer, the name, address, and so on are entered into a new record in CUSTOMER and a code is assigned.

2. The order number and date are entered into SUMMARY.

3. For each item, the part number and quantity ordered are entered into ORDER.

Now the program processes the order:

4. The relevant record was located in the CUSTOMER file in step 1; this file is consulted again, and the customer data is printed at the top of the order form.

5. The order number and the date, as entered into SUMMARY, are printed in the report heading.

6. The program searches the ORDER file and locates the group of records with the current order number.

7. For each part ordered, the relevant record is located in the PARTS file, and the description and unit price are retrieved.

8. The data for each part ordered is listed in the body of the report. For each item, dBASE multiplies the quantity by the unit price to generate the total price.

9. dBASE calculates the total cost of the order, stores it in SUMMARY, and prints it at the bottom of the report.

You could also have this data sent to the screen so that you could give a total price to a customer who phoned in an order.

These processes — accepting data, looking up related data in reference files, and generating a screen report or a printed order form — can be done by a simple dBASE application program. Once the databases are established and the program is running correctly, entering orders into this system becomes very simple: you enter the customer code and the specific parts being ordered, and the program takes care of the rest of the work for you.

2.05 Tip: *Plan each database file around a key field (or fields combined into a key expression) that uniquely identifies each individual record.*

The key field (or expression) is the part of each record that identifies the particular data contained in the record. For instance, in the preceding example,

- Each record in CUSTOMER is uniquely identified by the entry in CUST_CODE; the customer's name, address, and phone number must be placed in the record with the correct CUST—CODE. CUST—CODE is the key field for this file.

- Each record in PARTS is uniquely identified by the entry in PART—NO; the description and unit price must be placed in the entry with the proper PART—NO. PART—NO is the key field for this file.

In a mailing-list database, the key expression is *last name + first name.* The last name is not enough to identify each particular record, since several people on your list may have the same last name, but the combination of last name and first name is usually unique.

 2.06 Trap: *If you include fields in your database file that are not related to the key field, you can have problems editing records and you can accidentally lose important data.*

Consider the following database plan, intended to keep track of a staff of sales personnel. Each salesperson is assigned to one of four regions, North, South, East, or West, and each region is divided into territories made up of one or two states. Each region has a central office that is shared by the salespeople who work in that region.

SALESPER	REGION	OFFICE	TERRITORY	STATE_1	STATE_2
BROWN	SOUTH	DALLAS	22	TENNESSEE	MISSISSIPPI
CAMP	EAST	BOSTON	12	MAINE	VERMONT
DAVISON	SOUTH	DALLAS	19	TEXAS	ALABAMA
JONES	WEST	PHOENIX	31	ARIZONA	NEW MEXICO

This plan presents the potential for two problems:

- If the location of a regional office is changed, the OFFICE field will have to be updated for each salesperson in the region. The OFFICE field is determined by the REGION, not by each individual salesperson.

- If several salespeople resign and their records are removed from the file, there will be no record of how their territories were defined. The fields STATE—1 and STATE—2 are determined by the TERRITORY, not by each individual salesperson.

See the following tip.

2.07 Tip: *Whenever one field determines the possible entries in other fields, plan a separate file with the determining field as its key.*

Let's continue with the example given in the trap above. The database plan includes information about several different categories of data: salesperson, region, and territory. Each salesperson has an assigned region and territory, each region has its own office, and each territory consists of two states. A more effective plan uses each of these determining fields as the key expression in a separate file:

SALESPER NAME REGION TERRITORY	SALESPER contains the name of each sales- person and the region and territory assigned.
REGION REGION OFFICE	REGION contains the name of each region and the location of its office. The address and phone number of each office can be added to this file.
TERRIT TERRITORY STATE_1 STATE_2	TERRIT contains the name of each territory and its assigned states.

Now each file contains one distinct type of data, and each field is determined by the key field of the file. Deleting a salesperson will not cause data about regions or territories to be lost, and a change in data about a region or a territory will require only one entry to update the entire system.

You can confirm that each of your files contains one specific type of data by checking that each field of the file is determined by the key expression. In this example, each state belongs to a particular territory, so the STATE fields are determined by TERRITORY and belong in the file that has TERRITORY for its key field.

Your goal is a separate file for each category of information, with a key field or expression that uniquely identifies each record; the file should include all of the dependent data that is determined by the contents of the key field.

Designing a Database File

2.08 Tip: *After you have designed your overall system, plan the structure of each database file.*

A database file has two parts: the *header,* which contains a description of the structure of the file, and the *records,* which contain the actual data stored in the file. Here is an example of a small database file:

```
. DISPLAY STRUCTURE
Structure for database : B:SAMPLE.DBF
Number of data records :        6
Date of last update    : 08/13/85
Field  Field name  Type       Width    Dec
    1  L_NAME      Character     12
    2  F_NAME      Character     12
    3  DATE_IN     Date           8
    4  AMOUNT      Numeric        6      2
** Total **                      39

.
. LIST
Record#  L_NAME      F_NAME     DATE_IN   AMOUNT
      1  WARREN      DAVID      02/01/82   12.58
      2  ROSENBERG   ELSIE      04/17/82   12.34
      3  ROSEN       SYLVIA     10/03/82    8.00
      4  BENNETT     JERRY      02/12/82   11.75
      5  AMES        SIDNEY     04/17/82    8.00
      6  AMES        MARTHA     11/01/82   11.62
.
```

Notice that dBASE displays the header when you enter DISPLAY STRUCTURE.

You will use the CREATE command to define the structure of your database file. The key elements of the file structure are the field names, data types, and widths; you specify each of these when you CREATE the file.

2.09 Tip: *When you design a database file, think carefully about how the file will be used.*

The structure of each database file should be determined by the various ways in which it will be used. As guidelines for construction, you need to consider these questions:

- What key fields will you need to help you locate a particular record?

- What groups of records will you want to work with?

- What types of reports will you generate?

You'll make many of your dBASE tasks easier if you use a separate field for each discrete piece of data that you'll need to manipulate. It is possible to place several data items in one field and access them individually with the SUBSTR function (this approach was sometimes necessary in dBASE II because of restrictions in file size). dBASE III allows as many as 128 fields in a single file, more than enough for a well-planned application. See the previous section, "Designing an Application System," for tips and traps on deciding what data should be placed in an individual database file.

Here is the structure of a mailing-list file:

```
. DISPLAY STRUCTURE
Structure for database : B:MAIL_LST.dbf
Number of data records :      105
Date of last update    : 08/31/85
Field  Field name  Type       Width    Dec
    1  TITLE       Character      4
    2  L_NAME      Character     18
    3  F_NAME      Character     18
    4  CO_NAME     Character     20
    5  STREET      Character     20
    6  CITY        Character     15
    7  STATE       Character      2
    8  ZIP         Character      5
    9  USE_FIRST   Logical        1
   10  PHONE       Character     13
** Total **                     117
```

The three guidelines listed earlier in this tip were used to plan the fields:

- *Locating records.* Last names are placed in a separate field so that individual records can be located by last name.

- *Working with groups of records.* Company name, city, state, and ZIP code are each placed in a separate field. This makes it possible to print a list of all the people in California; a set of mailing labels for all the people in a certain ZIP code region; or a form letter for all people in the same company.

- *Reports.* Last names and first names are placed in separate fields so that alphabetical listings can be printed with the last name first and so that mailing labels can be generated with the first name first. The logical field USE_FIRST will tell a program whether to address a letter "Dear Tom" or "Dear Mr. Smith," based on the data in the TITLE field.

2.10 Tip: *Choose filenames and field names that are as descriptive as possible.*

Choose a filename that will clearly identify the unique function of a particular database file. For instance, ACC_REC and ACC_PAY are better names for accounts receivable and accounts payable files than are the names ACC1 and ACC2; it's much easier to tell exactly which records are in each file. (See the following tip for suggestions on naming groups of files in an application system.)

Descriptive field names are also important. Your programs will be much easier to read if each field name clearly indicates which part of the data is found in that field. F_NAME and L_NAME are better field names than NAME1 and NAME2; if you come back to modify your program two years from now, you'll be able to tell exactly what part of the data is being manipulated.

2.11 Tip: *If you plan to use more than one database file in your application system, identify the system in the filenames.*

You can make it easier to work with your application system if you set up all the files in the system so that they can be easily recognized and processed as a group. An effective method is to use the first two letters of each filename to represent the system. If you follow them with the underscore character, your filenames will be easier to read and you'll be able to distinguish the system files from others that begin with the same two letters. The remaining five letters can be used to describe the unique function of this particular file.

In a purchasing/inventory system, you could use these names:

Name	Meaning
IN‗ORDER	orders placed
IN‗VEND	vendor names and addresses
IN‗PRICE	prices of parts
IN‗PARTS	parts on hand

If you see these files listed in a disk directory, you will know which files belong to this system; and you will also know that a file named **INCOME** is not part of the system.

To list all of the files in the system from within dBASE, just enter

```
DIR IN_*.*
```

To list all of the index files in the system, use

```
DIR IN_*.NDX
```

 2.12 Trap: *If you name a file or a field with a dBASE reserved word, you might not be able to access that file or field.*

To be effective, a filename or field name must let dBASE know exactly what you are referring to when you use it. If you use dBASE reserved words, which have predefined meanings in the dBASE language, you can run into communication problems. Here are some examples:

- dBASE uses the first ten letters of the alphabet, A through J, as aliases for the ten available workspaces (see the section "Related Databases" in Chapter 5). If you name a file A or any letter through J, you will not be able to use the file once you create it. dBASE interprets USE A as a reference to the alias for the first workspace and responds with an error message.

- If you use FIELD, FOR, WHILE, or TO as field names, you will get a syntax error when you try to LIST or DISPLAY the field.

- If you name a field with a word that appears in a dBASE command phrase with LIST, such as FILE, STATUS, STRUCTURE, or MEMO, dBASE will not LIST that field for you. LIST FILE is interpreted as the command phrase and gives you a disk directory, not a listing of the field named FILE.

Never use a word that is a dBASE command or function name for your field names or filenames. Even if you manage to avoid the types of problems in the foregoing examples, your programs will be confusing to read. If the best word to describe a file or a field is a dBASE reserved word, either choose a synonym, such as COMMENT for MEMO, or alter the word slightly; MEMOS will work for a field name, and AA or A1 will work for a filename.

Numeric, Logical, and Memo Fields

 2.13 Trap: *To simplify indexing your file, do not use the numeric field type unless you will be doing calculations with the contents of the field.*

You want to set up your databases so that finding and retrieving data is as easy as possible. The most efficient tools for these tasks work with indexed files (see Chapter 4). Indexing is possible with all types of fields, but it is easiest with character fields.

The best guideline is this: Fields that contain numbers should be defined as character fields unless the numbers will be used in calculations, as in account balances or amounts of an item on hand in your inventory.

ZIP codes, for instance, are made up of numbers but are best entered into a character field. You can still process records selectively based on ZIP codes. dBASE can make comparisons between character data, so that you can process, for instance, all records with ZIP codes greater than 09999 or with ZIP codes between 40000 and 49999.

 2.14 Trap: *If your numeric fields are too small, your entries will be truncated.*

A numeric field must be long enough to hold the largest number that will be entered into the field. Keep these points in mind:

- The decimal point takes up one space in the field, which must be included in the length. A field of length 5 with two decimal places can hold numbers up to 99.99.

- Numbers less than 1 need a leading zero before the decimal point. dBASE requires that the decimal width be at least two less than the field width to allow for the leading zero. If you try to define a field that does not meet this requirement, dBASE will display the message "Illegal decimal length" and refuse to accept the field width.

- If your field might have a negative entry, you will need one space for the negative sign.

2.15 Trap: *A numeric field that is not defined to have decimal places will not accept numbers with fractional parts.*

If a field is not defined to have decimal places, dBASE will accept only the integer portion of each entry. If there's any chance you will need to enter numbers with decimal places into your field, define it appropriately.

You can use **MODIFY STRUCTURE** to add decimal places to a numeric field, and you will not lose your existing data if you do not try to change any field names at the same time. See the section called "Changing the Structure of a File" later in this chapter for tips and traps on adding decimal places to a numeric field.

2.16 Trap: *You cannot enter commas into the numbers in numeric fields.*

The only symbols dBASE will accept into a numeric field are the digits 0 through 9, a decimal point, and a positive or negative sign. If you try to enter any other character, dBASE will beep and will not write the character into the field.

However, it is easy to have dBASE insert commas into the numbers on your screen displays and printed reports. (See the tips and traps on PICTURE in Chapter 6.)

2.17 Tip: *Use logical fields for items that can only have one of two possible values.*

A logical field is one column wide, and it contains either .T. or .F. Use a logical field when there are only two possible choices for the entries, such as yes/no, male/female, or positive/negative. For instance, in your mailing-list file you might include the logical field USE—FIRST, which would contain .T. if letters are to be written "Dear Tom" and .F. if "Dear Mr. Smith" should be used.

If you define a field to be logical, dBASE will do some important data-entry validation for you, since only T/t, F/f, Y/y, or N/n will be accepted into the field.

 2.18 Trap: *Logical fields can cause problems during the transfer of data from dBASE to other software.*

If you plan to use your file with a spreadsheet program or with other software packages, you may want to avoid using logical fields. (See Chapter 8 for specific traps concerning data transfer.) You can always use a character field of length 1 to hold the same kind of data as a logical field, and you can write a program routine to validate the entries (described in Chapter 3).

2.19 Tip: *Name a logical field with the condition that must be true or false for each record.*

A logical field name is often used as part of an expression that dBASE will evaluate as true or false. To help you remember what information is in a particular logical field and to make your programs easier to read, name each logical field with the condition that must be met for a record to have .T. in the field.

For example, in a checkbook system, IS—CLEAR would be a convenient field. It contains .F. for each check as it is written, which is changed to .T. when the check clears the bank. Then a program segment like this can be written:

```
IF IS_CLEAR
  <processing of a cleared check>
ELSE
  <processing of an uncleared check>
ENDIF
```

2.20 Tip: *When you are entering new data records, you can just press RETURN if you need .F. in a logical field.*

dBASE uses a default value of .F. in a logical field; as soon as you begin to append a new record, dBASE places .F. in any logical fields in the record.

If you add a logical field to an existing file with **MODIFY STRUCTURE** (see the section "Changing the Structure of a File" later in this chapter), dBASE will automatically place .F. in the field for all existing records.

2.21 Tip: *Use a memo field to hold information associated with a data record that is too long to store in a character field.*

A character field can hold as many as 254 characters. You can store longer entries in a memo field. Each memo field has two parts:

- The text of the memo, which is stored in a separate file on your disk. This file has the same name as the database file, with the extension .DBT (database text). It holds all the memos for the file.

- A pointer, which tells dBASE where to find the memo for this particular record in the .DBT file. The pointer occupies ten spaces and is stored in the memo field of your database file.

2.22 Tip: *dBASE provides a word processor to use when you write in memo fields.*

To access the contents of a memo field, place the cursor on that field on the data-entry screen and press CTRL-PGDN. The screen will clear, and you'll see "dBASE Word Processor" at the top of the screen.

The arrow keys and the INS, DEL, TAB, PGUP, and PGDN keys all work as usual in this mode. You can also use END to move to the next word and HOME to move to the previous word. Each line is limited to 70 characters; once that limit has been reached, dBASE automatically begins a new line as you write.

See the following trap.

2.23 Trap: *The dBASE Word Processor does not automatically correct line lengths when you make changes in a memo field using INS or DEL.*

You can overcome this limitation by placing the cursor in the paragraph and pressing CTRL-KB; dBASE will then reformat all lines from the cursor position to the end of the paragraph.

 2.24 Trap: *If your entry into a memo field is too long, you will lose data.*

The dBASE Word Processor can only handle files up to 4000 characters long, about two full screens of data. If you enter more than this, dBASE will display this warning at the top of the screen: "File too large—some data may be lost". However, the program will not beep or stop accepting input. If you are not watching the top line of the screen, you can very easily miss this message. When the memo is saved, it will be truncated to 4000 characters.

See the following tip.

 2.25 Tip: *If you configure dBASE to use an external word processor, you can avoid the risk that memo entries will be truncated and you can take advantage of the editing features of the word processor.*

You can get around the limitations of the dBASE Word Processor—the 4000-character file-size limit, the lack of block editing, the absence of search and replace functions, and the like—by configuring dBASE to use an external word processor whenever you access a memo field. See Chapter 1 for a discussion of the use of an external word processor with dBASE.

2.26 Trap: *dBASE cannot SORT or INDEX a file using a memo field for the key field.*

If you tell dBASE to INDEX ON a memo field, you will get the error message "Operation with MEMO-type field invalid". If you tell dBASE to SORT ON a memo field, you will be told "Data type mismatch".

See the following two tips.

2.27 Tip: *If you'd like to access records in your file by the contents of a memo field, use a KEY__WORDS field to indicate the contents of the memo.*

Suppose you want to store references to journal articles, including title, author, publication, date, page, and an abstract of the contents, in a database file. The abstracts will be stored in a memo field.

In order to locate references to various topics, you need to be able to access records by the contents of this memo field. When you create the file structure (using the **CREATE** command), include a **KEY__WORDS** field, which is a character field containing a list of the topics covered in each article. Then you can ask dBASE to

```
DISPLAY FOR "ELEPHANT" $ KEY_WORDS
```

and dBASE will show you all records with "ELEPHANT" contained in the list of topics. (See Chapter 4 for tips and traps on accessing data.)

2.28 Trap: *You cannot access a memo field in BROWSE mode or with @...SAY...GET under program control; you cannot use REPLACE or UPDATE to change the contents of a memo field.*

Access to memo fields is limited; you must be in **APPEND, EDIT, CHANGE,** or **INSERT** mode, and you must press CTRL-PGDN, which clears the rest of the record from the screen and displays only the contents of the memo field. You cannot use **REPLACE** or **UPDATE** to change the contents of a memo field; you must access the field as explained above and enter data directly from the keyboard.

Choose a memo field only when you need to store long data entries and you don't need frequent access to the data.

 2.29 Trap: *Memo fields use a lot of disk space.*

dBASE stores memo fields in a separate disk file that is associated with the database file. It takes much more disk space to use memo fields than character fields. Use a memo field only when this seems to be an appropriate use of disk space. See the following tip.

2.30 Tip: *Use a character field instead of a memo field anytime you can limit entries to fewer than 255 characters.*

A character field can be as many as 254 characters long, and it is easy to display, edit, search for, and so on. Consider this **CONTACTS** database:

```
. DISPLAY STRUCTURE
Structure for database : B:contacts.dbf
Number of data records :      84
Date of last update    : 01/01/80
Field  Field name  Type       Width    Dec
    1  L_NAME      Character     15
    2  F_NAME      Character     15
    3  COMPANY     Character     18
    4  STREET      Character     18
    5  CITY        Character     15
    6  STATE       Character      2
    7  ZIP         Character      5
    8  AREA_CODE   Character      3
    9  PHONE       Character      8
   10  DATE_1      Date           8
   11  CALL_1      Character    254
   12  DATE_2      Date           8
   13  CALL_2      Character    254
** Total **                    624
.
```

The file structure includes two maximum-length character fields to hold notes on phone calls. Here is the custom screen used to append and edit data (see Chapter 6).

```
Date: [ /  / ] Notes: [

                                                                        ]

Date: [ /  / ] Notes: [

                                                                        ]

Last Name: [              ]       First Name: [           ]

   Company: [               ]
    Street: [               ]
      City: [           ]       State: [ ] Zip: [       ]

 Area code: [    ]     Phone: [    -    ]
```

There is enough room in each Notes field to include a lot of information. Character fields are easy to access and edit, and you can view all of the data in the record at once, rather than having to move in and out of the memo field to see the phone number (as indicated in Trap 2.28).

Using Another File's Structure or Data

2.31 Tip: *If you have a database file with the fields that you need for a new file, create the new file in one step with COPY STRUCTURE.*

COPY STRUCTURE will create a new database file that contains no records and has the same structure as all or part of an existing file.

Let's say you have a file named CLIENTS that contains fields for the last name, first name, company name, address, and phone number of each of your clients. You would like to create another database file to hold the same information about prospective clients.

The file in use must be the *source file,* the file with the structure you want to copy. Enter the following:

```
USE CLIENTS

COPY STRUCTURE TO PROSPECT
```

dBASE will create a new file named PROSPECT, with exactly the same fields as CLIENTS but without any records.

If you have several clients at each company, you might decide to keep the company name and address data in a separate file, and use a company code to relate the COMPANY file to CLIENTS. (See the section called "Designing an Application System" earlier in this chapter for tips and traps on deciding which data items should be placed in separate, related files.) You can use COPY STRUCTURE to copy selected fields from the CLIENTS database file:

```
USE CLIENTS

COPY STRUCTURE TO COMPANY FIELDS CO_NAME, STREET, CITY, STATE,;
   ZIP
```

This time, dBASE will create a file named COMPANY that contains the five fields listed in the command.

2.32 Tip: *To duplicate all or part of the structure and data of an existing file, use COPY TO.*

Here is the structure of a database file named IN—PRICE, which is part of a purchasing/inventory system:

```
. DISPLAY STRUCTURE
Structure for database : B:IN_PRICE.dbf
Number of data records :      50
Date of last update    : 08/15/85
Field  Field name  Type         Width    Dec
    1  PART_CODE   Character       6
    2  VEND_CODE   Character       6
    3  PRICE       Numeric         6      2
** Total **                      19
```

This file is used to keep a current price for each inventory item. There are 3 fields, as shown, and 50 records in the file.

The application system will use another file, called IN—PARTS, which will contain a brief description of each inventory item and the quantity on hand. This file will be related to IN—PRICE by the PART—CODE field. If you use COPY TO, you can begin to create IN—PARTS from the structure and data of IN—PRICE:

```
. USE IN_PRICE
.
. COPY TO IN_PARTS FIELD PART_CODE
     50 records copied
.
. USE IN_PARTS
.
. DISPLAY STRUCTURE
Structure for database : B:IN_PARTS.dbf
Number of data records :        50
Date of last update    : 08/15/85
Field  Field name  Type       Width    Dec
    1  PART_CODE   Character      6
** Total **                       7
.
```

A new file is created, named IN_PARTS, which has one field called PART_
CODE and already contains 50 records: the PART_CODE field was copied from
each record in the source file.

Use MODIFY STRUCTURE to add the other fields you want in your new
file (see the next section, "Changing the Structure of a File").

Be sure to read the following trap.

 2.33 Trap: *If you try to use COPY TO to add records or fields to an
existing file, you will lose the contents of that file.*

You cannot use COPY TO to add data to a file that already has records in it, even
if the files have the same structure. If you try to use COPY TO to add to a file that
is already on your disk and SET SAFETY is ON, dBASE will warn you that the
file already exists and ask if you want to overwrite it. If you answer yes, the file
will be erased. If SET SAFETY is OFF, the file will be erased with no warning
message. In either case, a new file containing the fields and records specified in
your COPY TO command will take its place.

If you need to add data to an existing file, see the tips and traps on APPEND
FROM, beginning with the following tip.

You also cannot use COPY TO to add fields to a file that already has a
defined structure. If you need to add fields to an existing file, see the next section,
"Changing the Structure of a File."

COPY TO is effective as a tool only for transferring data from an existing
database file to a new file.

2.34 Tip: *To add data from another file without overwriting the
existing database file receiving it, use APPEND FROM.*

Planning Applications and Establishing Databases

APPEND FROM is used to copy selected data from another file to the one in use (the target file). Such copying has no impact on the structure of the target file; instead, APPEND FROM fits the new data into the existing structure of the target file. The copied records are added to the end of the file.

To use APPEND FROM effectively, keep in mind that the structure of the target file determines which fields will be copied from the source file. Only fields that have the same name and are of the same data type in both files will be copied.

Use the following to copy the common fields of all records in the source file:

```
USE <target file>

APPEND FROM <source file>
```

You can also use APPEND FROM to copy selected records, as the following example shows. In a checkbook system, each check is entered into the file named CHECKS when it is written:

```
. DISPLAY STRUCTURE
Structure for database : A:CHECKS.dbf
Number of data records :      15
Date of last update     : 12/17/85
Field  Field name  Type       Width    Dec
    1   CHK_NO      Character     4
    2   CHK_DATE    Date          8
    3   PAY_TO      Character     15
    4   CHK_AMOUNT  Numeric       8       2
    5   IS_CLEAR    Logical       1
    6   CATEGORY    Character     15
** Total **                      52

.
. LIST FOR RECNO() < 7
Record#  CHK_NO CHK_DATE PAY_TO          CHK_AMOUNT IS_CLEAR CATEGORY
    1    501    02/11/85 CORNER STORE          2.85 .F.      INCIDENTALS
    2    502    02/12/85 MARCY'S             259.01 .F.      CLOTHES
    3    503    02/12/85 SMITH'S               8.15 .F.      ALLOWANCE
    4    504    02/13/85 DB DRUGS              9.38 .F.      INCIDENTALS
    5    505    02/13/85 XYZ SUPERMARKET      71.65 .F.      FOOD
    6    506    02/14/85 KATHY REED           72.00 .F.      HOUSECLEAN
.
```

When each check is written the logical field IS—CLEAR contains .F., which is changed to .T. when the check clears the bank.

After each bank statement is reconciled, the cleared checks are moved to another file, CL—CHECK, which has exactly the same structure as CHECKS. The following procedure moves the cleared checks from CHECKS to CL—CHECK:

```
USE CL_CHECK

APPEND FROM CHECKS FOR IS_CLEAR
```

```
USE CHECKS

DELETE FOR IS_CLEAR

PACK
```

Be sure to read the following trap and tip.

 2.35 Trap: *You cannot use APPEND FROM with a FOR condition that involves a field that is not common to both files.*

Let's look again at the checkbook system just discussed. Here is the structure of **CHECKS** and a listing of the first six records:

```
. DISPLAY STRUCTURE
Structure for database : A:CHECKS.dbf
Number of data records :        15
Date of last update    : 12/17/85
Field  Field name    Type         Width    Dec
    1  CHK_NO        Character       4
    2  CHK_DATE      Date            8
    3  PAY_TO        Character      15
    4  CHK_AMOUNT    Numeric         8       2
    5  IS_CLEAR      Logical         1
    6  CATEGORY      Character      15
** Total **                        52
```

```
.
. LIST FOR RECNO() < 7
Record#  CHK_NO  CHK_DATE  PAY_TO           CHK_AMOUNT  IS_CLEAR  CATEGORY
    1     501    02/11/85  CORNER STORE          2.85  .F.       INCIDENTALS
    2     502    02/12/85  MARCY'S             259.01  .T.       CLOTHES
    3     503    02/12/85  SMITH'S               8.15  .F.       ALLOWANCE
    4     504    02/13/85  DB DRUGS              9.38  .T.       INCIDENTALS
    5     505    02/13/85  XYZ SUPERMARKET      71.65  .F.       FOOD
    6     506    02/14/85  KATHY REED           72.00  .F.       HOUSECLEAN
.
```

There are two checks with .T. in IS—CLEAR. These checks have cleared the bank and need to be moved to CL—CHECK by the procedure in the preceding tip.

Let's try to Append the records using **CL—CHECK** without the IS— CLEAR field:

```
. DISPLAY STRUCTURE
Structure for database : B:CL_CHECK.dbf
Number of data records :        0
Date of last update    : 12/12/85
Field  Field name    Type         Width    Dec
    1  CHK_NO        Character       4
    2  CHK_DATE      Date            8
    3  PAY_TO        Character      15
    4  CHK_AMOUNT    Numeric         8       2
    5  CATEGORY      Character      15
```

```
** Total **                        51


.
. APPEND FROM CHECKS FOR IS_CLEAR
Variable not found
                                      ?
APPEND FROM CHECKS FOR IS_CLEAR
Do you want some help? (Y/N)
```

The APPEND FROM is unsuccessful because the FOR *condition* involves the
IS—CLEAR field; dBASE will accept only common fields in APPEND FROM
...FOR *condition*.

You can modify the structure of CL—CHECK (see the next section, "Changing the Structure of a File") to include the logical field, and the APPEND FROM procedure will then be successful:

```
. DISPLAY STRUCTURE
Structure for database : C:CL_CHECK.dbf
Number of data records :        0
Date of last update    : 12/17/85
Field   Field name  Type        Width    Dec
    1   CHK_NO      Character       4
    2   CHK_DATE    Date            8
    3   PAY_TO      Character      15
    4   CHK_AMOUNT  Numeric         8      2
    5   IS_CLEAR    Logical         1
    6   CATEGORY    Character      15
** Total **                       52


.
. APPEND FROM CHECKS FOR IS_CLEAR
     2 records added
.
. LIST
Record#  CHK_NO CHK_DATE PAY_TO          CHK_AMOUNT IS_CLEAR CATEGORY
     1   502    03/20/85 MARCY'S            259.01  .T.      CLOTHES
     2   504    03/24/25 DB DRUGS             9.38  .T.      INCIDENTALS
.
```

If you want to append selected records by using APPEND FROM with a FOR *condition*, be sure all fields involved in the condition are common to both files. See the following tip.

2.36 Tip: *If the field involved in APPEND FROM with FOR condition is not needed in your new file, APPEND in two steps with a TEMP file.*

As explained in the preceding trap, using the field IS—CLEAR in the FOR *condition* forces you to include the field IS—CLEAR in CL—CHECK. But it's inefficient to keep IS—CLEAR in CL—CHECK; all of the checks in this file have cleared the bank, so every record would have .T. in this field. You can avoid keeping an unnecessary field by appending in two steps with a TEMP file.

When you create the CL—CHECK file, do not include IS—CLEAR:

```
USE CHECKS

COPY STRUCTURE TO CL_CHECK FIELDS CHK_NO, CHK_DATE, PAY_TO,;
 CHK_AMOUNT, CATEGORY
```

To move the cleared checks into this file, first copy them into TEMP by using the COPY command:

```
USE CHECKS

COPY TO TEMP FOR IS_CLEAR
```

Now move the checks from TEMP to CL—CHECK:

```
USE CL_CHECK

APPEND FROM TEMP
```

You can APPEND everything in TEMP, since the only records in that file are the ones with .T. in IS—CLEAR. APPEND copies data into matching fields only; since CL—CHECKS has no IS—CLEAR field, that data will be skipped during the APPEND procedure.

Finally, remove the cleared checks from CHECKS:

```
USE CHECKS

DELETE FOR IS_CLEAR

PACK
```

You can write a dBASE program that will move the cleared checks for you (see Chapter 9); dBASE can do all of these steps under program control.

 2.37 Trap: *If you try to APPEND data into fields that are too small, you will lose data.*

If a field in your target file is shorter than its corresponding field in your source file, you will lose data:

- If a character field is too short, the copied data will be truncated.

- If a numeric field is too short, the numbers will be replaced with asterisks.

- If a numeric field has too few decimal places to hold the copied numbers, the digits to the right of the decimal point will be truncated.

Be sure to double-check the lengths of the fields in your files before you use the APPEND command on your data. Here is an easy way to do this:

```
USE <source file>
DISPLAY STRUCTURE TO PRINT
USE <target file>
DISPLAY STRUCTURE TO PRINT
```

Now you can compare the lengths of the common fields.

If you need to increase the size of a field in your target file, use MODIFY STRUCTURE (see the next section, "Changing the Structure of a File.)".

 2.38 Trap: *You cannot use APPEND FROM with a WHILE condition.*

Both the dBASE manual and the HELP screen for APPEND FROM show optional FOR and WHILE *condition* clauses in the command structure.

If you try using a WHILE *condition* with APPEND FROM, dBASE will respond with "Unrecognized phrase/keyword in command" and will not append data. Instead, use a FOR *condition*, as explained earlier in this section.

 2.39 Trap: *If you have records that are marked for deletion, they will not be copied by either COPY TO or APPEND FROM.*

COPY TO and APPEND FROM both skip records that are marked for deletion. Before using either of these commands, you can check your source file to see if there are entries marked for deletion (with *). Just use the source file and tell dBASE to

```
DISPLAY FOR DELETED()
```

You will see a listing of all the records that are marked; if you want any of these records to be copied to the target file, just RECALL them before you COPY TO or APPEND FROM.

See the section called "Deleting Records" in Chapter 3.

Changing the Structure of a File

2.40 Tip: *You can add or delete fields, or change the structure of a field, with MODIFY STRUCTURE.*

As you work with a database file, you may realize that certain tasks would be easier if you added another field to the file, or that a particular field should have a different name, a different length, or even a different data type. The tool for these changes is MODIFY STRUCTURE.

Figure 2-1 shows the structure of a database file named CHECKS. To see how MODIFY STRUCTURE works, let's make some changes in CHECKS.

When you tell dBASE to MODIFY STRUCTURE, you are presented with the screen that you used to create the file, with the current structure listed:

```
B:checks.dbf                                Bytes remaining:    3950
                                            Fields defined:        6

        field name   type      width  dec     field name   type      width  dec

     1  CHK_NO       Char/text     3
     2  DATE         Date          8
     3  PAY_TO       Char/text    15
     4  CHK_AMOUNT   Numeric       8    2
     5  IS_CLEAR     Logical       1
     6  CATEGORY     Char/text    15




Names start with a letter; the remainder may be letters, digits, or underscore
```

You can move freely around this screen, making the changes you need. A small HELP menu will be displayed if you press F1.

When you begin MODIFY STRUCTURE, dBASE creates a backup copy of

```
Structure for database : B:CHECKS.dbf
Number of data records :      15
Date of last update    : 12/12/85
Field  Field name  Type        Width    Dec
    1  CHK_NO      Character      3
    2  DATE        Date           8
    3  PAY_TO      Character     15
    4  CHK_AMOUNT  Numeric        8      2
    5  IS_CLEAR    Logical        1
    6  CATEGORY    Character     15
** Total **                      51
```

Figure 2-1. The CHECKS database file

your database file—in this example, CHECKS.BAK. The records are stored in the .BAK file while you make changes in the file structure.

When you are finished, you have three options: press CTRL-END or CTRL-W, or with the cursor on a new field, press RETURN, and the data records will be appended back into the modified file. The .BAK file remains on your disk; after you are sure the MODIFY STRUCTURE operation was successful, you can delete this file if you need the disk space.

Using MODIFY STRUCTURE to make changes in existing fields can be tricky; be sure to read the rest of the traps and tips in this section.

 2.41 Trap: *If you try to use MODIFY STRUCTURE to make more than one type of change in existing fields at the same time, you risk losing data.*

There are two distinct categories of changes that can be made to existing fields with MODIFY STRUCTURE:

- Field name
- Field width, decimal width, or data type.

If you try to make both types of changes in your file structure at the same time — even if you do not make both types of changes to any one field — you will lose the data in any field whose name was changed.

2.42 Tip: *Always read the message line before you complete the execution of a MODIFY STRUCTURE command; dBASE will warn you if there is a chance you might lose data.*

When you finish making changes on the MODIFY STRUCTURE screen, dBASE displays a message at the bottom of the screen, giving you the option of changing your mind. There are two possible messages.

Figure 2-2 shows the response to changing the width of field 1, with no other changes: "Database records will be COPIED from backup for all fields". When you get this message, you can be confident that no data will be lost unless you are trying to make changes involving a memo field. (See the trap that follows the next tip.)

Figure 2-3 shows the response to changing the name of field 2 and the width of field 1: "Database records will be APPENDED from backup fields of the same name only!!" This message is always displayed if you make changes in field width, decimal width, or data type. If you have not changed any field names or made changes involving a memo field, you will not lose data. If your modifications include changes to field names or involve a memo field, the data in each renamed field will be lost.

Press RETURN if you want dBASE to go ahead and change your file structure; press another key to go back into the MODIFY STRUCTURE screen, followed by ESC if you want to abandon the process altogether.

See the following tip.

```
   B:CHECKS.dbf                              INSERT    Bytes remaining:   3949
                                                       Fields defined:       6

          field name   type     width  dec        field name   type     width  dec

       1  CHK_NO       Char/text    4
       2  CHK_DATE     Date         8
       3  PAY_TO       Char/text   15
       4  CHK_AMOUNT   Numeric      8    2
       5  IS_CLEAR     Logical      1
       6  CATEGORY     Char/text   15








   Database records will be COPIED from backup for all fields
   Hit RETURN to confirm--any other key to resume
```

Figure 2-2. Using MODIFY STRUCTURE to change a field name

2.43 Tip: *You can make more than one type of change in a field structure without losing data if you use MODIFY STRUCTURE more than once, making single changes in succession.*

If you need to make changes in a field name and in another field property (see the preceding trap), you can avoid losing data by making each type of change separately.

Figure 2-1 shows the structure of a database file named CHECKS. Two changes need to be made, as shown in the MODIFY STRUCTURE screen in Figure 2-2:

- The check-number field, CHK__NO, needs to be made wider to hold check numbers with four digits.

- The name of the field DATE in Figure 2-1 needs to be changed to CHK__ DATE to distinguish check dates from deposit dates.

Notice what happens in Figure 2-3, when both modifications are attempted at once: the message at the bottom of the screen ("Database records will be APPENDED from backup fields of the same name only!!") indicates that the data in the DATE field will be lost.

```
 B:CHECKS.dbf                                Bytes remaining:   3949
                                             Fields defined:       6

        field name   type      width  dec    field name   type     width  dec

    1  CHK_NO       Char/text     4
    2  CHK_DATE     Date          8
    3  PAY_TO       Char/text    15
    4  CHK_AMOUNT   Numeric       8     2
    5  IS_CLEAR     Logical       1
    6  CATEGORY     Char/text    15




 Database records will be APPENDED from backup fields of the same name only!!
 Hit RETURN to confirm--any other key to resume
```

Figure 2-3. Using MODIFY STRUCTURE to change a field width

To avoid this, press any key except RETURN to go back up into the MODIFY STRUCTURE screen, and temporarily restore the name DATE to field 2. Press CTRL-END or CTRL-W and then press RETURN. All data will be appended back into the file, since all of the fields have their original names.

Now tell dBASE to MODIFY STRUCTURE again, and this time change the field name DATE to CHK—DATE. dBASE will respond as shown in Figure 2-2, and again no data will be lost.

 2.44 Trap: *If you change a memo field to a character field, or a character field to a memo field, you will lose the data in that field.*

Here is the structure of TEST:

```
. DISPLAY STRUCTURE
Structure for database : B:TEST.dbf
Number of data records :        3
Date of last update    : 12/12/85
Field  Field name  Type       Width     Dec
    1  CHAR_FIELD  Character     10
    2  MEMO_FIELD  Memo          10
** Total **                      21


.
. LIST CHAR_FIELD, MEMO_FIELD
Record#   CHAR_FIELD MEMO_FIELD
       1  little 1   small 1
       2  little 2   small 2
       3  little 3   small 3
.
```

Note the character field named CHAR—FIELD of length 10, and the memo field named MEMO—FIELD. There are three records in the file.

You can change the type of each field, as shown here:

```
B:TEST.dbf                            INSERT    Bytes remaining:  3980
                                                Fields defined:      2


    field name  type    width  dec       field name   type     width  dec

 1  CHAR_FIELD  Memo      10
 2  MEMO_FIELD  Char/text 10
```

```
Database records will be APPENDED from backup fields of the same name only!!
Hit RETURN to confirm--any other key to resume
```

No field names were changed, and the entries in MEMO—FIELD are short enough to fit into a character field of length 10.

However, this is one situation where the message from dBASE is inaccurate: you are told that data will be appended from fields of the same name, but it is not:

```
. DISPLAY STRUCTURE
Structure for database : B:TEST.dbf
Number of data records :        3
Date of last update    : 12/12/85
Field  Field name  Type      Width     Dec
    1  CHAR_FIELD  Memo         10
    2  MEMO_FIELD  Character    10
** Total **                     21


.
. LIST CHAR_FIELD, MEMO_FIELD
Record#   CHAR_FIELD                                   MEMO_FIELD
    1
    2
    3
.
```

All data was lost.

2.45 Tip: *If you are not satisfied with the results of a MODIFY STRUCTURE command, you can get the original file back by renaming the .BAK file.*

Whenever you enter MODIFY STRUCTURE, dBASE creates a backup copy of your file on the default disk, with the same filename and the extension .BAK. This file remains on your disk unless you erase it.

If you are not pleased with the results of a MODIFY STRUCTURE command, use the .BAK file to get back to the file you had before you began the modifications:

1. Erase the unsatisfactory file:

```
USE       (to close the file; dBASE will not delete
           an open file)

ERASE <filename>.DBF
```

2. Rename your backup file:

```
RENAME <filename>.BAK TO <filename>.DBF
```

3

Entering and
Updating Data

Entering your information into database files and keeping records updated are two critical steps in data management. dBASE III enables you to do both quickly and efficiently.

The previous chapter discussed the processes of getting a database file ready to accept records: planning a system of related databases, setting up each individual file, and working with different types of fields within a file. This chapter focuses on the processes of getting your data into the file and keeping it current once it's there.

dBASE provides several operating modes of data entry, and you will work most efficiently if you choose the best mode for a particular task. The chapter presents tips and traps on writing your own dBASE programs to perform data-entry and updating tasks; these programs can limit the user's access to confidential data and test the data that is entered before it is placed into your files.

Guidelines for Entering and Updating Data

3.01 Tip: *Any one of several commands puts you in full-screen oper-ating mode in data-entry and editing functions.*

dBASE places you in full-screen operating mode whenever you enter APPEND, EDIT, BROWSE, INSERT, or CHANGE. All of the data-entry areas that appear on the screen are available to you; you can use the cursor keys to move around the screen, making entries or changes wherever you need them. You can change the contents of a field by writing over it or by inserting and deleting letters with the INS and DEL keys. dBASE also provides control codes to speed up movement around the screen and through your file. If you press F1, dBASE will display a small menu of these codes on part of the screen.

3.02 Trap: *Don't exit from a data-entry or editing mode with ESC or CTRL-Q unless you do not want dBASE to save the entry you just made.*

dBASE offers two ways to exit the various full-screen operating modes, and it is imperative to use them appropriately:

- ESC and CTRL-Q are used to abort and exit. Either command has the following consequences. If you are adding data records to your file, the new record that is on the screen will not be saved. If you are editing records, no changes you have made to the record on the screen will be saved. If you are writing in a memo field, nothing you have entered since you accessed that field will be saved. Use ESC or CTRL-Q only if you want the current display to revert to its original contents.

- CTRL-END and CTRL-W are used to SAVE and exit. In all situations, your work will be saved.

It's a good idea to form a habit of using one of these commands every time you exit a data-entry or update mode. CTRL-END is easy to remember as the correct way to end your work, and it is effective in all modes of dBASE, including MODIFY COMMAND.

■ *3.03 Trap: Never make changes to your data without first having backed up your file.*

Whenever a file is open, it is vulnerable to error — human error, hardware malfunction, software bugs, fluctuations in the power supply, and the like. Always protect your data by making a backup copy of your file before you change the data. The only time dBASE automatically makes a backup copy of a database file is when you use MODIFY STRUCTURE; the rest of the time, it's up to you. The first time the unexpected happens, you'll be very glad you consistently made backups.

■ *3.04 Trap: If you enter data into your file immediately after you CREATE it, you lose the option of having dBASE automatically index the records for you.*

When you CREATE a file, dBASE will give you the option of entering data records after all of the fields are defined. If you choose to do so, you will have lost the chance to INDEX your new file most efficiently. See the following tip.

3.05 Tip: INDEX your database file before you enter any data.

An *index* is a special file created and maintained in association with a database file. The index file allows you to quickly locate and process a particular record or group of records. See Chapter 4 for a detailed discussion of index files.

The quickest way to establish an index file is to create it when the database is empty. Then dBASE does not have to spend time indexing existing records, but can quickly place each record in the index as it is entered.

Let's say you have just finished creating the structure of MAIL—LST (to hold your mailing list), and you want the records ordered alphabetically by last name, with duplicate last names in order by first name. Tell dBASE to

```
INDEX ON L_NAME + F_NAME TO ML_NAME
```

on the empty file, and the index will quickly be created. Each time you enter or update data, tell dBASE to

```
USE MAIL_LST INDEX ML_NAME
```

and the index will be automatically updated with each entry.

✋ *3.06 Trap:* *If you make changes in or additions to your database file without activating the index, your index file will not be updated to include the changes or additions.*

Whenever you add new records or make changes in existing records, you want dBASE to update the index to reflect these changes. If you forget to keep the index file current, you won't be able to use it for finding and processing selected data.

Whenever you work with a database file that has an index, tell dBASE to

```
USE <filename> INDEX <indexname>
```

and your index file will be updated as you work.

If you think an index is not correct (this may be the case if you cannot list all of the records, or if you get a "Record is out of range" message), tell dBASE to REINDEX, and the index file will be recreated for you.

💡 *3.07 Tip:* *Use a custom input screen to make data entry and updating easier and more accurate.*

You can design a custom input screen to suit your particular database application. To make it easier for an inexperienced dBASE user to enter and update data, you can supply expanded prompts for each field or even design the screen to look like

```
      Record No.      19
      CHK_NO      [    ]
      CHK_DATE    [  /  /  ]
      PAY_TO      [              ]
      CHK_AMOUNT  [     .   ]
      IS CLEAR    [?]
      CATEGORY    [              ]
```

Figure 3-1. The standard dBASE APPEND screen

the input documents. You can include any messages you wish on a custom screen, and you can provide preformatted data-entry guides to help in validating the data.

Figures 3-1 and 3-2 show two screens using the file CHECKS in APPEND mode. Figure 3-1 shows a standard dBASE screen, and Figure 3-2 shows a custom screen. Several points are worth noticing about the custom screen:

- A brief heading is displayed that identifies the purpose of this screen.

- The prompts are expanded from field names to full English words.

- The $ sign is placed in front of the data-entry area for the amount of the check. Since CHK_AMOUNT is a numeric field, dBASE will not accept $ as part of the entry; having $ already on the screen reminds the user to enter only numbers.

- The IS_CLEAR field is omitted; all new checks require .F. in this field, and dBASE will enter .F. into a logical field automatically (see the tips and traps on logical data in Chapter 2). There is no need to see this field when checks are entered, and leaving it off the screen saves the typist some time.

- An instruction line clearly describes the procedure for an inexperienced user.

Custom input screens can be very helpful in data entry and updating, particularly if you are setting up a system for someone else to use.

See Chapter 6 for tips and traps on designing and using custom input screens.

```
        **ENTER A NEW CHECK**


   Check number: [    ]    Date of check: [  /  /  ]


   Check written to: [               ]


   Amount of check: $ [     .   ]


   Expense Category: [   ]



   **PRESS Ctrl-End WHEN ALL NEW CHECKS HAVE BEEN ENTERED**
```

Figure 3-2. A custom input screen in APPEND mode

3.08 Tip: *Most data-entry and update modes can use a custom screen defined by a format file.*

If you begin working with the file CHECKS by telling dBASE to

```
SET FORMAT TO CHECK_IN
```

then every time you enter APPEND, EDIT, INSERT, or CHANGE mode, dBASE will use the custom screen defined by the format file CHECK_IN.FMT.

See Chapter 6 for tips and traps on writing and using format files.

3.09 Tip: *Use SET CARRY ON to avoid repetitive typing.*

If you are entering data records with a lot of repetition, such as a mailing list with many addresses in the same city, you will save time if you use the SET CARRY ON command. Each time you enter a new record, dBASE will display the contents of the previous record, and you only need to change those fields in which different data must be entered.

Suppose you are entering names into your mailing list, and you have a number of addresses in Alameda. Figures 3-3 and 3-4 show two different approaches to this task. Both figures show the same custom screen in APPEND

```
                   *** EDITING MAILING LIST ***

    Title (Mr.,Ms.,etc.): [    ]
    First Name: [            ]     Last Name: [            ]


    Company: [            ]

    Street Address: [            ]
      City: [          ]        State: [  ]    Zip: [      ]


    Phone: [ (   )   -     ]      Use first name? (y/n) [?]

            *** Enter ^END When Finished Editing ***
```

Figure 3-3. An APPEND screen

mode; the screen is defined in a format file and activated with SET FORMAT TO. (See Chapter 6 for tips and traps on using custom input screens.) Figure 3-3 shows the input screen without CARRY; you must enter data into all of the fields. Figure 3-4 shows the screen with SET CARRY ON; a new record is displayed with the contents of the previous record. You can skip over the CITY, STATE, and ZIP fields by just pressing RETURN.

Be sure to read the following trap.

3.10 Trap: *If you have SET CARRY ON, don't press* RETURN *at the beginning of a record unless you are finished entering data, or dBASE will exit APPEND mode.*

Figure 3-4 shows the screen at the start of entering a new record with SET CARRY ON; each field contains the entry from the previous record, and the cursor is in the first position of the first field (under the "M" in "Mr."). If you want this first field to remain the same as in the last record, you must move the cursor out of this position with an arrow key before you press RETURN. dBASE interprets a RETURN at the beginning of the first field as a signal that you are finished entering data records.

You can use the down arrow key to move the cursor into the FIRST NAME field, and enter the new data for this record. When the cursor moves to the CITY field, just press RETURN to keep "Alameda" for this record.

```
┌─────────────────────────────────────────────────────────────────────┐
│              *** EDITING MAILING LIST ***                            │
│                                                                       │
│   Title (Mr.,Ms.,etc.): [MR. ]                                       │
│   First Name: [JAMES          ]       Last Name: [WILLIAMS        ]  │
│                                                                       │
│                                                                       │
│   Company: [AMERICAN TIRE CO.   ]                                    │
│                                                                       │
│   Street Address: [3422 EAST ST.      ]                             │
│     City: [ALAMEDA       ]            State: [CA]    Zip: [93826]    │
│                                                                       │
│                                                                       │
│   Phone: [(415)987-6543]              Use first name? (y/n) [T]      │
│                                                                       │
│           *** Enter ^END When Finished Editing ***                   │
└─────────────────────────────────────────────────────────────────────┘
```

Figure 3-4. An APPEND screen with SET CARRY ON

You must type an entry into at least one field of each new record; if you press RETURN on the first field, or on all subsequent fields, you signal that you have finished entering data into the file.

3.11 Tip: *If certain words or phrases will be entered many times, you can save time by entering an abbreviation and using REPLACE.*

This tip can save you lots of typing time. Say you are entering records into your mailing list, and many of the people on your list live in San Francisco, Los Angeles, or Sacramento. If your source documents list the records in alphabetical order by name, these cities appear scattered throughout the records, and SET CARRY ON (see the preceding tip and trap) will not be helpful.

Enter SF for San Francisco, LA for Los Angeles, and SAC for Sacramento into the CITY field. When all of your records have been entered, tell dBASE to

```
REPLACE ALL CITY WITH "San Francisco" FOR CITY = "SF"

REPLACE ALL CITY WITH "Los Angeles" FOR CITY = "LA"

REPLACE ALL CITY WITH "Sacramento" FOR CITY = "SAC"
```

Be sure to include "ALL" after the REPLACE command so that dBASE will make the change in all records with the matching abbreviation.

See Tip 3.22 and Trap 3.23 for more information on using REPLACE.

Data-Entry and Update Modes

3.12 Tip: *If you want to add new records and edit existing records in the same session, use APPEND.*

When you enter APPEND mode, dBASE positions you in a new record at the end of your database file. You can add new records, or by pressing PGUP you can move into the file to edit existing records.

APPEND is the only mode that offers you both of these options with a custom input screen. You can also edit existing records and add new records in BROWSE mode, but you are limited to the dBASE BROWSE screen. See the tips and traps on BROWSE mode later in this section.

✋ **3.13 Trap:** *If you try to add new records in EDIT mode, you will get an error message or be returned to the dot prompt.*

You cannot append new records to a file in EDIT mode; if you press PGDN at the last record in the indexed order, you will be returned to the dot prompt. If you tell dBASE to EDIT a record number that has not been assigned to a record, you will be told "End of file encountered".

Use APPEND mode to add records while using a custom input screen; use BROWSE mode to add records while viewing several records at once. See the tips and traps on each of these modes in this section.

💡 **3.14 Tip:** *If you want to review or change records in the order of the active index, use EDIT.*

When you enter EDIT mode, dBASE gives you access to the current record, that is, the record indicated by the record pointer. You can use the PGUP and PGDN keys to move through the file, and if an index file is active (see Trap 3.06), you will move in the indexed order.

You can also move the record pointer to a particular record before entering EDIT mode, as discussed later in this section.

💡 **3.15 Tip:** *If you want to review or change records in the order in which they were entered into the file, use the APPEND command with PGUP.*

Sometimes it is useful to access the records in an indexed file in the order in which they were entered into the file, rather than in the indexed order. For example, you might want to review the most recent entries or make a change in several records that were entered at the same time. dBASE assigns record numbers as the data is entered, so the earliest entries have the lowest numbers, and the most recently entered records have the highest numbers.

You could access records in record-number order by using EDIT without activating the index, but then none of the changes you made would be reflected in the index file. You would have to REINDEX and SET INDEX TO *indexname* before continuing to work with the file.

A better approach is to use APPEND with PGUP, which allows you to access records in record-number sequence while the index is active. APPEND with PGUP takes you through the file from the most recently entered records to the oldest records, and any changes that you make will be reflected in the active index file.

3.16 Tip: *To change records or add new records while viewing several records at once, use BROWSE.*

Figure 3-5 shows the screen that is displayed while you are in BROWSE mode. Notice that 11 different records are displayed, but only the first 5 fields of each record are displayed. BROWSE will fill the screen with as many fields as possible; you can access the other fields by using CTRL-right arrow and CTRL-left arrow. To access other records, just move the cursor with the arrow keys or with RETURN. If you press F1, a menu of cursor control keys and insert and delete codes will be displayed at the top of the screen, as shown in Figure 3-5.

If you try to move below the last record in the indexed order, dBASE will ask if you want to append records to the file. If you choose to do so, you will enter the records into the BROWSE screen display; you cannot use BROWSE with a custom input screen.

Be sure to read the following tip and trap on BROWSE mode.

3.17 Tip: *BROWSE has functions that make editing faster and easier.*

If you press CTRL-HOME in BROWSE mode, you will see a list of special functions on the top line of the screen. Just place the cursor on the function you want and press RETURN; if a function requires specific input, dBASE will prompt you

```
Record No.     116    MAIL_LST

CURSOR    <-- -->           UP  DOWN      DELETE       Insert Mode:   Ins
  Char:     ← →    Record:     ↑    ↓ Char: Del   Exit:        ^End
  Field: Home End   Page:  PgUp PgDn    Field: ^Y    Abort:          Esc
  Pan:       ^^     Help:   F1           Record: ^U  Set Options: ^Home

  TITLE L_NAME--------  F_NAME--------- CO_NAME------- STREET--------
  MR.   BUCKLEY         THOMAS          DIABLO WRECKERS 630 HILL AVE.
  MRS.  CASPER          CAROLYN         QUALITY TUNE-UP 124 MARKET ST.
  MRS.  CLARK           CATHERINE       SUPERTUNE      710 A ST.
  MR.   COOPER          HARRY           VALLEY IMPORT  31 BETA CT.
  MS.   CRAIG           DIANE           AMERICAN TIRE  3422 EAST ST.
  MISS  CRANDELL        LUCILLE         PIONEER TIRE   121 CAMINO REAL
  MR.   DAILEY          JIM             DANVILLE IMPORT 67 FRONT ST.
  MR.   DE VIRA         WILLIAM         A-1 SERVICE    1433 MAZDA DR.
  MR.   DEEGAN          LEROY           AUTO CLINIC    411 AMADOR ST.
  MR.   DEWALL          TIMOTHY         THE REPAIR SHOP 7102 TICE WAY
  MS.   DOUGLAS         BARBARA         ADAMS & BOSCH  3105 IVY DR.
```

Figure 3-5. The BROWSE screen

for it. The available functions are

- *Bottom.* Move to the last record in the indexed order.

- *Top.* Move to the first record in the indexed order.

- *Lock.* Fix one or more fields on the left side of the screen while the other fields pan right or left. (In Figure 3-5, for example, it would be helpful to fix the two left-hand fields so the last names remain on the screen while you move through the other fields of the records.)

- *Record#.* Move to a particular record.

- *Freeze.* Make changes in one field only. Freeze restricts the cursor to the specified field; without Freeze, the cursor can move to another field when you press RETURN.

- *Seek.* Locate a specific record by its entry in the index file. dBASE will ask you what to search for, and if it finds a match in the index file, it will move the cursor to that record. See the following trap.

You can use more than one of these functions to customize the screen for a particular task. For example, if you need to update a field that does not appear on the screen with L—NAME, use Lock to keep L—NAME on the screen, move the field you want to change into the position next to L—NAME, and Freeze the cursor to that field.

✋ *3.18 Trap:* *In BROWSE mode, the Seek function does not work like the dBASE command SEEK.*

To use the BROWSE Seek function, enter the contents of the key field of your active index for the record you want to locate. The Seek function differs from the SEEK command in that, with the BROWSE Seek function, you

- Do not use quotes around a character string
- Cannot search for the contents of a memory variable.

If you need more flexible searching options, locate records from the dot prompt and access them in EDIT mode (see the following tip).

3.19 Tip: *To access a particular record, locate the record with FIND, SEEK, or DISPLAY FOR and then use EDIT mode.*

EDIT gives you access to the record at the position of the record pointer; to update a particular record, just move the pointer to that record and enter EDIT mode. See Chapter 4 for tips and traps on locating a particular record.

Let's use some examples to demonstrate efficient ways to move the record pointer in different situations. Figure 3-6 shows the structure of a database file named IN __PRICE, part of a purchasing/inventory system. Each record contains the part code, vendor code, and price of an item in the inventory. The file is indexed on PART__CODE, and the index file is active.

Your first task is to change the price of an item whose part code is WI-108. Tell dBASE to

```
FIND WI-108
```

and the record pointer will be moved to the desired record. Enter EDIT to access the record.

When you know the contents of the index's key field for the record you want to locate, use FIND if the contents are a character string or SEEK if they are a numerical expression. (See the tips and traps on FIND and SEEK in Chapter 4.)

Now you want to change the price of another part, but this time you don't remember the part code. You do know that the part is purchased from XEC Company. Since the file is not indexed on vendor code, FIND will not work here; instead, tell dBASE to

```
DISPLAY FOR VEND_CODE = "XEC"
```

dBASE will show you each record that has XEC for the vendor code; if there are more than enough of them to fill the screen, dBASE will pause for a key press before continuing.

Find the record you want to access in the list, note the record number, and tell dBASE to

```
EDIT <record#>
```

This will move the record pointer and then place you in EDIT mode.

See the rest of the tips in this section for information on updating groups of related records.

3.20 Tip: *To access records that are grouped together in an indexed file, move the record pointer to the first record in the group and enter EDIT mode.*

When you need to access a group of related records, all of which have the same entry in the key field of your active index file, use EDIT with FIND or SEEK. For example, Figure 3-6 shows the structure of IN—PRICE, part of a purchasing/inventory system. The file is indexed on PART—CODE, and the index file is active.

If you need to update the prices of all of the widgets in your inventory, as shown in Figure 3-6, you can take advantage of their being grouped together in the indexed file, since each widget has a part code that begins with WI-. Tell dBASE to

```
FIND WI-
```

The record pointer will move to the first widget in the index. Use EDIT to access this record and PGDN to access each of the other widgets in your database file.

```
. DISPLAY STRUCTURE
Structure for database : B:IN_PRICE.dbf
Number of data records :       50
Date of last update    : 08/15/85
Field  Field name  Type        Width   Dec
    1  PART_CODE   Character       6
    2  VEND_CODE   Character       6
    3  PRICE       Numeric         6       2
** Total **                      19

.
. LIST FOR "WI" $ PART_CODE
Record#  PART_CODE  VEND_CODE   PRICE
      1  WI-102     ALAM         0.78
      2  WI-104     ALAM         0.97
      3  WI-105     ALAM         1.03
      4  WI-108     ALAM         1.16
      5  WI-111     ALAM         1.35
      6  WI-203     EBAY         1.67
      7  WI-211     EBAY         2.04
.
```

Figure 3-6.   The IN—PRICE file and selected records

3.21 Tip: *To access related records that are not grouped together by the index, use CHANGE FOR.*

Say you need to update records that all have a field with the same entry, but your file is not indexed on that field. The most efficient tool is **CHANGE FOR**.

Let's continue with the example that has been developed in the last two tips. Now your task is to update the prices for all inventory items purchased from the East Bay Company. Since the file is not indexed by vendor code, these records will not be grouped together in the indexed file. Tell dBASE to

```
CHANGE FOR VEND_CODE = "EBAY"
```

dBASE will present you in turn with each of the records that meet this condition.

3.22 Tip: *To make an identical change to the contents of specified fields in specified records, use REPLACE.*

If you need to make an identical change to many records, **REPLACE** is often the most efficient tool. Here are some situations in which **REPLACE** will save a lot of editing time:

- *Changing one field in all records.* Say your company has just raised all salaries 6%, and you would like to update your personnel records. The salaries for all employees are listed in a numeric field named SALARY. You don't have to access each record separately; just tell dBASE to

```
REPLACE ALL SALARY WITH SALARY*1.06
```

and each salary entry will be changed for you.

- *Changing one field in certain records.* Tom Smith, one of your salespeople, has been promoted, and Susan Parker has taken over Tom's clients. You need to update your CLIENTS file. The field S_PERSON holds the last name of the salespeople assigned to each client. You don't have to access each record separately; just enter

```
REPLACE ALL S_PERSON WITH "PARKER" FOR S_PERSON = "SMITH"
```

Note that you need to use the scope ALL to have dBASE check all of the records against the condition; if you omit ALL, dBASE will only check the current record.

- *Changing more than one field.* The XEC Company has put in a new, toll-free telephone line, and several of its people are in your CONTACTS database. All of these people have the same entry in the field CO—NAME, which holds company names, so you don't have to access each record separately. Tell dBASE to

```
REPLACE ALL AREA_CODE WITH "800", PHONE WITH "555-1111" FOR ;
CO_NAME = "XEC Co."
```

Note that the two different field changes are separated by a comma; more than one field change can be included in a REPLACE command as long as a comma is used to separate each one from the preceding one.

Be sure to read the following trap.

3.23 Trap: *If you use REPLACE ALL to change the contents of the key field of your index file, some—and perhaps many— of your records may not be processed.*

Figures 3-7 and 3-8 illustrate this trap. The database file CHECKS is indexed on the field CATEGORY, as shown in Figure 3-7. The two checks to ROP Catering

```
. USE CHECKS INDEX CHK_CAT
.
. LIST
Record#  CHK_NO CHK_DATE PAY_TO            CHK_AMOUNT IS_CLEAR CATEGORY
      3  503    03/21/85 SMITH'S                 8.15 .F.      ALLOWANCE
      7  507    03/25/85 ROP CATERING           21.35 .F.      ALLOWANCE
     10  511    03/30/85 ROP CATERING            4.53 .F.      ALLOWANCE
     12  513    03/30/85 READ 'EM BOOKS          9.05 .F.      ALLOWANCE
     14  515    03/31/85 SARAH WILLIAMS          7.50 .F.      BABYSITTING
      2  502    03/20/85 MARCY'S               259.01 .T.      CLOTHES
      5  505    03/24/85 XYZ SUPERMARKET        71.65 .F.      FOOD
      9  509    03/26/85 CORNER STORE           22.12 .F.      FOOD
     15  510    03/29/85 CORNER STORE           13.33 .F.      FOOD
      6  506    03/25/85 KATHY REED             72.00 .F.      HOUSECLEAN
      1  501    03/20/85 CORNER STORE            2.85 .F.      INCIDENTALS
      4  504    03/24/25 DB DRUGS                9.38 .T.      INCIDENTALS
      8  508    03/25/85 SMITH'S                13.75 .F.      INCIDENTALS
     11  512    03/30/85 XYZ DRUGS              10.10 .F.      INCIDENTALS
     13  514    03/31/85 CORNER STORE           10.78 .F.      INCIDENTALS
.
```

Figure 3-7.   The records in CHECKS.DBF

```
. REPLACE ALL CATEGORY WITH "FOOD" FOR PAY_TO = "ROP CATERING"
      1  record replaced
.
. LIST
Record#   CHK_NO  CHK_DATE  PAY_TO            CHK_AMOUNT  IS_CLEAR  CATEGORY
      3   503     03/21/85  SMITH'S                 8.15  .F.       ALLOWANCE
     10   511     03/30/85  ROP CATERING            4.53  .F.       ALLOWANCE
     12   513     03/30/85  READ 'EM BOOKS          9.05  .F.       ALLOWANCE
     14   515     03/31/85  SARAH WILLIAMS          7.50  .F.       BABYSITTING
      2   502     03/20/85  MARCY'S               259.01  .T.       CLOTHES
      5   505     03/24/85  XYZ SUPERMARKET        71.65  .F.       FOOD
      9   509     03/26/85  CORNER STORE           22.12  .F.       FOOD
     15   510     03/29/85  CORNER STORE           13.33  .F.       FOOD
      7   507     03/25/85  ROP CATERING           21.35  .F.       FOOD
      6   506     03/25/85  KATHY REED             72.00  .F.       HOUSECLEAN
      1   501     03/20/85  CORNER STORE            2.85  .F.       INCIDENTALS
      4   504     03/24/25  DB DRUGS                9.38  .T.       INCIDENTALS
      8   508     03/25/85  SMITH'S                13.75  .F.       INCIDENTALS
     11   512     03/30/85  XYZ DRUGS              10.10  .F.       INCIDENTALS
     13   514     03/31/85  CORNER STORE           10.78  .F.       INCIDENTALS
```

Figure 3-8. Incomplete REPLACE ALL

(records 7 and 10) were assigned to the wrong category, ALLOWANCE; we will try to use REPLACE to correct this.

Note the command entered at the top of Figure 3-8:

REPLACE ALL CATEGORY WITH "FOOD" FOR PAY_TO = "ROP CATERING"

dBASE will begin at the top of the file, searching the PAY—TO field for ROP CATERING. The first occurrence is record 7, so dBASE will REPLACE the category with the word "FOOD" in this record.

Now the index is updated; dBASE reindexes the file each time a key field entry is changed. So before the next record is looked for, record 7 is moved to the position shown in Figure 3-8, with the other records in the FOOD category.

Next dBASE continues to search for ROP CATERING in the PAY—TO field, but it starts from the new position of record 7. Figure 3-8 shows the result: dBASE never found record 10, and only one of the two relevant records was processed. In a large database file with many records to be updated, this trap could be repeated a number of times and many records might not be processed.

You are vulnerable to this type of error any time you use REPLACE ALL to change the entries in the key field of your index. A better approach would be to use the file without the index, execute the REPLACE command, and then use the reindex command to reindex the file.

Deleting Records

3.24 Tip: To remove records from your file, use DELETE followed by PACK.

Removing records from a database file is a two-step procedure. First the records are marked for deletion, indicated by an asterisk in the first position of the record when the file is LISTed, and then the records can be removed.

Figure 3-9 shows a listing of some of the records in the file MAIL—LST. Several records have been marked for deletion. Record 10 was marked by entering

```
DELETE RECORD 10
```

The four records in sequence, beginning with record 13, were marked by entering

```
GO 13      (to move the record pointer)
DELETE NEXT 4
```

Record 24 was marked by entering

```
DELETE FOR CO_NAME = "Clive Busch"
```

```
. USE MAIL_LST INDEX ML_NAME
.
. LIST L_NAME, F_NAME, CO_NAME FOR L_NAME > "B" .AND. L_NAME < "F"
Record#   L_NAME           F_NAME            CO_NAME
     6    CASPER           CAROLYN           QUALITY TUNE-UP
     8    CHARLES          DOLORES           JERRY OTT
    10   *CHARLES          ELLEN             J & B INTERIORS
     9    CLARK            CATHERINE         SUPERTUNE
    13   *COOPER           HARRY             VALLEY IMPORT
    11   *CRAIG            DIANE             AMERICAN TIRE
     2   *CRANDELL         LUCILLE           PIONEER TIRE
    15   *DAILY            JIM               DANVILLE IMPORT
    20    DE VIRA          WILLIAM           A-1 SERVICE
    19    DEEGAN           LEROY             THE REPAIR SHOP
    17    DEWALL           TIMOTHY           AUTO CLINIC
     4    DOUGLAS          BARBARA           ADAMS & BOSCH
    16    DRAPER           FRED              A/C UNLIMITED
    24   *EDWARDS          SHEILS            CLIVE BUSCH
     7    ERIKSEN          GRAHAM            MOTOR WORKS
    23    EVERETT          BUD               EAST BAY TOWING
.
```

Figure 3-9. Records marked for deletion

These marked records can be removed from the file by telling dBASE to PACK. Be sure to read the following trap and tip.

3.25 Trap: *If you tell dBASE to PACK only part of a file, the command will be accepted, but everything marked for deletion will be deleted.*

You cannot limit the action of PACK. dBASE will accept commands like these:

```
PACK FOR L_NAME = "Miller"

PACK NEXT 15

PACK RECORD 2

PACK WHILE RECNO() < 30
```

but in every case, the whole database file will be packed.
See the following tip.

3.26 Tip: *Before you PACK a file, check which records will be deleted and RECALL any records that you want to keep in the file.*

PACK removes all records that are marked for deletion in your file. There is no way to undo a PACK command, except by entering records once again.

Before you use PACK, double-check which records will be removed by entering

```
LIST FOR DELETED()
```

Here is the result of this command on the file shown in Figure 3-9:

```
. LIST L_NAME, F_NAME, CO_NAME FOR DELETED()
Record#  L_NAME          F_NAME          CO_NAME
     10 *CHARLES         ELLEN           J & B INTERIORS
     13 *COOPER          HARRY           VALLEY IMPORT
     11 *CRAIG           DIANE           AMERICAN TIRE
      2 *CRANDELL        LUCILLE         PIONEER TIRE
     15 *DAILY           JIM             DANVILLE IMPORT
     24 *EDWARDS         SHEILS          CLIVE BUSCH
     .
```

Now you can change your mind about removing any of these records. To keep record 10, enter

```
RECALL RECORD 10
```

To keep records 13, 11, and 2, which are grouped together in the indexed file as shown in Figure 3-9, tell dBASE to

```
GO 13      (to move the record pointer)
RECALL NEXT 3
```

To retain all of the marked records, enter

```
RECALL ALL
```

To recall all records with the company name American Tire that are scattered in different locations in the indexed file, tell dBASE to

```
RECALL ALL FOR CO_NAME = "American Tire"
```

Be sure to include the scope "ALL" so that dBASE checks all marked records against the condition.

3.27 Tip: *To remove all records from a database file, use ZAP.*

ZAP is an efficient way to DELETE ALL and PACK in one step, leaving you with an empty file. ZAP is irreversible, so it must be used carefully.

If you ZAP a file and then realize you need some of the records, you can access your most recent backup copy of the file.

3.28 Trap: *If you use PACK or ZAP to make your database files smaller, you will not be able to access the disk space.*

PACK and ZAP make files smaller, but dBASE does not release disk space after executing either of these commands. dBASE releases disk space from a database file only when it is copied with the COPY TO command. If you have just removed a number of outdated records from the file ACC—PAY, you can release the disk space in this way:

```
USE ACC_PAY
COPY TO TEMPFILE
```

Now rename the file:

```
USE      (to close the file; dBASE will not ERASE
           an open file)
ERASE ACC_PAY.DBF
RENAME TEMPFILE.DBF TO ACC_PAY.DBF
ERASE TEMPFILE.DBF
```

Limiting Access and Validating Data

3.29 Tip: You can protect specific data so that it can be viewed but not changed.

There are two ways to display the contents of a field on the screen (see Chapter 6):

- GET *field name* displays the current contents and allows the cursor into the field to make changes.
- SAY *field name* displays the current contents but does not permit changes.

Suppose you have a file named **CUSTOMER** that contains the fields CUST—CODE, NAME, STREET, CITY, STATE, ZIP, and PHONE. The name, address, and phone number of each customer must be available for updating, but you want to protect CUST—CODE from accidental changes. When you design your screen, use

```
@row,col SAY "Customer Code: " + CUST_CODE
```

This command will display the current contents of CUST—CODE after the prompt without placing the cursor in that field for updating. Each of the other fields can be accessed with a command like

```
@row,col SAY "Street Address:" GET STREET
```

which will permit editing.

3.30 Tip: *You can hide confidential data.*

Let's say you have a file named EMPLOYEE containing the name, address, phone number, and salary for each of your employees. You'd like one of your staff to be able to update addresses and phone numbers, but you do not want him or her to see the entries in the SALARY field.

Write a format file named EMP—UPDT.FMT with @...SAY...GET commands for each field except SALARY; leave the SALARY field out of the file altogether (see Chapter 6). Whenever someone else will be using the EMPLOYEE file, just enter

```
SET FORMAT TO EMP_UPDT
```

This can be done from the dot prompt or from within a program; either way, the SALARY field will not be displayed. The person using the EMPLOYEE file will not even realize that the SALARY field exists.

To access EMPLOYEE yourself, including the SALARY field, just use a different format file or no format file at all.

3.31 Tip: *Pay close attention to your needs for data-entry validation.*

When you plan your application system, you need to consider how data will be entered and updated. You can choose among the data-entry and update modes discussed in the second section of this chapter, or you can write your own programs. A key element in this decision is your need to validate the data that is entered. There are five general criteria for data validation.

1. Data must be of a certain type. dBASE checks the data type for you automatically. For example, if a field is defined as a date field, dBASE will not accept "Smith" into the field; a logical field will limit entries to T/t, F/f, Y/y, N/n, and so on. You set up this type of data validation when you define each field of your database file.

2. Data must be in a certain format. You can control the format of each entry into a field by using a custom screen with a PICTURE clause. For example, you can use

```
arow,col SAY "Phone:" GET PHONE PICTURE "(999)999-9999"
```

The parentheses and hyphen will be in place for each entry, and only the digits 0 to 9 will be accepted. See Chapter 6 for tips and traps on using PICTURE.

3. Data must be within a certain range. For entries into numeric or date fields, you can tell dBASE to accept input only within a certain range of values by using RANGE with @...SAY...GET. For example, you could use

```
arow,col SAY "Price: $" GET PRICE RANGE 0,100
```

This would limit acceptable entries to positive numbers less than or equal to 100. See Chapter 6 for a detailed discussion of using RANGE.

If you need to limit entries in a character field to a certain range, as in limiting ZIP codes to those beginning with 9, you'll need a dBASE program similar to the one described in the following tip.

4. Input must be one of a limited group of acceptable choices. If you have a field named OFFICE, for example, which contains the office assignment for each of your salespeople, you may wish to verify that all entries are one of the actual office locations.

This type of validation requires a dBASE program that accepts a proposed entry into a buffer memory variable, checks it against the acceptable entries, and places it into the field only if it matches one of the specified choices. Such programs are discussed in detail in the tips and traps in the rest of this section.

5. Input cannot duplicate another entry in the file. If you use the field CUST_CODE to link the data in your CUSTOMER file with the other files in your system, it's critical that each customer have a unique code. You don't want a new customer to be entered with the same code as an existing one, so the CUST_CODE entry for each new record must be checked to be sure it's not a duplicate code.

Such checking also requires a dBASE program to accept a new customer code into a buffer memory variable and to compare it to each code that is already in the file. Tip 3.41 describes checking for duplicate entries.

3.32 Tip: Use a validation loop to test entries.

When new records are entered into a database file under program control, a blank record is appended onto the file, data is entered and tested, and the validated entries are placed into this record, as described in the section "Entering and Updating Data Under Program Control" later in this chapter.

Figure 3-10 shows the general structure of a validation loop, and Figure 3-11 shows a program segment that uses this structure. The user is asked to enter the data for the field SIZE; the only valid sizes are P, S, M, or L. Let's look at each step of the validation process.

1. Initialize a memory variable to hold the data entry:

```
STORE " " TO M_SIZE
```

M __ SIZE will hold a data entry intended for the field SIZE, a character field of length 1. The STORE command establishes the memory variable as a blank string of that length, which will be displayed when GET puts the current contents of the memory variable on the screen.

2. Initialize a logical flag to control exit from the loop:

```
STORE .F. TO VALID
```

VALID will be .F. until a valid entry is made.

3. Start the validation loop:

```
DO WHILE .NOT. VALID
```

```
    Initialize memory variable to hold entry
    *
    Initialize logical flag to .F.
    *
    VALIDATION LOOP - repeat while .NOT. flag
    *
       Clear message lines
       *
       Get entry - uppercase
       *
       IF entry passes test
          Set flag to .T.
       *
       Otherwise
          Display error message
          Prompt for return
       *
    End of validation loop
```

Figure 3-10. General structure of a validation loop

The validation loop will repeat until VALID is changed to .T., which occurs when an acceptable entry is made.

4. Clear the lines where error messages are displayed:

```
@15,0
@17,0
```

If an entry is not valid, an error message will be displayed on row 15 and a prompt on row 17 will ask the user to press RETURN and to make another entry. These messages will remain on the screen even if the next entry is valid unless the program clears the lines.

5. Ask for the entry:

```
@5,3 SAY "Size (P/S/M/L):" GET M_SIZE PICTURE "!"
```

The PICTURE clause is used to convert whatever is entered to uppercase.

6. READ the input:

```
READ
```

```
    *** program is appending new record to file
    *
    *** procedure to validate SIZE
    *
    *
    STORE " " TO M_SIZE
    *
    STORE .F. TO VALID
    *
    DO WHILE .NOT. VALID
        *
        @15,0
        @17,0
        *
        @5,3 SAY "Size (P/S/M/L):" GET M_SIZE PICTURE "!"
        READ
        *
        IF M_SIZE $ "PSML"
            STORE .T. TO VALID
            *
        ELSE
            @15,3 SAY "*** INVALID SIZE.  Enter P, S, M, or L. ***"
            @16,0
            WAIT "     *** Press return to re-enter size. ***"
        *
        ENDIF ** M_SIZE $ "PSML"
        *
    ENDDO ** WHILE .NOT. VALID
    *
    REPLACE SIZE WITH M_SIZE
    *
    *
    *** program continues
```

Figure 3-11. Program segment using a validation loop

7. If the entry is acceptable, change VALID to .T.:

```
IF M_SIZE $ "PSML"

   STORE .T. TO VALID
```

8. If the entry is not acceptable, display the error message:

```
ELSE

   @15,3 SAY "*** INVALID SIZE. Enter P, S, M, or L ***"
```

9. Pause for return:

```
@16,0

   WAIT "     *** Press return to re-enter size ***"

ENDIF ** M_SIZE $ "PSML"
```

The program must pause here to let the user read the error message, look back at the entry, and understand what has happened.

10. End the validation loop:

```
ENDDO ** WHILE .NOT. VALID
```

When the program is being executed, dBASE will arrive at the ENDDO with .T. in VALID if an acceptable entry has been made; if the entry was not acceptable, VALID will still contain .F. dBASE now checks the beginning of the loop (at step 3) to see if it should repeat the procedure. If VALID is still .F., the loop will be executed again to get another entry. If VALID is now .T., dBASE will move on to step 11.

11. Place the validated entry into the field:

```
REPLACE SIZE WITH M_SIZE
```

See the remaining tips in this section for various ways to test the entry in the IF...ELSE part of the program.

3.33 Tip: *Use PICTURE to uppercase an entry to be tested.*

You can use a PICTURE clause to convert all keyboard entries to uppercase:

```
@row,col SAY "Enter a 3-letter word:" GET WORD PICTURE "!!!"

@row,col SAY "Enter any length word:" GET WORD PICTURE "@!"
```

The validation process will be made easier because you only need to check for the valid uppercase possibilities; you can use lowercase letters to trap incorrect entries.

3.34 Tip: *To test a one-letter entry, use the $ function.*

The $ sign (meaning "is contained in") is the dBASE substring-comparison function. For example, in the program segment in Tip 3.32, the SIZE entry is tested with

```
IF M_SIZE $ "PSML"
```

which is true if the contents of the variable M—SIZE are contained in the string PSML and is false otherwise.

Tip 3.32 explains in detail how to use this test within a program.

3.35 Trap: *If you use $ to test an entry that is more than one character long, you may allow invalid entries.*

Two possibilities govern entries that are more than one character long: all valid entries are the same length, or there are valid entries of different lengths. Each needs a different approach to validation. In either case, using the $ function may allow invalid entries to be accepted.

For instance, if the field **DAY** is intended to hold the first three letters of one of the days of the week, you could use

```
IF M_DAY $ "MONTUEWEDTHUFRISATSUN"
```

If you use PICTURE "!!!" when you GET M—DAY, you are guaranteed that M—DAY will be three characters long, but "NTU" or "HUF" will also pass this test. If you use

```
IF M_DAY $ "MON TUE WED THU FRI SAT SUN"
```

"N T", "E W", and the like will pass. See the following tip.

When valid entries vary in length, the possibility of error increases. Say the field OFFICE has four possible valid entries: VALLEJO, CONCORD, HAYWARD, and SAN JOSE. If you use

```
IF M_OFFICE $ "VALLEJOCONCORDHAYWARDSAN JOSE"
```

then entries like "JOCON", "SAN", or even "A" will pass the test. If you try

```
IF M_OFFICE $ "VALLEJO CONCORD HAYWARD SAN JOSE"
```

you are still open to invalid entries like "JO CON", "SAN", or "L".

See the tip on entries of varying length later in this section.

3.36 Tip: *To validate an entry of a fixed length greater than one, use a test string with lowercase separators.*

Let's continue the example begun in the preceding trap, in which an entry is valid if it contains the first three letters of one of the days of the week. If you use

```
@row,col SAY "Day:" GET M_DAY PICTURE "!!!"
```

the string in M—DAY will be three characters long; if the keyboard entry is shorter, dBASE will fill in with blanks, allowing the validation test to focus on accuracy of content.

The PICTURE clause guarantees that the contents of M—DAY are uppercase; if you use a lowercase letter as a separator, you can be certain that only valid entries will pass the test:

```
IF M_DAY $ "MONxTUExWEDxTHUxFRIxSATxSUN"
```

Tip 3.32 explains in detail how you can use this test within a program.

3.37 Tip: *To validate an entry with variable lengths, you will need to make more than one comparison.*

If valid entries into a particular field vary in length, you will have to make more than one comparison for precise validation. You can connect the comparisons with .OR. within a command line; if you need to make many comparisons, you may have to use DO CASE to have room for all of them.

Let's continue the example begun in the foregoing trap, where the field OFFICE has four possible valid entries, each of differing length. These can all be tested on one command line:

```
IF M_OFFICE = "VALLEJO" .OR. M_OFFICE = "CONCORD" .OR.;

    M_OFFICE = "HAYWARD" .OR. M_OFFICE = "SAN JOSE"
```

If there were six valid office locations — the four above, plus SAN FRANCISCO and STOCKTON — a DO CASE structure could be used:

```
DO CASE

    CASE M_OFFICE = "VALLEJO" .OR. M_OFFICE = "CONCORD"

        STORE .T. TO VALID

    CASE M_OFFICE = "HAYWARD" .OR. M_OFFICE = "SAN JOSE"

        STORE .T. TO VALID

    CASE M_OFFICE = "SAN FRANCISCO" .OR. M_OFFICE = "STOCKTON"

        STORE .T. TO VALID

    OTHERWISE

        <display error message and prompt for return>

ENDCASE
```

dBASE will act only on the first CASE that is true and will skip the others, so this program segment will execute quickly. Tip 3.32 explains in detail how you can use this test within a program.

If some of your valid entries have the same length, you can combine the approach given here with the one in the previous tip; see the following trap and tip.

3.38 Trap: *If you use a test involving LEN( ) and $ to validate entries with variable lengths, shorter valid entries will not pass the test.*

In the example developed in the preceding tip, three of the valid entries have the same length: VALLEJO, CONCORD, and HAYWARD. If you use

```
IF LEN(M_OFFICE) = 7 .AND. M_OFFICE $ "VALLEJOxCONCORDxHAYWARD"
```

none of these three valid entries will pass the test.

The memory variable M—OFFICE must be initialized to SPACE(13) to hold entries as long as SAN FRANCISCO. When a keyboard entry is shorter than 13 characters, dBASE stores the letters entered and enough blanks to keep the memory variable 13 characters long. Thus, the length of M-OFFICE will never be 7, and VALLEJO followed by 6 blanks is not a substring of VALLEJOxCON-CORDxHAYWARD. See the following tip.

3.39 Tip: *If you want to test a variable-length entry with LEN( ) or $, use TRIM.*

The TRIM function removes trailing blanks from character strings and solves the problems demonstrated in the preceding trap.

Now we can test the entry in M—OFFICE by combining the methods used in several of these tips. Just TRIM the entry after you READ it:

```
arow,col SAY "OFFICE:" GET M_OFFICE PICTURE "a!"
READ
STORE TRIM(M_OFFICE) TO M_OFFICE
```

Now you can use the LEN( ) and $ functions; here is an example:

```
IF LEN(M_OFFICE) = 7 .AND. M_OFFICE $ "VALLEJOxCONCORDxHAYWARD"
    STORE .T. TO VALID
ELSE
    IF LEN(M_OFFICE) = 8 .AND. M_OFFICE $ "SAN JOSExSTOCKTON"
        STORE .T. TO VALID
    ELSE
        <display error message and prompt for return>
    ENDIF ** LEN(M_OFFICE) = 8
ENDIF ** LEN(M_OFFICE) = 7
```

3.40 Tip: *To validate part of a character entry, use the SUBSTR function.*

Suppose you have a mailing list, and all of the addresses in it have ZIP codes that begin with 94. You can tell dBASE to allow only entries that begin with 94 into the ZIP field:

```
IF  SUBSTR(M_ZIP,1,2)  =  "94"

    STORE .T. TO VALID

ELSE

    <display error message and prompt for return>

ENDIF
```

Tip 3.32 explains in detail how you can use this test within a program. The SUBSTR function is discussed in Chapter 4.

3.41 Tip: *To check for duplicate records, use a loop with SEEK.*

Say you have a file named CUSTOMER that contains the name, address, and phone number of each of your customers. This file is related to other files in your application system by the field CUST_CODE. In order for your system to work smoothly, each customer must have a unique CUST_CODE; when a new custom-

```
    Initialize memory variable to hold entry
*
    Initialize logical flag to .F.
*
    DUPLICATE CHECK LOOP - repeat while .NOT. flag

        Clear message lines
        *
        Get entry - uppercase
        *
        SEEK entry
        *
        IF SEEK is unsuccessful
            Set flag to .T.
        *
        Otherwise
            Display error message
            Prompt for return
        *
    End of duplicate check loop
```

Figure 3-12. Program structure to check for duplicate record

er is entered, it is important to check that the CUST—CODE for this new customer is not already in use.

Figure 3-12 shows the structure of a program segment that checks for duplicate codes, and Figure 3-13 shows the dBASE code. The structure of this program segment is essentially the same as that of a validation loop; see Tip 3.32 for a step-by-step explanation of the program logic.

Let's look at the portion of this example that checks for an existing duplicate of the proposed code:

```
SEEK M_CODE
```

SEEK will search the file index on CUST—CODE to see if anything in CUST—CODE matches the contents of M—CODE. If it finds a match, it will move the record pointer to that record; if not, EOF( ) will be set to .T. (See Chapter 4 for tips and traps on locating a particular record.)

```
IF EOF()

   STORE .T. TO UNIQUE
```

```
*** checking CUST_CODE for duplicate before appending new record
*
*** index on CUST_CODE is active
*
*** procedure to check for duplicate CUST_CODE
*
*
STORE SPACE(5) TO M_CODE
*
STORE .F. TO UNIQUE
*
DO WHILE .NOT. UNIQUE
   *
   @15,0
   @17,0
   *
   @5,3 SAY "Customer Code:" GET M_CODE PICTURE "!!!!!"
   READ
   *
   SEEK M_CODE
   *
   IF EOF()
      STORE .T. TO UNIQUE
   *
   ELSE
      @15,3 SAY "*** CODE ALREADY IN USE -- SELECT ANOTHER CODE. ***"
      @16,0
      WAIT "    *** Press return to re-enter code. ***
   *
   ENDIF ** EOF()
*
ENDDO ** WHILE .NOT. UNIQUE
*
*** program continues
```

Figure 3-13.   dBASE code to check for duplicate records

If EOF( ) is true, dBASE has found no matching data in CUST__CODE, and the new entry can be accepted.

ELSE

If the record pointer has not passed beyond the last record, dBASE has found a match, and the proposed entry to CUST__CODE cannot be accepted. The appropriate message is displayed; and since UNIQUE is still false, the loop will be repeated. Be sure to read the following trap.

3.42 Trap: *If your data-validation test moves the record pointer, you will not be in position to REPLACE the fields of a new record.*

Look again at the check for duplicate customer codes in Figure 3-13. When a unique code is entered, the SEEK command leaves the record pointer at EOF, beyond the last record in the file. If you try to REPLACE data in the file at this point, dBASE will have no place to put the entry and will respond with an error message.

See Trap 3.53 and Tip 3.54 for a discussion of using REPLACE correctly with the fields of a new record.

Entering and Updating Data Under Program Control

Programs to control data entry and updating can make these functions easier for an inexperienced dBASE user and can protect against many errors. The dBASE data-entry and updating modes and tools discussed earlier in this chapter give the person who is entering data uncontrolled access to your files. That user may make incorrect entries, update the wrong data, or accidentally lose important records. dBASE gives very few instructions in BROWSE or APPEND modes; these built-in data-entry tools are best used by a person who understands how dBASE operates and who wants quick access to the data.

To set up your system with clear instructions for each step of data entry and updating and with built-in safeguards against various types of errors, you can use programs to control data-entry and updating functions. A menu-driven system allows the user to select the desired function from a list of available options; the program then sets up the files and relationships that are needed, and the user is free to concentrate on entering data accurately into the records.

3.43 Trap: *If you try to add a new record onto the end of a file without initializing the record, dBASE will display an error message and stop executing your program.*

If you move the record pointer past the last record in your database file and try to GET data for a new record, dBASE will respond "End of file encountered" and stop executing your program. dBASE will not accept input from the keyboard unless the program handles the input in two distinct steps, first establishing the record or memory variable where the entry will be placed, and then accepting data entry from the keyboard.

When you enter new records into your file in APPEND or BROWSE mode, dBASE automatically establishes a new record to accept your entries. If you will be adding records under program control, the program must add an empty record to the file before asking dBASE to accept data for that new record. See the following tip.

3.44 Tip: *To add new records to a file under program control, use APPEND BLANK.*

When you add records to a file in APPEND or BROWSE mode, dBASE takes care of one important step of the process for you: it opens up a blank record at the end of the file to hold the new data. If you want to enter new records under program control, your program must establish this blank record before the new data can be placed in the fields.

APPEND BLANK adds an empty record to the end of the database file that is in use and then moves the record pointer to this new record. After APPEND BLANK, dBASE is ready to accept data into the new record. Data can be entered directly into a field with GET *field name,* or it can be entered into a buffer memory variable with GET *memvar,* validated, and then placed into the field with

```
REPLACE <field name> WITH <memvar>
```

3.45 Tip: *To verify data entries before they are placed into your file, use a buffer memory variable.*

If you use GET *field name* to accept a new entry, the data is placed into the field as soon as your program executes READ. To test the entry before it is placed into the file,

1. Initialize a buffer memory variable.

2. Accept the input with GET *memvar.*

3. If the entry fails the test, display an error message, ask for a revised entry, and return to step 2.

4. If the entry passes the test, place the data in the record with REPLACE.

The previous section of this chapter, "Limiting Access and Validating Data," gives detailed examples of this procedure.

3.46 Trap: *If you try to GET an entry into a memory variable that has not been initialized, dBASE will display an error message and stop executing your program.*

If you try to GET a memory variable that does not yet exist because it has not been initialized, dBASE will say "Variable not found" and stop executing your program.

See the following five tips and traps.

3.47 Tip: *Initialize each memory variable with STORE before you GET the memory variable.*

To establish a memory variable, use STORE:

```
STORE SPACE(7) TO M_CITY

STORE 000.00 TO M_COST,M_TOTAL,M_TAX

STORE .F. TO UNIQUE
```

Each of these command lines tells dBASE to set aside a space in memory with the given name and with the given characteristics. M—CITY is established as a character memory variable of length 7, M—COST, M—TOTAL, and M—TAX as numeric memory variables of length 6 with 2 decimal places, and UNIQUE as a logical memory variable. Each of these is now available for access with GET or for use in conditional statements.

3.48 Tip: *Give each buffer memory variable a name that indicates which field the data will be placed in.*

You can make your program code easier to read and understand if you choose memory variable names that clearly communicate the purpose of that memory variable in the program. This approach also makes programs easier to write and debug, as well as making them easy to modify at a future time.

The method used throughout this chapter has been to name each buffer memory variable with the characters "M—" followed by as much of the field name as possible. For instance, the memory variable used with the field **OFFICE** is called **M—OFFICE**, and the memory variable used with **CUST—CODE** is called **M—CODE**.

If you come back in five years to modify a program, these names will clearly indicate how each memory variable is being used.

3.49 Tip: *If a memory variable will serve as a logical flag, name it with the condition that is true when the memory variable is set to .T.*

This tip does the same thing as the preceding one: it makes your program code easy to read, understand, write, and modify. Two logical flags are used in the examples in this chapter:

- VALID is set to .T. when a valid entry is made.

- UNIQUE is set to .T. when a unique entry is made.

Names like these make the logical conditions easy to read:

DO WHILE .NOT. VALID   The loop is to be repeated until a valid entry is made.

DO WHILE .NOT. UNIQUE   The loop is to be repeated until the entry is unique.

3.50 Trap: *If you don't initialize a buffer memory variable to match the corresponding field, you may lose data or dBASE may display an error message and stop executing your program.*

If your memory variable is longer than its corresponding field, the entry will be truncated to fit the field; if it is shorter than the field, dBASE will add trailing blanks. If a numerical memory variable is not initialized with decimal places, it will not accept entries with fractional parts; it accepts exactly the number of decimal places it was given when it was initialized.

See the following tip.

3.51 Tip: *Your memory variables will match their corresponding fields perfectly if you APPEND BLANK first and then initialize the memory variables with the empty fields.*

This technique is illustrated by the program in Figure 3-14, which shows the program structure, and Figure 3-15, which shows the dBASE code.

APPEND BLANK places an empty record at the end of the file. Each entry to the field CUST_CODE will be checked for duplicates before it is placed into the field, so a buffer memory variable is needed. After the empty record has been appended, just

```
STORE CUST_CODE TO M_CODE
```

M_CODE is now initialized as precisely the same length and data type as the field CUST_CODE.

3.52 Tip: *You can speed up data entry by accepting all fields of a record at one time and then testing only those entries that require validating.*

There are two methods of placing data into a record in your database file:

- GET *field name* followed by READ places the entry directly into the field.

- GET *memvar* followed by READ allows the entry to be tested. When a valid entry has been made, REPLACE places the contents of the memory variable into the field.

You can combine these methods on the same screen so that data entry will go quickly and smoothly. Figure 3-15 illustrates the combination of methods. A new

```
Have file in use with index active
*
Add a blank record
*
Save the record number of the blank record
*
Initialize memory variable to hold entry to be tested
*
Get entry to be tested - uppercase
*
Get all other entries directly into fields
*
Initialize logical flag to .F.
*
DUPLICATE CHECK LOOP - repeat while .NOT. flag
*
   Clear message lines
   *
   READ data entered above
   *
   Search for duplicate
   *
   If duplicate not found
      Set flag to .T.
   *
   Otherwise
      Display error message
      Prompt for return
      *
      Get new entry - uppercase
   *
End of duplicate check loop
*
Move record pointer to new record
*
Place validated entry into field
```

Figure 3-14. *Program structure to APPEND a record and check for duplicate code*

record will be added to the file CUSTOMER, and the entry in the CUST_CODE field will be tested for its uniqueness in the file. Let's look at each step of the code:

1. The test for duplicate codes uses the SEEK command, which requires that the file be indexed on he field being searched; the program begins with

```
USE CUSTOMER INDEX CUST_CODE
```

to ensure that the index is active.

2. A blank record is needed to accept the new data:

```
APPEND BLANK
```

```
USE CUSTOMER INDEX CUST_CODE
*
APPEND BLANK
*
STORE RECNO() TO POSITION
*
STORE CUST_CODE TO M_CODE
*
@3,3 SAY "Customer Code:" GET M_CODE PICTURE "!!!!!"
*
@5,3 SAY "Last Name:" GET L_NAME
@5,35 SAY "First Name:" GET F_NAME
@7,3 SAY "Company Name:" GET CO_NAME
@9,5 SAY "Street:" GET STREET
@11,5 SAY "City:" GET CITY
@11,35 SAY "State:" GET STATE PICTURE "!!"
@11,45 SAY "Zipcode:" GET ZIP PICTURE "99999"
@13,3 SAY "Phone:" GET PHONE PICTURE "(999)999-9999"
*
STORE .F. TO UNIQUE
*
DO WHILE .NOT. UNIQUE
    *
    @17,0
    @19,0
    *
    READ
    *
    SEEK M_CODE
    *
    IF EOF()
       STORE .T. TO UNIQUE
       *
    ELSE
       @17,3 SAY "*** CODE ALREADY IN USE -- SELECT ANOTHER CODE. ***"
       @18,0
       WAIT      "*** Press return to re-enter code. ***"
       *
       @3,3 SAY "Customer Code:" GET M_CODE PICTURE "!!!!!"
       *
    ENDIF ** EOF()
    *
ENDDO ** WHILE .NOT. UNIQUE
*
GO POSITION
*
REPLACE CUST_CODE WITH M_CODE
*
```

Figure 3-15. dBASE code to APPEND and check for validation

3. The location of the new record is saved in a memory variable:

```
STORE RECNO() TO POSITION
```

(See the following trap and tip for a discussion of the need to keep careful track of the record pointer in this program.)

4. The buffer memory variable must be initialized:

```
STORE CUST_CODE TO M_CODE
```

This establishes a memory variable that exactly matches the corresponding field (as described in the preceding tip).

5. The data to be tested is entered into the memory variable:

```
a3,3 SAY "Customer Code:" GET M_CODE PICTURE "a!"
```

6. All of the other data in the record is written directly into the fields with GET *field name*.

7. The code is tested in a DO WHILE loop. This portion of the program is explained in detail in Tip 3.41.

8. The line

```
GO POSITION
```

is reached only when a unique customer code has been entered. The record pointer will be beyond the last record in the file, because SEEK did not find a match. This command takes the record pointer back to the new record so the validated code can be entered into CUST—CODE.

See the following trap and tip.

3.53 Trap: *If you use a data-validation test that moves the record pointer, you will not be in position to REPLACE data into your new record.*

Figure 3-15, explained in the preceding tip, shows an example of this situation: a proposed customer code is entered and the program checks to see if the code is already in use in the file. The procedure uses SEEK; when a new code is valid — that is, not already in the file — SEEK leaves the record pointer at EOF, beyond the last record of the file.

You cannot use REPLACE to store the validated data into your file until the record pointer is positioned at the new record. If you APPEND BLANK and then run a validation test using SEEK, the record pointer will not be in the required position.

See the following tip.

3.54 Tip: *Save the position of the record pointer before you use a test that will move the pointer.*

Usually you would use APPEND BLANK to make a new record available before your program asked for a new entry, and then you would accept entries, testing those that require validation. If you want to READ any entries directly into the fields or if you want to use the blank fields of the new record to initialize memory variables (see Tip 3.51), you must use APPEND BLANK first.

If all entries will be placed in buffer memory variables and tested before they are placed in the record, you can APPEND BLANK after the tests are done. This will ensure that the record pointer is in the correct position for the REPLACE command to replace the data into the record—but you lose the option of initializing your memory variables from the blank record. A better approach is to save the position of the record pointer before you test the new data, and then move the record pointer back to the new record before you place the validated data into the field with REPLACE.

Figure 3-15, explained in detail in Tip 3.52, illustrates this procedure:

```
APPEND BLANK

STORE RECNO() TO POSITION
```

These commands are executed before any data is entered. Several fields receive entries directly from the keyboard, and one entry is tested with SEEK. After this entry is validated,

```
GO POSITION
```

moves the record pointer to the incomplete new record, and the validated data is entered into the proper field.

3.55 Trap: *You cannot access a memo field under program control.*

See the section called "Numeric, Logical, and Memo Fields" in Chapter 2.

✋ *3.56 Trap:* *If your program does not remove error messages, they will remain on the screen even when an entry is valid.*

dBASE does not clear any part of the screen during program execution unless the program includes the command to do so. When you are testing an entry from the keyboard, any error messages that you display will remain on the screen until you clear the message lines. This situation is very confusing to the person using your program.

Each testing loop illustrated in this chapter begins with commands to clear the message lines by telling dBASE to write an empty row at that location. For instance, to clear rows 17 and 19, use

```
a17,0
a19,0
```

This ensures that an error message will not be on the screen when it is no longer an accurate response to an entry.

✋ *3.57 Trap:* *Your error messages will flash by too quickly to read if your program does not include a delay.*

Because it is necessary for a testing loop to clear the message lines on the screen (see the preceding trap), unless your program explicitly prevents it, error messages will be erased almost as soon as they are displayed. This can be very disconcerting to the person using your program.

The error message presents information and instructions to a user who has made an incorrect entry; you want the user to have time to read the message, check the entry, and understand why it is not acceptable. To allow enough time to do this, build in a delay that is controlled by the user.

The program segments in this chapter use the following technique:

```
<entry fails validation test>

arow,col <display error message>

arow,col

WAIT "    *** Press return to re-enter ***"
```

First the error message is displayed: it includes a reason if possible, such as "Code already in use" when a duplicate customer code is rejected. The blank row is printed to position the WAIT message two lines below the error message.

WAIT tells dBASE to display the given string and then pause until a key is pressed. This allows the user time to read the error message and to understand what has happened. Once a key is pressed, dBASE returns to the top of the testing loop and the error message and WAIT message are erased.

3.58 Tip: *To edit records under program control, move the record pointer to the particular record and GET the current field entries.*

The procedure for editing records under program control is similar to the steps used to append a record:

1. Ask the user which record to edit, and move the record pointer to that record. (See Chapter 4 for tips and traps on locating a particular record.)

2. GET the current contents of the fields. This is the same procedure that was used to add a new record; when you edit, the current contents will not be blank strings, but rather,

```
GET <field name>
```

will display those contents and allow corrections.

3. If you want to test a particular entry, use a buffer memory variable. You can initialize the memory variable with the current field contents by using

```
STORE <field name> TO <memvar>
```

exactly as explained in Tip 3.51 on initializing memory variables from a blank record.

All of the various techniques that have been described for testing data and placing it into a record can be used in an editing program as well. The example in Figure 3-15, explained in detail in Tip 3.52, could be changed to an editing program simply by replacing the line

```
APPEND BLANK
```

with a procedure that asks the user which record to edit and then moves the record pointer to that record.

4

Ordering and
Retrieving Data

dBASE III is a powerful tool for managing information — storing, organizing, and processing data in a wide variety of ways. The last chapter described how to get your data into dBASE files and how to keep the files up to date. You also want to be able to access the information in your files quickly and flexibly — to print out a list of customer names in alphabetical order, to find out which accounts receivable are more than 90 days past due, to see the current inventory levels of certain parts, and so on. The key to easy, effective access is the proper organization of the records within each file. In this chapter you will learn how to order the records in your database files. You will also learn how to locate and process selected data in them.

SORT Versus INDEX

It is important to understand the difference between SORT and INDEX. Figure 4-1 shows the structure of a small database file named SAMPLE and its six records. Note that the records are in order by record number. This example will be used to illustrate the two different ways to order the records in a file: SORT and INDEX.

SORT rearranges a file, placing each record in the position determined by the ordering criterion that you have entered. Say you use SORT to order the records in SAMPLE alphabetically by last name:

```
. SORT ON L_NAME, F_NAME TO SAMPLE_2
  100% Sorted              6 Records sorted
.
. USE SAMPLE_2
.
. LIST
Record#   L_NAME        F_NAME        DATE_IN   AMOUNT
      1   AMES          MARTHA        11/01/82   11.62
      2   AMES          SIDNEY        04/17/82    8.00
      3   BENNETT       JERRY         02/12/82   11.75
      4   ROSEN         SYLVIA        10/03/82    8.00
      5   ROSENBERG     ELSIE         04/17/82   12.34
      6   WARREN        DAVID         02/01/82   12.58
.
```

A new database file, SAMPLE—2, has been created. It has the same records as SAMPLE, but each record now has a different record number from the one it had before. Now, when the records are listed in order by record number, they are in alphabetical order by last name (and by first name if last names match).

By contrast, INDEX does not reassign record numbers; instead, a separate index file is created, with the file extension .NDX, which tells dBASE how to access the records in order according to the INDEX criterion. Say you again order

```
. DISPLAY STRUCTURE
Structure for database : B:SAMPLE.dbf
Number of data records :       6
Date of last update    : 08/13/85
Field   Field name   Type         Width    Dec
    1   L_NAME       Character       12
    2   F_NAME       Character       12
    3   DATE_IN      Date             8
    4   AMOUNT       Numeric          6      2
** Total **                          39

.
. LIST
Record#   L_NAME        F_NAME        DATE_IN   AMOUNT
      1   WARREN        DAVID         02/01/82   12.58
      2   ROSENBERG     ELSIE         04/17/82   12.34
      3   ROSEN         SYLVIA        10/03/82    8.00
      4   BENNETT       JERRY         02/12/82   11.75
      5   AMES          SIDNEY        04/17/82    8.00
      6   AMES          MARTHA        11/01/82   11.62
.
```

Figure 4-1.   The SAMPLE database file

the records in SAMPLE alphabetically by last name, but this time you use INDEX:

```
. INDEX ON L_NAME + F_NAME TO SA_NAMES
      6 records indexed
.
. LIST
Record#   L_NAME        F_NAME       DATE_IN   AMOUNT
      6   AMES          MARTHA       11/01/82  11.62
      5   AMES          SIDNEY       04/17/82   8.00
      4   BENNETT       JERRY        02/12/82  11.75
      3   ROSEN         SYLVIA       10/03/82   8.00
      2   ROSENBERG     ELSIE        04/17/82  12.34
      1   WARREN        DAVID        02/01/82  12.58
.
```

As before, the records have been reordered; however, the record numbers have not been changed and are now listed out of order. The records are displayed in name order, regardless of record number. When an index file is active, it determines the order of access to the records in the database file.

See the following trap and tip.

 4.01 Trap: *The SORT command is not the most efficient tool for ordering your files.*

Using SORT to order your files presents a number of disadvantages:

- The SORT process is slow, particularly if the database file is large.

- SORT uses a lot of disk space. During the SORT process, dBASE creates two files: the new file that your database is being sorted into, and a temporary working file. Your default disk must have enough space to hold two files as large as the file being processed by SORT.

- If you want to access your data in more than one order—for instance, by name and by amount—with SORT you need a separate sorted file for each application.

- Each time the database is updated, you must SORT the file again.

- Keeping records in order by using SORT slows the process of locating particular records.

See the following tip.

4.02 Tip: *Always use INDEX to order your files.*

The INDEX approach resolves the problems with SORT that were listed in the preceding trap:

- An index file can be built quickly. You can establish one or more indexes on an empty file in a short time, and then you can have dBASE automatically place the records in the index or indexes as you add them to the file. There is no need to repeat the INDEX command.

- INDEX uses less disk space than SORT. Most index files are smaller than their related databases, and no temporary working files are needed to build an index.

- A database file can have more than one index file; as many as seven index files can be kept current at a time.

- dBASE automatically updates all open index files as you make additions or changes to the database file.

- dBASE structures an index file so that you can locate particular records as quickly as possible. The searching commands that can be used with indexed files never take more than one or two seconds, even with large database files.

INDEX is a powerful dBASE tool, and it is always a more efficient choice than SORT. See the following tip.

4.03 Tip: *If you need your records in sorted order, using COPY TO with an active index is faster and more flexible than SORT.*

Sometimes it is helpful to have your database file in sorted order, so that the record-number order corresponds to the logical order of the records. This speeds up the execution of many dBASE commands (see Trap 4.26 and Tip 4.27), particularly with a large database file.

There are many disadvantages to using SORT with database files (see Trap 4.01); if your objective is a file in SORTed order, INDEX is still a better tool. Using COPY TO with an active index file is faster than using SORT, and the entire range of indexing options is still available.

To create a file with the same record-number order as the INDEXed order,

1. USE the file with the index file open:

```
USE YOURFILE INDEX YOUR_NDX
```

2. Copy the file:

```
COPY TO TEMP
```

The new file created by COPY will have record numbers assigned in the indexed order.

3. Close the file, erase the old file, and rename the new one:

```
USE
ERASE YOURFILE.DBF
RENAME TEMP.DBF TO YOURFILE.DBF
```

4. Reestablish the index or indexes to correspond to the new order of the file:

```
USE YOURFILE INDEX <up to seven index files>
REINDEX
```

Getting Started With Indexes

 4.04 Tip: Create an index file with the INDEX command.

Each index file has a key field or expression that is used to order the records. To establish an index file, tell dBASE to **INDEX ON** *key expression* **TO** *indexfile*. This command establishes the index file and automatically activates it.

You can use the INDEX command on a database file at any time, but the most efficient approach is to create the index file before any records are entered into your database. See Chapter 3 for tips and traps on keeping index files open while you enter or update data. See the section called "Indexing Options" later in this chapter for tips and traps on choosing the best key expression for your index file.

4.05 Tip: *Choose a name for each index file that tells you which database file it corresponds to and identifies its unique function within the system.*

Say you have a mailing-list database named MAIL—LST, which you will use to generate alphabetical lists, to print out letters to people in selected cities, and to print mailing labels in order by ZIP code. You can use these indexes:

> ML—NAMES   Index by last name + first name
> ML—ZIP   Index by ZIP code
> ML—CITY   Index by city

dBASE assigns each index file the extension .NDX, so you can list all of the indexes associated with MAIL—LST with

```
DIR ML_*.NDX
```

The name of each index clearly indicates its function, and you can tell at a glance which index file is needed for a particular task.

4.06 Tip: *An index file is activated when you USE the database, or if the database file is already in use, when you enter SET INDEX TO.*

If you start working with your file by entering

```
USE MAIL_LST INDEX ML_NAMES
```

dBASE will keep the index ML—NAMES up to date for you while you work with MAIL—LST. This is usually the most efficient way to work with an index file.
Sometimes you may choose to work with a file without the index, or if you

have more than one index file, you may want to change the master index (see the following tip and trap). To activate an index file when the database file is already in use, tell dBASE to

```
SET INDEX TO <index file>
```

4.07 Tip: *You can have as many as seven index files open at the same time.*

dBASE allows you to keep up to seven index files open at once. Just enter

```
USE YOURFILE INDEX INDEX_1, INDEX_2, INDEX_3, . . .
```

The first index file in the list is the master index. It will determine the order for processing data, but all of the index files listed will be updated as you make changes in your file. You can change the master index with

```
SET INDEX TO MASTER, OTHER_1, OTHER_2, OTHER_3, . . .
```

See the following trap.

4.08 Trap: *If you have more than seven index files for a database, you will have a hard time keeping them updated.*

dBASE allows a maximum of seven open index files; if there are more than seven for a database, they won't all be updated automatically. You can USE the file with seven indexes, update the file, USE the file with the remaining indexes, and then REINDEX, but this approach is time-consuming.

If a file requires more than seven indexes, consider splitting it into more than one database. See the "Application Systems" section in Chapter 2.

4.09 Trap: *If you forget to open an index file when you use the data-base, the index can become out-of-date.*

Every time a change is made to a field that is involved in the key expression of an index file, the index must be updated to reflect the change. If you do not open an index file, dBASE will not update it for you and the index file will not correspond to the database file.

See the following tip.

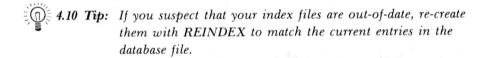 *4.10 Tip:* *If you suspect that your index files are out-of-date, re-create them with REINDEX to match the current entries in the database file.*

There are several signs that your index files may be out-of-date: you are unable to access a particular record or you get a "Record is out of range" or "Record is not in index" message.

Tell dBASE to REINDEX, and all open index files will be re-created to correspond to the current records in the database file.

Indexing Options

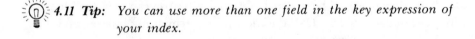 *4.11 Tip:* *You can use more than one field in the key expression of your index.*

Each index file orders the records in your database file according to their entries in the key field or key expression. The following examples use the file SAMPLE with the structure and records shown in Figure 4-1.

You can INDEX ON one field of a file:

```
. INDEX ON L_NAME TO SA_LAST
       6 records indexed
.
. LIST
Record#    L_NAME        F_NAME         DATE_IN   AMOUNT
      5    AMES          SIDNEY         04/17/82   8.00
      6    AMES          MARTHA         11/01/82  11.62
      4    BENNETT       JERRY          02/12/82  11.75
      3    ROSEN         SYLVIA         10/03/82   8.00
      2    ROSENBERG     ELSIE          04/17/82  12.34
      1    WARREN        DAVID          02/01/82  12.58
.
```

This creates an index file that processes the records in alphabetical order by last name. This ordering is not completely satisfactory, since Sidney Ames is listed before Martha Ames.

A better approach is to **INDEX ON** both name fields:

```
. INDEX ON L_NAME + F_NAME TO SA_NAMES
       6 records indexed
.
. LIST
Record#    L_NAME        F_NAME         DATE_IN   AMOUNT
      6    AMES          MARTHA         11/01/82  11.62
      5    AMES          SIDNEY         04/17/82   8.00
      4    BENNETT       JERRY          02/12/82  11.75
      3    ROSEN         SYLVIA         10/03/82   8.00
      2    ROSENBERG     ELSIE          04/17/82  12.34
      1    WARREN        DAVID          02/01/82  12.58
.
```

Now the first names are in order within matching last names.

You can also use a date field or a numeric field for an index:

```
. INDEX ON DATE_IN TO SA_IN
       6 records indexed
.
. LIST
Record#    L_NAME        F_NAME         DATE_IN   AMOUNT
      1    WARREN        DAVID          02/01/82  12.58
      4    BENNETT       JERRY          02/12/82  11.75
      2    ROSENBERG     ELSIE          04/17/82  12.34
      5    AMES          SIDNEY         04/17/82   8.00
      3    ROSEN         SYLVIA         10/03/82   8.00
      6    AMES          MARTHA         11/01/82  11.62
.
.
. INDEX ON AMOUNT TO SA_AMT
       6 records indexed
.
. LIST
Record#    L_NAME        F_NAME         DATE_IN   AMOUNT
      3    ROSEN         SYLVIA         10/03/82   8.00
      5    AMES          SIDNEY         04/17/82   8.00
      6    AMES          MARTHA         11/01/82  11.62
      4    BENNETT       JERRY          02/12/82  11.75
      2    ROSENBERG     ELSIE          04/17/82  12.34
      1    WARREN        DAVID          02/01/82  12.58
.
```

A file indexed by date displays the records in chronological order, and a file indexed by numeric field displays records from smallest entry to largest.

Both of these indexes have limited usefulness; if the entries in DATE__IN or AMOUNT are the same for two records, they are listed in record-number order. Often it is important to have records in a particular order within each major category, such as an overall order by city, with names in order within each city. You can accomplish this by combining fields into a key expression:

```
INDEX ON CITY + L_NAME + F_NAME TO CIT_NAME
```

You must be careful when combining fields that are not character fields into the key expression of an index. See the following seven traps and tips.

4.12 Trap: *You'll get an error message if you try to INDEX ON a combination of character and date or numeric fields.*

Here are two attempts to INDEX ON a combination of fields of different data types using the SAMPLE file:

```
. INDEX ON AMOUNT + L_NAME TO TRY_AMT
Data type mismatch
                        ?
INDEX ON AMOUNT + L_NAME TO TRY_AMT
Do you want some help? (Y/N) No
.
.
.
. INDEX ON DATE_IN + L_NAME TO TRY_DATE
Data type mismatch
                        ?
INDEX ON DATE_IN + L_NAME TO TRY_DATE
Do you want some help? (Y/N) No
.
```

When dBASE creates an index, the contents of the key expression for each record in the database file are stored in the index file. dBASE can only store one type of data at a time, so the key expression of each index must be one data type.

The following six tips and traps explain how you can work around this limitation.

4.13 Tip: *If you need to combine a numeric field with other fields in a key expression, use STR( ) to convert the numbers to character data.*

The key expression of an index file must be one data type (see the preceding trap). Here is an example of the technique for combining numeric fields with character fields:

```
. INDEX ON STR(AMOUNT, 6, 2) + L_NAME TO SA_AMT
      6 records indexed
.
. LIST
Record#   L_NAME      F_NAME      DATE_IN   AMOUNT
      5   AMES        SIDNEY      04/17/82    8.00
      3   ROSEN       SYLVIA      10/03/82    8.00
      6   AMES        MARTHA      11/01/82   11.62
      4   BENNETT     JERRY       02/12/82   11.75
      2   ROSENBERG   ELSIE       04/17/82   12.34
      1   WARREN      DAVID       02/01/82   12.58
.
```

The records are ordered by amount paid, with matching amounts ordered alphabetically by name. Because the STR( ) function converts numeric data to a character string, dBASE can combine the amount with the last name to serve as the key expression of the index file.

In general, STR( ) is used in the form STR(*numeric expression, length, decimals*), where:

• *numeric expression* is the number to be converted to a character string.

• *length* is the length of the character string (including a space for the decimal point, if there is one).

• *decimals* is the number of decimal places in the numeric expression that should be included in the string.

The *decimals* parameter is optional; if you omit it, dBASE will convert only the integer portion of your number to a character string.

The length specified must be at least equal to that of the string that results. A greater length will work, but if the length given will not hold the number, dBASE will convert your number to a row of asterisks.

Be sure to read the following trap.

4.14 Trap: *If you use STR( ) without specifying a length in the key expression of an index file, you will be unable to access records when the index is active.*

If you tell dBASE to

```
INDEX ON L_NAME + STR(AMOUNT) TO AMT_NAME
```

it will create the index and tell you that all of your records have been indexed; if you LIST the file, the index appears to order the records correctly. However, when you try to access a record with a command like **GO 12**, **EDIT RECORD 14**, or **DELETE RECORD 3**, dBASE will respond with "Record is not in index", even though the record appears in the listing. To avoid this, you must include the length parameter when you use STR( ) in the key expression of an index (see the preceding tip).

4.15 Tip: *If you need to combine a date field with other fields in a key expression, and all the dates are in the same year, use DTOC( ) to convert the dates to character data.*

The key expression of an index file must be of one data type (see Trap 4.12), so the entries in a date field must be converted to character data if they will be combined with other fields in a key expression. If all of the dates are in one calendar year, you can use the DTOC( ) function to convert the dates to character strings:

```
. INDEX ON DTOC(DATE_IN) + L_NAME + F_NAME TO SA_DATE
       6 records indexed
.
. LIST
Record#   L_NAME      F_NAME      DATE_IN   AMOUNT
      1   WARREN      DAVID       02/01/82  12.58
      4   BENNETT     JERRY       02/12/82  11.75
      5   AMES        SIDNEY      04/17/82   8.00
      2   ROSENBERG   ELSIE       04/17/82  12.34
      3   ROSEN       SYLVIA      10/03/82   8.00
      6   AMES        MARTHA      11/01/82  11.62
.
```

The records are ordered by date, with matching dates ordered alphabetically by name.

Be sure to read the following trap and tip.

✋ *4.16 Trap:* *If the entries in a date field are not all in the same*
calendar year, an index using DTOC( ) will not order the
dates correctly.

If your date field includes dates in more than one year, an INDEX ON DTOC( )
will not order the dates chronologically; the dates will first be grouped together by
month, and then ordered by day and by year within each month. You could end
up with an order like this:

01/12/80

01/12/82

01/28/80

02/04/81

02/05/82

dBASE represents dates in the form MM/DD/YY, so when dates are converted to character data, the numbers representing the month come first. Because
dBASE indexes character strings from left to right, it gives the month highest
priority when ordering character strings obtained with DTOC( ).

See the following tip.

💡 *4.17 Tip:* *If you need to combine a date field with other fields in a*
key expression, and the dates are in more than one
calendar year, index on the number of days from a fixed
date.

The DTOC( ) function is not an effective tool for indexing on dates in more than
one calendar year (see the preceding trap). If you want a chronological ordering of
dates spanning more than one year, use date arithmetic to generate a number
corresponding to each date.

dBASE will calculate the number of days between two dates: DATE1 −
DATE2 is evaluated as the number of days between DATE1 and DATE2. This is
an effective tool for indexing on combined key expressions like customer name
and transaction date. The number of days from a fixed date will correspond to the
chronological order of the entries; just choose a date that is earlier than all the
entries in the file.

Say you have a transaction file that includes records for more than one year, with the earliest records in 1980. You want the records grouped by customer and in date order for each customer; the date of each transaction is in the field TR__DATE. Tell dBASE to

```
INDEX ON CUSTOMER + STR(TR_DATE - CTOD("12/31/79"), 4) TO CU_DATE
```

The phrase TR__DATE $-$CTOD("12/31/79") evaluates to a number—the number of days between 12/31/79 and the entry in TR__DATE. Then STR( ) is used to convert that number to a character string of length 4, so that it can be combined with the entry in CUSTOMER (see Tip 4.13).

4.18 Trap: *If you combine fields in the key expression of your index, you may get misleading results when you use SEEK or FIND to access a certain record.*

Trap 4.44 explains this trap, and Tips 4.45 and 4.46 help you avoid it.

4.19 Trap: *If you use TRIM( ) within the key expression of your index, dBASE may not be able to position on some of your records.*

If you tell dBASE to

```
INDEX ON TRIM(L_NAME) + F_NAME TO NAMES
```

it will create an index file and indicate that all of the records have been indexed; but you can run into problems when you try to locate particular records.

When dBASE creates an index file, it sets aside a certain fixed length for the key expression. If you use TRIM( ) within your key expression, dBASE will use the result of TRIM( ) on the first record in your file to determine this length. If subsequent records are longer, their key expressions will not be stored in their entirety in the index file, and they may not be located or processed correctly when the index file is open.

Your index file will work properly if the key expression is the same length for all records in the database file. When you combine fields, the length remains constant, since dBASE fills any unused spaces in a field with blanks. TRIM( ) eliminates these blanks and results in variable-length strings.

Trap 4.44 and Tips 4.45 and 4.46 discuss blank spaces within the key expression of an index.

4.20 Tip: *You can use any valid dBASE expression that does not change the length of a string in the key expression of an index file.*

As the preceding trap explains, dBASE requires the key expression of an index file to be the same length for all records. As long as you meet this requirement, you can INDEX ON any valid dBASE expression.

See the following three tips for examples.

4.21 Tip: *You can INDEX ON a numeric field in descending order.*

dBASE creates all index files in ascending order, so numeric fields are processed from smallest entry to largest. You can reverse this order by indexing on the opposite of the numbers. For example, to order your records from largest amount to smallest, tell dBASE to

```
INDEX ON AMOUNT * -1 TO AM_DESC
```

This method will not work if you try to combine a descending numerical order with other fields in your key expression. The numbers will have to be converted to character strings (see Trap 4.12 and Tip 4.13), and character strings are not indexed the same way as positive and negative numbers.

To combine a field in decreasing numeric order with other fields, INDEX ON an expression that first subtracts each entry from the largest number that would fit into the field and then converts it to character data with STR( ). Say you want to generate a sales report that lists the sales of each of your salespersons in the order of highest amount to lowest. The AMOUNT field is length 6 with two decimal places. To order your records for this report, just

```
INDEX ON SALESPER + STR(999.99 - AMOUNT, 6, 2) TO SPER_AMT
```

4.22 Tip: *You can INDEX ON date fields in descending order.*

To process date fields in descending order, with the most recent dates first, INDEX ON an expression that subtracts each entry from a date in the future. For instance, with a date field named DATE—IN, just tell dBASE to

```
INDEX ON CTOD("12/31/99") - DATE_IN TO DATE_DEC
```

If you want to combine descending date order with another order, you will have to convert to character data. Since the result of subtracting one date from another is a number (the number of days between the dates), this numeric part of the key expression must be converted with STR( ). (See Tip 4.13.)

As an example, suppose you want a list of sales to each customer in date order, with the most recent sale first. The date of each sale is stored in S—DATE, a date field. Tell dBASE to

```
INDEX ON CUSTOMER + STR(CTOD("12/31/99") - S_DATE, 8) TO CUS_DATE
```

4.23 Tip: *You can keep the most recently entered records at the top of your database file.*

If you'd like the record pointer to go to the most recent record every time you USE your database file, you can

```
INDEX ON RECNO() * -1 TO RECENT
```

The file will appear to operate upside-down, with new records appended to the top of the file.

4.24 Trap: *dBASE will not accept a key expression that is longer than 100 characters.*

If you try to INDEX ON an expression that is more than 100 characters long, dBASE will respond "Index is too big (100 char maximum)".

See the following tip.

4.25 Tip: *You can use part of a character field in your key expression with SUBSTR( ).*

If you would like to INDEX ON an expression that includes long character fields, SUBSTR( ) lets you use just part of the entry in a field. For example, to use L_NAME, F_NAME, and the first five letters of CO_NAME for a key expression, tell dBASE to

```
INDEX ON L_NAME + F_NAME + SUBSTR(CO_NAME, 1, 5) TO NAME_CO
```

SUBSTR( ) is used to access part of a character string. The general form is SUBSTR(*character string, start, length*), where

- *character string* is the original string.

- *start* is a number, the position in the original string of the first letter to be used for the new string.

- *length* is the number of characters to be used.

If no length is specified, dBASE will take all of the characters from the starting position to the end of the original string.

When you are creating an index, be sure to include the length parameter with SUBSTR( ); as explained in Trap 4.19, dBASE requires that the key expression of an index file have a fixed length.

4.26 Trap: *If you are working with a large indexed file in which many records have been updated, dBASE will process your operations on the file more slowly.*

Many dBASE commands proceed through a file in the sequence of the indexed order: AVERAGE, COUNT, DISPLAY FOR, LIST, REPORT, SUM, TOTAL, UPDATE, and so on. When a large file has been heavily updated, the indexed order will differ greatly from the record-number order and dBASE will be slow in executing these sequential-access commands.

See the following tip.

4.27 Tip: *You can speed up the processing of a heavily updated indexed file by copying the file with the index in use.*

All sequential-access commands work more quickly on a file whose record-number order is close to its indexed order. Files that are heavily updated should be copied with the index open periodically. This will reassign the record numbers to correspond to the indexed order. Then the record pointer can move rapidly from record to record, saving you much time when your database file is large.

See Tip 4.03 for the COPY procedure used to copy a file with an open index.

4.28 Tip: *To quickly check a file for duplicate entries, create an index with SET UNIQUE ON.*

If you have entered SET UNIQUE ON before you create an index, dBASE will ignore duplicates of the key expression. For example, the file CUSTOMER is related to other files by the key field CUST_CODE; it is imperative that each customer have a unique CUST_CODE or the relations will not work correctly. To check that all codes are unique, enter

```
USE CUSTOMER

SET UNIQUE ON

INDEX ON CUST_CODE TO CODE_CHK
```

When dBASE builds an index file it displays a message telling you how many records have been indexed. Use the LIST STRUCTURE command to quickly see how many records are in CUSTOMER, and compare this number to the final count of indexed records. If the numbers are the same, you can be confident that each customer has a unique code; if not, the difference between the numbers will tell you how many duplicate codes are in the file.

Be sure that SET UNIQUE is OFF after you use it; see Trap 4.30.

4.29 Tip: *To eliminate duplicate entries from a file, use the INDEX command with SET UNIQUE ON, and then use COPY TO with the index file active.*

When an index file is active, COPY TO will copy the records in the indexed order. If a record is not included in the index file, it will not be copied.

Suppose you have two files, CUSTOMER and PROSPECT, with the same structure. Some of the entries in CUSTOMER are also listed in PROSPECT. You'd like to combine the records into a file called MAIL_LST for your mailings, and you don't want any duplicate records.

1. First, get all the records into the combined file:

```
USE CUSTOMER

COPY TO TEMP

USE TEMP

APPEND FROM PROSPECT
```

2. Create an index file that will have no entries for duplicate records:

```
SET UNIQUE ON

INDEX ON L_NAME + F_NAME TO NO_DUP
```

3. Create the MAIL_LST file by copying with the index file active:

```
COPY TO MAIL_LST
```

Be sure to read the following trap.

4.30 Trap: *If you create an index file while SET UNIQUE is ON, the index will not be updated reliably when you make changes in the database file.*

An index file created while SET UNIQUE is ON will not include entries for duplicated key expressions, which means it may not have an entry for each record number that is used in your file. This can create problems when the file is updated.

Consider index files created when SET UNIQUE is ON as tools for specific tasks, as detailed in the two preceding tips. Don't try to use them to keep your database file in order.

If you create an index file with SET UNIQUE ON, be sure to enter SET UNIQUE OFF after you finish the task that required the index. You don't want other index files accidentally created or updated while SET UNIQUE is ON.

Locating and Processing Selected Data

As dBASE moves from record to record within a database file, it keeps the record number of its current location in a record pointer. Whenever you have a file open, dBASE has access to one record at a time, as indicated by the position of this pointer. If you want to process a particular record, you must first move the record pointer to its location within the file.

When you open a file, the record pointer is positioned at the top of the file. This will be record 1 if no index is in use; when an index file is active, the top of the file will be the first record in the indexed order. Here is how you can move around in the file:

- To return to the first record, tell dBASE to GO TOP.

- To move to the last record in the file, use GO BOTTOM.

- To move the record pointer to the next record in the file or the next record in index order if an index file is open, tell dBASE to SKIP.

- You can move a specific number of records ahead in the file with SKIP *number*.

- Move back a specific number of records by using SKIP − *number*.

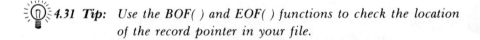 **4.31 Tip:** *Use the BOF( ) and EOF( ) functions to check the location of the record pointer in your file.*

Two built-in dBASE functions are related to the record pointer:

- BOF( ) is .T. (true) when the record pointer is positioned above the first record in the file and is .F. (false) otherwise.

- EOF( ) is .T. when the record pointer has passed beyond the last record in the file, and is .F. otherwise.

You can check for each of these positions from the dot prompt. Enter

`?BOF()`

and dBASE will respond .T. only if the pointer is at the beginning of the file (that is, above the first record). Similarly,

```
?EOF()
```

will return .F. unless the record pointer has passed beyond the last record in your file.

These functions are useful within dBASE application programs. To process all records in a file, use this:

```
GO TOP

DO WHILE .NOT. EOF()

   <processing of a single record>

   SKIP

ENDDO
```

After each record is processed, the SKIP command moves the record pointer to the next record. If you omit SKIP, the same record will be processed over and over; dBASE needs to be explicitly told to move the record pointer within a program. The preceding program structure will process every record in the file, since EOF( ) is not true (.T.) until the record pointer passes beyond the last record.

To process records by starting at the bottom of the file and continuing backwards through the entire file, use a similar approach:

```
GO BOTTOM

DO WHILE .NOT. BOF()

   <processing of a single record>

   SKIP -1

ENDDO
```

Again, since BOF( ) is not true until the record pointer passes above the first record, every record in the file will be processed.

4.32 Tip: *You can display selected data on the screen and on paper.*

Figure 4-2 shows a database file, called CHECKS, with its 15 records indexed on the field CATEGORY. The LIST command allows you to specify particular records to be displayed.

You can use the **LIST FOR** commands to select all records that meet a certain condition, as shown here:

```
. LIST FOR CHK_AMOUNT > 20
Record#    CHK_NO CHK_DATE PAY_TO            CHK_AMOUNT IS_CLEAR CATEGORY
      7    507    03/25/85 ROP CATERING           21.35 .F.      ALLOWANCE
      2    502    03/20/85 MARCY'S               259.01 .F.      CLOTHES
      5    505    03/24/85 XYZ SUPERMARKET        71.65 .F.      FOOD
      9    509    03/26/85 CORNER STORE           22.12 .F.      FOOD
      6    506    03/25/85 KATHY REED             72.00 .F.      HOUSECLEAN
.
```

dBASE checks each record to see if **CHK__AMOUNT** is greater than 20 and then lists the records that meet the condition.

You can combine more than one condition by using **.AND.**:

```
. LIST FOR CATEGORY = "INCIDENTALS" .AND. CHK_AMOUNT > 10
Record#    CHK_NO CHK_DATE PAY_TO            CHK_AMOUNT IS_CLEAR CATEGORY
      8    508    03/25/85 SMITH'S                13.75 .F.      INCIDENTALS
     11    512    03/30/85 XYZ DRUGS              10.10 .F.      INCIDENTALS
     13    514    03/31/85 CORNER STORE           10.78 .F.      INCIDENTALS
.
```

dBASE again checks each record, this time listing only the ones that meet both conditions.

```
. USE CHECKS INDEX CHK_CAT
.
. LIST
Record#    CHK_NO CHK_DATE PAY_TO            CHK_AMOUNT IS_CLEAR CATEGORY
      3    503    03/21/85 SMITH'S                 8.15 .F.      ALLOWANCE
     10    511    03/30/85 ROP CATERING            4.53 .F.      ALLOWANCE
     12    513    03/30/85 READ 'EM BOOKS          9.05 .F.      ALLOWANCE
      7    507    03/25/85 ROP CATERING           21.35 .F.      ALLOWANCE
     14    515    03/31/85 SARAH WILLIAMS          7.50 .F.      BABYSITTING
      2    502    03/20/85 MARCY'S               259.01 .F.      CLOTHES
      5    505    03/24/85 XYZ SUPERMARKET        71.65 .F.      FOOD
      9    509    03/26/85 CORNER STORE           22.12 .F.      FOOD
     15    510    03/29/85 CORNER STORE           13.33 .F.      FOOD
      6    506    03/25/85 KATHY REED             72.00 .F.      HOUSECLEAN
      1    501    03/20/85 CORNER STORE            2.85 .F.      INCIDENTALS
      4    504    03/24/25 DB DRUGS                9.38 .F.      INCIDENTALS
      8    508    03/25/85 SMITH'S                13.75 .F.      INCIDENTALS
     11    512    03/30/85 XYZ DRUGS              10.10 .F.      INCIDENTALS
     13    514    03/31/85 CORNER STORE           10.78 .F.      INCIDENTALS
.
```

Figure 4-2. The CHECKS database file

You can also combine conditions by using .OR. Any record that meets either or both of the conditions will be listed:

```
. LIST FOR CATEGORY = "BABYSITTING" .OR. CATEGORY = "HOUSECLEAN"
Record#   CHK_NO CHK_DATE PAY_TO           CHK_AMOUNT IS_CLEAR CATEGORY
    14    515    03/31/85 SARAH WILLIAMS         7.50 .F.      BABYSITTING
     6    506    03/25/85 KATHY REED            72.00 .F.      HOUSECLEAN
.
.
. LIST FOR PAY_TO = "CORNER STORE" .OR. CHK_AMOUNT < 10
Record#   CHK_NO CHK_DATE PAY_TO           CHK_AMOUNT IS_CLEAR CATEGORY
     3    503    03/21/85 SMITH'S                8.15 .F.      ALLOWANCE
    10    511    03/30/85 ROP CATERING           4.53 .F.      ALLOWANCE
    12    513    03/30/85 READ 'EM BOOKS         9.05 .F.      ALLOWANCE
    14    515    03/31/85 SARAH WILLIAMS         7.50 .F.      BABYSITTING
     9    509    03/26/85 CORNER STORE          22.12 .F.      FOOD
    15    510    03/29/85 CORNER STORE          13.33 .F.      FOOD
     1    501    03/20/85 CORNER STORE           2.85 .F.      INCIDENTALS
     4    504    03/24/25 DB DRUGS               9.38 .F.      INCIDENTALS
    13    514    03/31/85 CORNER STORE          10.78 .F.      INCIDENTALS
.
```

If you include the command TO PRINT after the condition, the selected records will be printed out for you.

To display selected data in an indexed file you can move the record pointer to the first record that makes the condition true and then use LIST WHILE:

```
. FIND FOOD
.
. LIST WHILE CATEGORY = "FOOD"
Record#   CHK_NO CHK_DATE PAY_TO           CHK_AMOUNT IS_CLEAR CATEGORY
     5    505    03/24/85 XYZ SUPERMARKET       71.65 .F.      FOOD
     9    509    03/26/85 CORNER STORE          22.12 .F.      FOOD
    15    510    03/29/85 CORNER STORE          13.33 .F.      FOOD
.
```

FIND is used here to move the record pointer to the first record in the FOOD category, and LIST WHILE displays each record that has the entry FOOD in CATEGORY.

FIND followed by LIST WHILE *condition* can only be used when the file is indexed on the field(s) involved in the condition. Use this approach whenever you can; it is much faster than LIST FOR, which checks every record in the file to see if it meets the condition. This can be time-consuming, particularly with a large file.

LIST WHILE will process all of the records that meet the condition, and it will stop as soon as one record does not. See Tip 4.36 and Trap 4.37 for a discussion of using FIND to locate a particular record or group of records.

4.33 Trap: *If you use LIST to display many records, they will scroll off the screen before you can read them.*

The LIST command keeps displaying the specified records and does not pause until all of them have been displayed. This often results in more than one screenful of data. To stop the scrolling, press CTRL-S; press any key to resume scrolling.

4.34 Tip: *To see one screenful of records at a time, use DISPLAY ALL.*

If you enter DISPLAY, dBASE will show you the current record only. If you enter DISPLAY ALL, dBASE will show the entire file, one screenful at a time, with a pause between screens until you press RETURN.

To view certain records, use FOR or WHILE *condition* with DISPLAY ALL, exactly as they are used with LIST (see Tip 4.32). In every case, DISPLAY ALL will show the requested records with pauses between screenfuls.

4.35 Tip: *Choose the most appropriate dBASE tool to locate a particular record or group of records.*

To work with a specified record or with a group of related records, you have to move the record pointer to each record before you can process it. dBASE provides several tools for locating records; if a file is indexed on the criterion you use for your search, records can be located with amazing speed, even in a very large database.

To choose the best tool for a particular task, you need to consider the following questions. Each item listed here is treated in detail in the tips and traps following this one.

- Is the file indexed on the field or fields involved? FIND and SEEK work very quickly with indexed files. If your search involves an expression that is not the key for an index file, FIND and SEEK will not work; use LOCATE FOR instead.

- Are you working in interactive mode, or are you writing a program? FIND works effectively with character strings from the dot prompt, but it has limited use within programs. SEEK is often a better choice. See Tip 4.38 for details on the use of SEEK or FIND in application programs.

- Do you need to locate records that match a particular entry, or records that compare in a certain way with your criterion? FIND and SEEK are limited in that they can locate only matching entries; LOCATE FOR can be used for comparisons or logical relationships.

4.36 Tip: *Use FIND or SEEK to locate a record by its entry in the key expression of the active index file.*

One of your customers has moved, and you need to change the address data in your CUSTOMER file. The file is indexed on the character field CUST—CODE, and the code for American Tire Company is AMTIRE. Tell dBASE to

```
USE CUSTOMER INDEX CU_CODE

FIND AMTIRE
```

dBASE moves the record pointer to the first record that has AMTIRE in the CUST—CODE field.

If there is no record with a key expression that matches AMTIRE, dBASE responds with "No find". Otherwise, the dot prompt appears and the record pointer is positioned at the matching record. Enter DISPLAY to view the record.

You could use the SEEK command to find the record as well; SEEK requires quotes around character data, so you would enter

```
SEEK "AMTIRE"
```

If you were not sure of the code for American Tire, you could use FIND AM or SEEK "AM". Either command would locate the first record in which the beginning of the character field matched the search string.

If you are searching a numeric field, both commands require a perfect match. Neither FIND 24 nor SEEK 24 would locate a record with 24.5 in the key field.

See the following three tips and traps.

4.37 Trap: *You will receive a "No find" message if you use FIND memvar or if you use FIND &memvar with numeric or date fields, even when there are matching records in the file.*

If you enter FIND XXX, dBASE assumes that XXX is a string to be matched and searches for XXX in the key expressions of the index. If you enter FIND &*memvar*, dBASE assumes *memvar* is a character variable and searches for the contents of the memory variable as character data.

See the following tip.

4.38 Tip: *Use SEEK rather than FIND in your dBASE application programs.*

Many dBASE application programs need to position the record pointer on a particular record requested by the user. Suppose you are writing a program that will find the code of a desired customer in your CUSTOMER file and will then position the record pointer to that record.

The CUSTOMER file is in use, and the index on CUST_CODE is active; CUST_CODE is a character field of length 6. The program will initialize a memory variable to hold the requested code and then will ask for the code:

```
STORE SPACE(6) TO M_CODE
@7,3 SAY "Enter code of customer to be edited:" GET M_CODE
```

Now you want the program to locate the entry made at the keyboard and stored in the memory variable M_CODE. SEEK can do this directly:

```
SEEK M_CODE
```

FIND, however, requires a macro:

```
FIND &M_CODE
```

Each command makes different assumptions about the character data and handles it differently. When you enter FIND XXX, dBASE assumes that XXX is a string; when you enter SEEK XXX, dBASE assumes that XXX is the name of a memory variable. These assumptions force you to use quotes with SEEK "string" so that dBASE does not identify "string" as a memory variable, and to use the macro with FIND &*memvar*, so that dBASE does not identify *memvar* as a string.

SEEK can search for the contents of a character, numeric, or date memory variable without requiring macro expansion. FIND requires a macro, and can search only for the contents of a character memory variable.

FIND and SEEK also differ in their ability to process expressions like CTOD( ) and TRIM( ), as explained in Trap 4.47 and Tip 4.48. Because of these differences, it's most efficient to use FIND only with a particular string, such as FIND "SMITH", and SEEK with the contents of a memory variable, such as SEEK M_NAME, or an expression like SEEK TRIM (M_CITY).

 4.39 Trap: FIND and SEEK can position the record pointer only at the first matching record in the indexed order of the file.

Both FIND and SEEK use the structure of the index file to locate a particular entry in the key expression field or fields. Both commands position the record pointer at the first match in the indexed order of the file, regardless of where the record pointer was positioned when the FIND or SEEK command was given. This means that you cannot use SEEK or FIND to move to subsequent records that have a matching key expression.

However, since the INDEX command grouped all records with matching key expressions together in the file, you can move consecutively through the file to find all of the matching records. In your dBASE application programs you will need to move the record pointer with SKIP and test each new record to see if the key expression is still a match. See the following tip.

 4.40 Tip: Use SKIP with SEEK in your dBASE application programs to process all records that have the same key expression.

If your program used SEEK to move the record pointer to the first record with the desired key expression, you can use SKIP to process all matching records. The file has to have been indexed on the key expression for SEEK to work, so all of these records will be grouped together. You can process them in order until all the matching records have been processed.

Here is the general procedure:

```
SEEK <memvar>

DO WHILE <key expression> = <memvar> .AND. (.NOT. EOF())

   <processing of a single record>

   SKIP

ENDDO
```

SEEK *memvar* finds the first record in the file that has a key expression matching the entry in the memory variable. The DO WHILE loop begins at this record and processes it; then SKIP moves the record pointer to the next record. At ENDDO, dBASE returns to the top of the loop and checks to see whether the key expression of this new record is still a match. If it is a match, it is processed; if not (or if the end of the file has been reached), control moves to the program line after ENDDO.

Be sure to read the following trap and tip.

 4.41 Trap: *If your program uses SEEK, don't forget to tell the user if no matching record was found.*

SEEK has two possible results: a match is found and the record pointer is moved to the matching record, or no match is found. In dBASE programs, SET TALK is usually OFF, which prevents dBASE messages from appearing on the screen. When SET TALK is OFF, the "No find" message will not be displayed when a search is not successful. If your program doesn't display a message when a match is not found, the person using the program will not know why no records are being processed.

See the following tip.

4.42 Tip: *If your program locates records with SEEK, use the EOF( ) function to control what happens when no matching record is found.*

When SEEK does not find a match, the record pointer moves beyond the last record in the file and EOF( ) is set to .T. Figures 4-3 and 4-4 show how this is used in a program. Figure 4-3 gives the general structure, and Figure 4-4 gives the sample dBASE code.

Let's look at the key steps of the program:

1. The file is in use, and the relevant index is active (as it must be anytime you use SEEK).

2. STORE SPACE(15) TO M—CAT

M—CAT is a memory variable that will contain the user's request for a category to locate in the file. Since the CATEGORY field has length 15, M—CAT is initialized to match it.

3. STORE .F. TO FOUND

The program will continue asking for a category to search for until a search is successful; FOUND is a logical variable that keeps track of whether a search has been successful. Before any attempts have been made to locate a record, no match has been found, so FOUND is initialized to .F.

```
Have database file in use with index active
*
Initialize memory variable to hold search request
*
Initialize logical flag to .F.
*
Repeat until search is successful - until flag is .T.
    *
    Clear error message rows
    *
    Ask for search request - upper case
    *
    Search for requested entry
    *
    IF search is successful
        Change flag to .T.
        *
    Otherwise
        Display error message
        WAIT for return to re-enter
        *
End of search loop
*
Clear screen
*
Repeat for each record that matches search request
    *
    process a record
        *
    move to next record
    *
End of processing loop
```

Figure 4-3. Using EOF( ) with SEEK (program structure)

4. DO WHILE .NOT. FOUND

This portion of the code will be repeated until a search is successful.

5. @15,0
   @17,0

Rows 15 and 17 are used to display messages after an unsuccessful search. These lines must be cleared before each search to clear messages from a prior search from the screen (see the tips and traps in Chapter 3 on displaying error messages).

6. @3,5 SAY "Budget Category:" GET M__CAT PICTURE "@!"
   READ

The search criterion is requested and taken in; the PICTURE function converts whatever is entered to uppercase. The file being searched has all entries in upper-case letters, so dBASE needs the search string in uppercase as well (see the following tip).

7. SEEK M__CAT

dBASE will locate a matching record if there is a match in the file.

8. IF .NOT. EOF( )
       STORE .T. TO FOUND

If SEEK finds a match, the record pointer is moved to that record, and EOF( ) is .F. Since there is no need to repeat the search, the flag FOUND is changed to .T. so that dBASE will not repeat the searching loop.

9. ELSE
       @15,3 SAY "*** CATEGORY NOT FOUND--ENTER ANOTHER
   CATEGORY ***"
       @16,0
       WAIT "   *** Press return to re-enter category ***"

When a matching record is not found, these messages are displayed to let the user know that the requested category is not in the file. The WAIT line adds a pause to give the user time to read the message and understand what has happened.

10. ENDDO ** WHILE .NOT. FOUND

This is the end of the search loop. Program control returns to the beginning of the loop, and the **DO WHILE** condition is checked to see whether the loop should be executed again. If a search has been successful, FOUND is now .T. and the loop will not repeat. If no matching record has been located, FOUND is still .F. and dBASE will execute the loop again, requesting another category to search for, and the process repeats.

11. DO WHILE CATEGORY = M—CAT .AND. (.NOT. EOF( ))

This is the loop for processing all records that match the search criterion. dBASE will not execute this loop until it has finished with the searching loop; that is, until a matching record has been found. Tip 4.40 explains the **DO WHILE** loop.

```
*** file in use with index on CATEGORY active
*
CLEAR
*
STORE SPACE(15) TO M_CAT
*
STORE .F. TO FOUND
*
DO WHILE .NOT. FOUND
    *
    @15,0
    @17,0
    *
    @3,5 SAY "Budget Category:" GET M_CAT PICTURE "@!"
    READ
    *
    SEEK M_CAT
    *
    IF .NOT. EOF()
        STORE .T. TO FOUND
    *
    ELSE
        @15,3 SAY "*** CATEGORY NOT FOUND -- ENTER ANOTHER CATEGORY. ***"
        @16,0
        WAIT "    *** Press return to re-enter category. ***"
    *
    ENDIF ** .NOT. EOF()
    *
ENDDO ** WHILE .NOT. FOUND
*
CLEAR
*
DO WHILE CATEGORY = M_CAT .AND. (.NOT. EOF())
    *
    <processing of a single record >
    *
    SKIP
    *
ENDDO ** WHILE CATEGORY = M_CAT
*
*** program continues
```

Figure 4-4. Using EOF( ) with SEEK (dBASE code)

4.43 Tip: *Locating particular records is easier if you keep all charac-ter entries in uppercase letters.*

When an index file is created on a key expression of the character type, dBASE orders the entries according to the ASCII values of the characters. "AMTIRE" does not match "Amtire": uppercase letters do not match lowercase letters.

If you keep all your data records entirely in uppercase (by using the CAPS LOCK key from the dot prompt and PICTURE clauses in custom screens), you can be confident that your records will be indexed with all matching key expressions together. You can then always use uppercase with search strings, and if the result is "No find", you can be certain no other entry has the same letters as your search string.

4.44 Trap: *If a key expression incorporates more than one field, FIND or SEEK might not locate matching entries.*

FIND and SEEK locate records that match the searching criterion. With character strings, the entire search string must match the beginning of the entry in the field; numeric data requires that all of the digits in the field match.

The form of the data in the key field of the index file is very important here: if the key expression for a record contains blank spaces between the contents of two fields, a search will be unsuccessful unless the searching criterion also contains exactly the same number of blanks.

Consider a mailing-list file indexed on L_NAME + F_NAME. If each name field is of length 12, the record for PAUL JOHNSON is represented in the index file by "JOHNSON   PAUL   ", and FIND JOHN-SON PAUL will not match this key expression.

See the following two tips.

4.45 Tip: *To use FIND or SEEK with a key expression incorporating more than one field, your searching criterion must be con-structed the same way the key expression was constructed.*

The SEEK and FIND commands are successful only if the searching criterion has exactly the same form as the entry in the key field of the index file (see the preceding trap). You need to choose your searching criterion to ensure this match.

If you want to use FIND to search your file from the dot prompt, you can create an index file with no spaces between the fields. Thus, in MAIL—LST, which is indexed by last name and first name, FIND JOHNSONPAUL will locate the record for Paul Johnson. (See the following tip.)

If you want to use SEEK within a dBASE program, there is an easy way to ensure that the searching criterion matches the form of the index file. Say you write a program segment to locate records indexed on L—NAME + F—NAME, where each field is of length 12.

First, for each field initialize a memory variable of the same length as the field:

```
STORE SPACE(12) TO M_LAST, M_FIRST
```

Now ask the user for the name to be searched for, and use GET to obtain the input:

```
a5,3 SAY "Last Name:" GET M_LAST PICTURE "a!"

a7,3 SAY "First Name:" GET M_FIRST PICTURE "a!"

READ
```

The STORE command gives M—LAST and M—FIRST length 12. When dBASE executes READ, the keyboard input will be stored in each memory variable, followed by as many blanks as are needed to fill the 12 spaces. Since GET with a memory variable uses blanks to fill any spaces after the entry, you can use GET to create a memory variable that will precisely match the data in a field.

Now you can use SEEK with an expression that will match the structure of the index file's key expression:

```
SEEK M_LAST + M_FIRST
```

This command tells dBASE to combine the 12 characters (including any blanks) of M—LAST with the 12 characters of M—FIRST, in exactly the same way as the command INDEX ON L—NAME + F—NAME created the index file.

Leading blanks in a numeric field require a similar solution. Suppose a file named SALES has a record for each sale; the record includes fields containing the salesperson's initials and the amount of the commission. To generate a report that lists each salesperson's sales in order of increasing commissions, you would need an index created with

```
INDEX ON S_PER + STR(COM, 6, 2) TO SP_COMM
```

The STR( ) function converts each commission to a string of length 6; if the amount of a commission does not fill all six spaces, dBASE will add leading blanks. Thus, entries in the index can have key expressions with embedded blanks, such as DF 78.50, as well as entries without blanks, such as HP212.00.

To search this index from the dot prompt, you must construct the string to match the key expression of the index file. Within a program, the approach used previously for character strings will construct the matching string for you:

```
STORE SPACE(2) TO M_SPER

STORE 000.00 TO M_COMM

@5,3 SAY "Salesperson's Initials:" GET M_SPER PICTURE "!!"

@7,3 SAY "Amount of Commission:" GET M_COMM

READ

SEEK M_SPER + STR(M_COMM, 6, 2)
```

To use SEEK successfully with a key expression created from more than one field,

1. Create memory variables that match the fields used in the key expression.

2. Use GET to input the search request.

3. Combine the memory variables in the SEEK command exactly as the fields were combined in the **INDEX ON** *expression*.

4.46 Tip: *If you will be searching your file on a key expression that contains character fields, you can join the fields with "-" when you use the INDEX command.*

This approach can be particularly useful if you will be searching your database file from the dot prompt. dBASE has two ways to concatenate strings:

* STRING1 + STRING2 adds STRING2 onto the end of STRING1; if there are blanks at the end of STRING1, they will be embedded in the combined string:

"JOHNSON " + "PAUL " results in "JOHNSON PAUL "

* STRING1 − STRING2 adds STRING2 onto the end of STRING1 and moves any blanks at the end of STRING1 to the end of STRING2:

"JOHNSON " − "PAUL " results in "JOHNSONPAUL   "

If you index on FIELD1 + FIELD2, a search string must have the correct number of blanks between the field entries in order for SEEK or FIND to match the key expression (see Trap 4.44). Within a program, this is easy to do, as explained in the preceding tip, but you would have to insert the correct number of blank spaces yourself from the dot prompt.

If you index on FIELD1—FIELD2, the search string should contain the field entries with no blank spaces between them. At the dot prompt, just enter the strings this way; within a program, search on *memvar1—memvar2*.

4.47 Trap: *If you try to use FIND expression with an expression that involves a dBASE function other than "+" or "—", matching records will not be found.*

FIND cannot handle dBASE functions, such as TRIM( ) or CTOD( ), that may be essential for constructing a search criterion. The response will be "No find" every time, even when there are matching records in the file.

See the following tip.

4.48 Tip: *Use SEEK to search on an expression that involves dBASE functions.*

SEEK can handle a wide variety of dBASE functions. Here are some examples:

- SEEK TRIM(*memvar*) finds records in which the beginning of the key expression matches the contents of the memory variable with any trailing blanks removed.

- SEEK CTOD("12/02/85") finds a record with 12/02/85 in a file indexed on a date field.

- SEEK CTOD(*memvar*) — 90 finds a record containing a date that is 90 days prior to the date entered at the keyboard and stored in the memory variable.

Use SEEK instead of FIND anytime you want to use a dBASE function other than "+" or "—" to construct your searching criterion.

✋ 4.49 Trap: *You cannot use FIND or SEEK with fields that are not indexed.*

Both FIND and SEEK are designed to take advantage of the special structure of an index file; they automatically search your database file on the key expression of the index, and they cannot be used to search on any other field or expression.

See the following tip.

💡 4.50 Tip: *LOCATE FOR enables you to access records on fields that are not indexed.*

The LOCATE command begins at the top of a database file and examines each record in turn (or by the indexed order if an index file is active) to see if the record matches the given criterion. LOCATE can examine any field or combination of fields, as specified in the command:

```
LOCATE FOR <condition>
```

Suppose your **CHECKS** database is indexed on a combination of the CATE-GORY field and the CHK_DATE field but not on PAY_TO, and you need a listing of all the checks written to Ace Supply. These records will not be grouped together by the index file, so SEEK or FIND will not work; instead, enter

```
LOCATE FOR PAY_TO = "ACE SUPPLY"
```

LOCATE FOR has the same results as FIND and SEEK: if a matching record exists, the record pointer will be moved to that record; if no match is found, EOF( ) becomes .T. In interactive mode, LOCATE will display the record number of a successful match or "End of locate scope" if no match is found. In an application program, you must test for the result of the search, as explained in Trap 4.41 and Tip 4.42.

You can combine more than one condition with LOCATE FOR. Let's say you want to see a list of all checks written to Ace Supply for more than $20.00. To move the record pointer to the first of the desired records, tell dBASE to

```
LOCATE FOR PAY_TO = "ACE SUPPLY" .AND. CHK_AMOUNT > 20
```

Since LOCATE FOR moves the record pointer in the same way as SEEK, it can be used in dBASE programs with essentially the same structure as that of programs using SEEK. See Tip 4.42 for a detailed example of this structure.

There is one way in which LOCATE FOR must be handled differently from SEEK or FIND; be sure to read the following trap and tip.

4.51 Trap: *If you follow LOCATE FOR with SKIP, or if you access records sequentially from the dot prompt, you will not be guaranteed access to all records that meet the searching criterion.*

When records have matching entries in the key expression of an index file, they are grouped together by the index. Once the record pointer has been moved to the first record in the group, each of the others can be reached by moving the record pointer sequentially in the indexed order.

When you use LOCATE FOR to find records by means of an expression that is not the key expression of the active index file, other matching records might be scattered through the rest of the file. Accessing records in sequential order will not find other matching records for you; dBASE needs to be told to continue searching for the specified LOCATE condition in the rest of the file.

See the following tip.

4.52 Tip: *Use the CONTINUE command with LOCATE FOR to process all of the records that meet the LOCATE condition.*

When the LOCATE command is issued, dBASE starts searching at the top of the file, so repeating a LOCATE command won't help you find all the records that meet a certain condition.

CONTINUE tells dBASE to search on the same condition as the most recent LOCATE command, but to begin the search at the record following the current position of the record pointer. CONTINUE allows you to proceed through the file, moving the record pointer to each record that meets the searching criterion and reaching the end of the file when all of the specified records have been found.

A dBASE program using LOCATE FOR will use CONTINUE to move to the next desired record; otherwise, the structure is the same as the one used with SEEK:

```
<LOCATE the first of the desired records>
DO WHILE <LOCATE condition> .AND. (.NOT. EOF())
    <processing of a single record>
    CONTINUE
ENDDO
```

See Tip 4.42 for an explanation of this loop.

✋ **4.53 Trap:** *LOCATE FOR is not the most efficient dBASE tool with which to search for an exact match on the key expression of an index file.*

LOCATE FOR is substantially slower than the SEEK and FIND commands when searching for entries in the key expression of an index. SEEK and FIND take advantage of the unique logical structure of a dBASE index file, which is designed to make very rapid searching possible; LOCATE FOR simply checks each record in the file against the search condition. The time difference can be significant with large database files.

Use SEEK or FIND whenever possible; use LOCATE FOR only when the searching task is beyond the scope of those commands.

✋ **4.54 Trap:** *SEEK and FIND cannot be used to compare records to a searching criterion.*

SEEK and FIND can locate only records that match a search criterion; you can only give SEEK or FIND an expression to be matched. You cannot FIND or SEEK, say, the first record with less than 20 in a certain field. Neither command will accept expressions involving either inequalities or the logical operators .AND., .NOT., and .OR.

See the following tip.

4.55 Tip: *If you want to process records that compare in a certain way to a searching criterion, use LOCATE FOR.*

LOCATE FOR *condition* is the most flexible of the dBASE searching commands; you can use comparisons, like <, >, or # (not equal to) or logical expressions that join more than one condition.

You can use LOCATE FOR with any valid dBASE expression that is either true or false for each record in your file. For example, to move the record pointer to the first record with an entry that is less than 50 in the numeric field CHK__ AMOUNT, you would enter

```
LOCATE FOR CHK_AMOUNT < 50
```

To locate the first check written to Ace Supply for more than 20 dollars, you would enter

```
LOCATE FOR PAY_TO = "ACE SUPPLY" .AND. CHK_AMOUNT > 20
```

To find the first check in the UTILITIES category that is not written to P BELL or PG&E, enter

```
LOCATE FOR CATEGORY = "UTILITIES" .AND. (PAY_TO # "PBELL" .AND. PAY_TO;
# "PG&E")
```

To move the record pointer to the first record with a company name that contains AUTO, enter

```
LOCATE FOR "AUTO" $ CO_NAME
```

Finally, to locate the first record that has .F. in the logical field named IS__ CLEAR, enter this:

```
LOCATE FOR .NOT. IS_CLEAR
```

In each of these cases, subsequent records that meet the condition can be located with CONTINUE (see Tip 4.52).

5

Working With More Than One Database File

The first section of Chapter 2, "Designing an Application System," discussed in detail how to design a system of database files that can hold large quantities of information with very little duplication of data entry or disk storage. The result is a group of files, each containing one particular category of data, related to one another by a common field or expression.

This chapter focuses on how dBASE allows you to work with an entire system of database files at once:

- You can access as many as ten files without repeatedly opening and closing them.

- You can move back and forth between files while you process data.

- You can update one file from the contents of another.

- You can establish a link between files so that related records in each file can be accessed together.

143

Using More Than One Workspace

5.01 **Tip:** *You can have more than one database file open at once, each in its own workspace.*

dBASE allows you to use as many as ten workspaces, each with an open database file and associated index and format files. You establish the workspaces with SELECT:

```
SELECT 1

USE ORDER

SELECT 2

USE CUSTOMER
```

Every time you use SELECT, you change the current workspace — in this case, to workspace 2, which contains the file CUSTOMER. Each workspace is independent, so you can move around in CUSTOMER, changing records or performing procedures, without affecting other files.

If you tell dBASE to

```
SELECT 1
```

then workspace 1 becomes current and you have full access to the ORDER file. When you have finished working with ORDER, you can return to workspace 2 and find CUSTOMER exactly the way you left it (see the following tip).

Any command that changes the data in a file or the structure of a file can be used only with the file in the current workspace. Moving the record pointer in the current workspace will not affect other open workspaces unless you have established a relation between the files (as described in "Using Related Databases" later in this chapter).

5.02 **Tip:** *You can move back and forth between database files without losing your place if you use multiple workspaces.*

If you remain in one workspace and you need to work with more than one file, you have to open the files with USE as you need them. When you do this, the record pointer is positioned at the top of the file.

Each workspace has an independent record pointer (unless you establish a relation between the files; see "Using Related Databases"). If you would like to move between files without moving the record pointer within a given file, have each file open in a different workspace and move between them with SELECT. Then when you process records in one file, you will not lose your place in an unselected file.

Say the ORDERS file is open in workspace 1 and the CUSTOMER file in workspace 2. You can locate the record for American Tire in CUSTOMER, move to workspace 1, and process several records in ORDERS. When you return to CUSTOMER, the record pointer will still be positioned at the record for American Tire.

5.03 Tip: *You can open a format file and as many as seven index files for the database file in each work area.*

Each workspace is a complete dBASE environment that you define. You can open a file with as many as seven indexes and a format file in each work area. There are two restrictions on opening files; see the following two traps.

5.04 Trap: *You cannot open the same file (whether it is a database file, index file, or format file) in more than one workspace.*

dBASE will not open a file in more than one workspace at a time. If you try to do so, you'll get the error message "ALIAS name already in use" or "File is already open".

But you can get around this limitation. Say you have a format file called NAME_IN.FMT that you use to add records to both your MAIL_LST and CUSTOMER files. You can have dBASE make a duplicate for you, giving each file a unique name:

```
RENAME NAME_IN.FMT TO MAIL_IN.FMT
COPY FILE MAIL_IN.FMT TO CUST_IN.FMT
```

Now you can have both MAIL＿LST and CUSTOMER open in different work-spaces, each with its own format file.

 5.05 Trap: *You cannot have more than 15 files open simultaneously.*

Because of the way dBASE III uses your computer's memory, you are limited to a total of 15 open files. This limit applies to all types of files—database, index, format, command, and procedure files. If you try to exceed this limit, you'll get the error message "Too many files open".

    Whenever you are working with dBASE III, open only the files that you will need to work on to accomplish the current task, and when you have finished working with them, close them (with USE).

5.06 Tip: *To save typing, use the ALIAS command to establish an alias filename.*

When you USE a dBASE file, you can assign it an *alias*. If you enter

```
USE CUSTOMER ALIAS CU
```

the file CUSTOMER is given the alias CU, which can be used in certain expressions to refer to this file (see the following tip). An alias created by the ALIAS command can be up to ten characters long and can contain letters, numbers, and the underscore character, but not blank spaces.

5.07 Tip: *You can refer to a workspace by its number, by its letter, or by the alias of the file that is open in that workspace.*

Each work area has a number from 1 to 10 and a letter from A to J to identify it. You can also identify the workspace by using the alias of the file opened in it.

    If the file CUSTOMER is open in workspace 3 and has the alias CU, any of these commands can be used to access the file:

```
SELECT 3

SELECT C

SELECT CU
```

If CUSTOMER was opened without assigning an alias, SELECT CU does not work (see Tip 5.08); you could use

```
SELECT CUSTOMER
```

When you refer to the fields in a file in an unselected workspace, dBASE will not accept the workspace numbers. You can use the workspace letter, or the alias of the file:

```
C->CO_NAME
```

```
CU->CO_NAME
```

If you do not assign an alias, you can use the name of the file to refer to a field:

```
CUSTOMER->CO_NAME
```

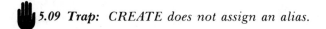 *5.08 Tip:* *If you don't assign an alias to a file, you can use the file-name every time you refer to the file.*

If you enter

```
USE CUSTOMER
```

dBASE will automatically assign the alias CUSTOMER to the file, so that the filename is the same as the alias. You can then use the filename whenever the alias can be used. As explained in the preceding tip, the alias is used to refer to files that are open in workspaces other than the currently selected workspace. If you would like to use the filename to refer to these files, just use the file without specifying an alias, and the filename will also be the alias.

5.09 Trap: *CREATE does not assign an alias.*

CREATE does not assign an alias to a new file and does not assign the filename to the alias. If you have a newly created file open in the current workspace and you need to assign it an alias, you must open the file again with USE. Otherwise, if you use the name of a newly created file in a command that requires an alias (see Tip 5.07), dBASE will respond "ALIAS not found". Whenever you know you will be using such commands with a file, be sure to open the file with USE. You can either specify an alias in your USE command, or allow dBASE to assign the filename to the alias (see the preceding tip).

5.10 Tip: *Use the DISPLAY STATUS command to check the alias assigned to a file.*

DISPLAY STATUS shows you the files that are open in each workspace and the alias assigned to each file:

```
. DISPLAY STATUS
Select area -  1, Database in use: B:IN_PARTS.dbf   Alias - PART
Select area -  2, Database in use: B:IN_PRICE.dbf   Alias - PRICE
Currently selected database:
Select area -  3, Database in use: B:IN_VEND.dbf    Alias - VENDOR
Press any key to continue...
```

You can change the alias by entering

```
USE YOURFILE ALIAS YOUR_ALIAS
```

or you can establish the filename itself as the default alias:

```
USE YOURFILE
```

5.11 Tip: *You can display or print data from the file in a workspace other than the currently selected workspace.*

Say you are processing a customer order; CUSTOMER is open in workspace A and ORDER in workspace B.

First you SELECT A, the CUSTOMER file, and locate the record of the customer placing the order. Next you move to the ORDER file with SELECT B and enter the details of the order, such as the parts ordered and the quantity.

You can display data from the CUSTOMER file without leaving workspace B. Preface each field name you want from the file with the letter representing the workspace that file is in (see Tip 5.07), followed by an arrow formed by a hyphen and a greater-than symbol (>):

```
LIST ORDER_NO, A->NAME, A->STREET, A->CITY, A->STATE, A->ZIP
```

dBASE will display the contents of the specified fields from the file in workspace A, even though workspace B is currently selected.

You can also use

```
@5,3 SAY A->NAME
```

to display the contents of a field from another workspace, but you cannot GET the contents of a field unless the file is in the currently selected workspace.

Be sure to read the following two traps.

5.12 Trap: *If you try to display the contents of a memo field in a workspace that is not currently selected, you'll get an error message.*

dBASE can read data from a file that is open in a workspace that is not currently selected (see the preceding tip), except for the contents of a memo field.

If you are in workspace A and you ask dBASE to

```
? B->MEMO_FIELD
```

you'll be told "Unrecognized phrase/keyword in command". If you try this:

```
LIST B->MEMO_FIELD
```

dBASE will respond with "No database in USE, enter filename:". To display the contents of a memo field, you must first select the workspace containing that file.

5.13 Trap: *You cannot change the records in a workspace that is not currently selected.*

The file in the current workspace (the one chosen in the most recent SELECT command) is the only file you can make changes in. You can read information from the files in other workspaces (as described in Tip 5.11), or you can use another open file to update the current file (see the next section of this chapter). But if a file is not in the current workspace, you cannot REPLACE data into its records, GET the contents of any of its fields, or use any other command that changes records. If you use one of these commands with a field name from an unselected file, dBASE will respond with "Variable not found".

To change the contents of a file, you must first SELECT the workspace containing that file.

5.14 Trap: *CONTINUE cannot be used with LOCATE in two different workspaces at the same time.*

If you use CONTINUE with LOCATE (see Chapter 4 for a discussion of these commands), you must remain in the same workspace while issuing these commands. Say you LOCATE a record in workspace 1, and then SELECT workspace 2 and LOCATE a record in it. When you return to workspace 1, CONTINUE will not move the record pointer to the next matching record. Instead, the record pointer will move to the next record in the file, even if this record does not meet the LOCATE condition.

To use LOCATE in more than one work area at once, enter the following:

```
SELECT 1
LOCATE FOR AMOUNT > 25
SELECT 2
LOCATE FOR QUANTITY < REORDER
SELECT 1
LOCATE NEXT 9999 FOR AMOUNT > 25
```

Instead of CONTINUE, a *scope* is used with LOCATE: the command NEXT tells dBASE to start with the next record in the file, and the number indicates how many records should be checked for a match. Choose a number larger than the highest record number in the file so that dBASE will search all records.

You can use this approach from the dot prompt or from within a dBASE program — in short, whenever you need to use LOCATE in more than one workspace and find all matching records.

5.15 Trap: *SELECT memvar will not select the work area whose name is stored in the memory variable.*

If you want to select a workspace named in a memory variable, use a macro (&) to explicitly tell dBASE to look inside the *memvar* (as described in Chapter 9).

Suppose you have written a program that asks the user which file to access and stores the alias of the file in the memory variable M_AREA. If you enter

```
SELECT M_AREA
```

it will result in the error message "Alias not found". Instead, you must use

```
SELECT &M_AREA
```

to choose the workspace stored in the memory variable.

5.16 Tip: *Keep an on-line notepad in workspace 10.*

Few applications require using all ten workspaces available. Keep a database file open in workspace 10 for notes to yourself. The file can have a date field and a memo field, or several long character fields — whatever would be useful. Then you can SELECT 10, jot down notes on a procedure, an idea, or a telephone call that interrupted your work, and return to your previous workspace to resume your work exactly where you left off.

Updating One File From Another

 5.17 Tip: *The UPDATE command can save you lots of editing time.*

Suppose the selling prices have changed for a number of items in your inventory, and you need to change the prices in your PARTS file accordingly. Here is the PARTS file:

```
. DISPLAY STRUCTURE
Structure for database : B:PARTS.dbf
Number of data records :      7
Date of last update    : 01/01/80
Field  Field name  Type       Width    Dec
    1  PART_CODE   Character      6
    2  DESCRIPT    Character     25
    3  UNIT_PRICE  Numeric        6       2
** Total **                     38

.
.
. LIST
Record#   PART_CODE  DESCRIPT                 UNIT_PRICE
      1   WI-104     2" COPPER WIDGET               1.17
      2   WI-111     3" COPPER WIDGET               2.50
      3   WI-102     2" RUBBER WIDGET               0.78
      4   WI-105     2-1/2" RUBBER WIDGET           1.03
      5   WI-108     3" RUBBER WIDGET               1.16
      6   WI-203     4" RUBBER WIDGET               1.87
      7   WI-211     4-1/2" RUBBER WIDGET           2.04
.
```

You could access the records one at a time by using EDIT mode or a custom editing program, thus making each change directly. But UPDATE can make the changes much more quickly:

1. Use the file with an index that uniquely identifies each record. In this file, PART_CODE is different for each record:

```
. SELECT 1
.
. USE PARTS
.
. INDEX ON PART_CODE TO PA_CODE
      7 records indexed
.
. LIST
Record#   PART_CODE  DESCRIPT                 UNIT_PRICE
      3   WI-102     2" RUBBER WIDGET               0.78
      1   WI-104     2" COPPER WIDGET               1.17
      4   WI-105     2-1/2" RUBBER WIDGET           1.03
      5   WI-108     3" RUBBER WIDGET               1.16
      2   WI-111     3" COPPER WIDGET               2.50
      6   WI-203     4" RUBBER WIDGET               1.87
      7   WI-211     4-1/2" RUBBER WIDGET           2.04
.
```

2. Open another workspace and create a new file with two fields — the key expression of the index on the file being updated, and the field to be updated:

```
. SELECT 2
.
. DISPLAY STRUCTURE
Structure for database : B:NU_PRICE.dbf
Number of data records :      4
Date of last update    : 01/01/80
Field  Field name  Type       Width     Dec
    1  PART_CODE   Character      6
    2  NU_PRICE    Numeric        6        2
** Total **                      13
.
```

3. Index the new file on the key expression field by using INDEX ON, and enter a record for each update:

```
. INDEX ON PART_CODE TO NU_CODE
     4 records indexed
.
. LIST
Record#   PART_CODE NU_PRICE
     2    WI-104       1.22
     3    WI-108       1.24
     1    WI-111       2.78
     4    WI-203       1.95
.
```

4. SELECT the workspace with the original file and then use the UPDATE command:

```
. SELECT 1
.
. UPDATE ON PART_CODE FROM NU_PRICE REPLACE UNIT_PRICE WITH B->NU_PRICE
     4 records updated
.
. LIST
Record#   PART_CODE DESCRIPT              UNIT_PRICE
     3    WI-102    2" RUBBER WIDGET          0.78
     1    WI-104    2" COPPER WIDGET          1.22
     4    WI-105    2-1/2" RUBBER WIDGET      1.03
     5    WI-108    3" RUBBER WIDGET          1.24
     2    WI-111    3" COPPER WIDGET          2.78
     6    WI-203    4" RUBBER WIDGET          1.95
     7    WI-211    4-1/2" RUBBER WIDGET      2.04
.
```

✋ *5.18 Trap:* *If the file undergoing the UPDATE procedure is not indexed on the key expression, some (or even many) of the records may not be updated.*

Let's use the same UPDATE command that is used in the previous tip, but without the necessary index on the target file (the file to be updated). We'll use very large numbers for the new prices, so the results of UPDATE will be easy to see:

```
. SELECT 1
.
. USE PARTS
.
. LIST
Record#    PART_CODE  DESCRIPT                     UNIT_PRICE
        1  WI-104     2" COPPER WIDGET                   1.22
        2  WI-111     3" COPPER WIDGET                   2.78
        3  WI-102     2" RUBBER WIDGET                   0.78
        4  WI-105     2-1/2" RUBBER WIDGET               1.03
        5  WI-108     3" RUBBER WIDGET                   1.24
        6  WI-203     4" RUBBER WIDGET                   1.95
        7  WI-211     4-1/2" RUBBER WIDGET              2.04
.
. SELECT 2
.
. USE NU_PRICE INDEX NU_CODE
.
. LIST
Record#    PART_CODE  NU_PRICE
        2  WI-104      33.33
        3  WI-108      44.44
        1  WI-111      55.55
        4  WI-203      66.66
.
```

dBASE will accept the UPDATE command with an unindexed target file. Here is the result:

```
. SELECT 1
.
. UPDATE ON PART_CODE FROM NU_PRICE REPLACE UNIT_PRICE WITH B->NU_PRICE
      3 records updated
.
. LIST
Record#    PART_CODE  DESCRIPT                     UNIT_PRICE
        1  WI-104     2" COPPER WIDGET                  33.33
        2  WI-111     3" COPPER WIDGET                  55.55
        3  WI-102     2" RUBBER WIDGET                   0.78
        4  WI-105     2-1/2" RUBBER WIDGET               1.03
        5  WI-108     3" RUBBER WIDGET                   1.24
        6  WI-203     4" RUBBER WIDGET                  66.66
        7  WI-211     4-1/2" RUBBER WIDGET              2.04
.
```

Record 5 was not updated.

When dBASE is told to UPDATE, it assumes the file in use is indexed (or sorted) on the key expression. The key expression entries in the target file are used to structure the UPDATE procedure.

dBASE begins at the top of PARTS, where the code entry is WI-104, and searches NU — PRICE for a match. The very first record matches, and record 1 in PARTS is updated. dBASE moves on to the next record in PARTS, where PART — CODE is WI-111. A match is found in NU — PRICE at the third record in the indexed order, and record 2 in PARTS is updated.

Note what happened to the record pointer in NU — PRICE: it skipped over the second record. Since dBASE assumes there are index files ordering the records, it will only search for a matching PART—CODE beginning with the current location of the record pointer. dBASE will never move backwards in the source file (in this case, NU—PRICE); the skipped record is missed entirely in the UPDATE process.

Whenever you use UPDATE, have your target file indexed on the key expression that relates it to the source file.

5.19 Tip: You can UPDATE from a source file that is not indexed on the key expression.

If you include the keyword **RANDOM** at the end of your **UPDATE** command line, dBASE will update from a source file that is not indexed on the common key expression. However, the target file (the file being updated) must be indexed on the key expression (see the preceding trap).

5.20 Tip: dBASE can UPDATE with a calculated expression.

Say your inventory system has a file, IN — PARTS, that contains in a field named ON — HAND the quantity of each part on hand. IN — PARTS is indexed on the PART—CODE field.

When a new shipment is received, the part codes and amounts received are entered into a file, IN — RECVD, and IN — PARTS is updated with

```
UPDATE ON PART_CODE FROM IN_RECVD REPLACE ON_HAND WITH;
   ON_HAND + B->AMT_RECVD
```

dBASE calculates each new quantity, adding the quantity received to the quantity on hand, and places the result into the file.

See the following trap.

5.21 Trap: *If you're not careful, you could UPDATE a file more than once with the same data.*

Let's continue with the example begun in the preceding tip. An order comes in on Monday, and you UPDATE your IN — PARTS file as previously described. So far everything is working fine. On Tuesday another shipment comes in.

Here is the potential problem: if you add the items received on Tuesday to IN—RECVD and repeat the UPDATE command without first removing the records for the items that were updated on Monday, the items received in the earlier shipment will have been added to the inventory levels twice.

See the following trap and tip.

5.22 Trap: *You cannot UPDATE from selected records in the source file; you cannot use a FOR or WHILE phrase with the UPDATE command.*

There is no way to use UPDATE on selected records in the source file; dBASE requires that the whole file be used.

If you try to limit the scope of UPDATE with a FOR or WHILE phrase, dBASE will respond "Syntax error".

See the following tip.

5.23 Tip: *Always UPDATE from a temporary source file.*

The UPDATE command uses every record in the source file to update the records in its target file (see the above two traps), so controlling the records in the UPDATE source file is of the utmost importance. An efficient approach is to use UPDATE only with a temporary source file.

If the data used to update a file does not need to be saved, you can ZAP the source file as soon as the UPDATE procedure has been accomplished. ZAP erases all the records but preserves the file structure, so you can use this empty file for your next UPDATE.

If the data in the source file needs to be saved, enter it first into a TEMP file, UPDATE from this TEMP file, and then APPEND the records to your permanent file.

5.24 Trap: *If you use UPDATE with a file that is indexed on a key field that is not unique for each record, only the first occurrence of a particular key expression will be updated.*

Each record in an UPDATE source file (the file updated from) is used to change only one record in the target file. Once dBASE has found a record with a matching key expression, it updates that record and moves to the next entry in the source file.

Because of this, UPDATE is not an effective tool for making the same change to a whole category of related records. For instance, suppose you are updating a file of merchandise prices in a clothing store that is having a sale. Various categories of merchandise have the same discount: all blouses are $5 off, all skirts are $7 off, and so on.

The file **PRICES** includes a field called **CATEGORY** that allows you to process records in groups by type of merchandise, but you cannot use UPDATE to accomplish this.

Here is an attempt to make these changes with UPDATE:

```
. SELECT 1
.
. LIST
Record#    ITEM_NO CATEGORY  PRICE
        1  A12-7   BLOUSE    13.49
        2  A12-9   BLOUSE    22.89
        3  A17-2   BLOUSE    24.98
        7  A21-3   JACKET    89.97
        8  A24-6   JACKET    48.99
        4  A19-1   SKIRT     17.49
        5  A19-5   SKIRT     28.99
        6  A19-8   SKIRT     34.99
.
. SELECT 2
.
. LIST
Record#    CATEGORY DISCOUNT
        1  BLOUSE       5.00
        3  JACKET       9.00
        2  SKIRT        7.00
.
.


. SELECT 1
.
. UPDATE ON CATEGORY FROM MARKDOWN REPLACE PRICE WITH PRICE - MARKDOWN->DISCOUNT

        3 records updated
.
```

```
. LIST
Record#   ITEM_NO  CATEGORY  PRICE
       1  A12-7    BLOUSE     8.49
       2  A12-9    BLOUSE    22.89
       3  A17-2    BLOUSE    24.98
       7  A21-3    JACKET    80.97
       8  A24-6    JACKET    48.99
       4  A19-1    SKIRT     10.49
       5  A19-5    SKIRT     28.99
       6  A19-8    SKIRT     34.99
.
```

As you can see, updating was performed only on the first record in the BLOUSE category, the first record in the SKIRT category, and so on.

To make changes to an entire category of records, use REPLACE ALL. In this example, you would have to use one REPLACE ALL command for each category:

```
REPLACE ALL PRICE WITH PRICE - 5.00 FOR CATEGORY = "BLOUSE"

REPLACE ALL PRICE WITH PRICE - 9.00 FOR CATEGORY = "JACKET"

REPLACE ALL PRICE WITH PRICE - 7.00 FOR CATEGORY = "SKIRT"
```

See Chapter 3 for tips and traps on using REPLACE ALL.

Using Related Databases

5.25 Tip: *You can link related records in different files with the SET RELATION command.*

Suppose your inventory system includes these three files:

```
Structure for database : B:IN_ORDER.dbf
Number of data records :      36
Date of last update    : 01/01/80
Field   Field name  Type       Width    Dec
    1   ORD_NUMBER  Character      5
    2   DATE        Date           8
    3   PART_CODE   Character      6
    4   ORD_AMT     Numeric        4
** Total **                       24
```

Working With More Than One Database File

```
Structure for database : B:IN_PARTS.dbf
Number of data records :     144
Date of last update    : 01/01/80
Field   Field name  Type       Width    Dec
    1   PART_CODE   Character      6
    2   VEND_CODE   Character      6
    3   DESCRIPT    Character     15
    4   UNIT_PRICE  Numeric        6      2
** Total **                      34
```

```
Structure for database : B:IN_VEND.dbf
Number of data records :      32
Date of last update    : 01/01/80
Field   Field name  Type       Width    Dec
    1   VEND_CODE   Character      6
    2   VEND_NAME   Character     20
    3   STREET      Character     25
    4   CITY        Character     15
    5   STATE       Character      2
    6   ZIP         Character      5
    7   PHONE       Character     13
** Total **                      87
```

You want to display a list of parts on order that consists of these fields:

PART_CODE	from IN_ORDER
ORD_AMT	from IN_ORDER
DESCRIPT	from IN_PARTS
VEND_NAME	from IN_VEND

The first step is to open the three files, each in its own workspace, with the appropriate index:

```
SELECT 1

USE IN_ORDER

SELECT 2

USE IN_PARTS INDEX PA_CODE

SELECT 3

USE IN_VEND INDEX VE_CODE
```

For each record in IN_ORDER, you want to display the related information from the other two files as well. If you try to use the DISPLAY command on the data from all three files, you will get the following result.

```
. DISPLAY ALL OFF PART_CODE, B->DESCRIPT, C->VEND_NAME, ORD_AMT
PART_CODE B->DESCRIPT      C->VEND_NAME        ORD_AMT
WI-121    3/4" COUPLER     AMERICAN TIRE CO.         5
WI-242    3/4" COUPLER     AMERICAN TIRE CO.        12
WI-012    3/4" COUPLER     AMERICAN TIRE CO.        24
WI-411    3/4" COUPLER     AMERICAN TIRE CO.         6
GA-101    3/4" COUPLER     AMERICAN TIRE CO.        12
GA-003    3/4" COUPLER     AMERICAN TIRE CO.        18
GA-411    3/4" COUPLER     AMERICAN TIRE CO.        24
CP-121    3/4" COUPLER     AMERICAN TIRE CO.         1
CP-117    3/4" COUPLER     AMERICAN TIRE CO.         8
WI-242    3/4" COUPLER     AMERICAN TIRE CO.       100
WI-316    3/4" COUPLER     AMERICAN TIRE CO.        12
GA-111    3/4" COUPLER     AMERICAN TIRE CO.        10
GA-118    3/4" COUPLER     AMERICAN TIRE CO.        12
CP-121    3/4" COUPLER     AMERICAN TIRE CO.        24
HF-103    3/4" COUPLER     AMERICAN TIRE CO.         5
HF-227    3/4" COUPLER     AMERICAN TIRE CO.         3
HF-289    3/4" COUPLER     AMERICAN TIRE CO.        12
WI-002    3/4" COUPLER     AMERICAN TIRE CO.        22
WI-367    3/4" COUPLER     AMERICAN TIRE CO.        18
WI-182    3/4" COUPLER     AMERICAN TIRE CO.        75
Press any key to continue...
```

As you can see, the record pointers in workspaces B and C are improperly related to workspace A, ORD_AMT, so the same description and vendor name were listed for each record. It looks like American Tire placed every order, and every order was for a coupler.

The record pointer in each workspace is independent of the others; DISPLAY by itself, with no relation set up, will not show related records from the three files. You could move between the work areas with SELECT and locate the related record in each area. Once all three record pointers were positioned correctly, you could display the related data. But this would require several commands for each line of your display.

There is a much faster way: dBASE can move the record pointers for you, easily and automatically. If you enter

```
SELECT 1

SET RELATION TO PART_CODE INTO IN_PARTS
```

dBASE will establish a link between IN_ORDER and IN_PARTS.

Whenever you move the record pointer in workspace A (that is, in the file IN_ORDER), dBASE will move the pointer in the related file, IN_PARTS, to the first record with a matching PART_CODE. You can thereby display the part codes and order amounts for several records in one file, and also the matching descriptions from another file, without leaving your selected workspace.

A second relation will make the vendor names automatically match up as well:

```
SELECT 2

SET RELATION TO VEND_CODE INTO IN_VEND

SELECT 1
```

Now you can display the related data from the three files for all records in IN — ORDER:

```
. DISPLAY ALL OFF PART_CODE, B->DESCRIPT, C->VEND_NAME, ORD_AMT
  PART_CODE B->DESCRIPT     C->VEND_NAME        ORD_AMT
  WI-121    3/4" RUB WIDGET AMERICAN TIRE CO.        5
  WI-242    1/4" COP WIDGET AMERICAN TIRE CO.       12
  WI-012    1/2" RUB WIDGET THE ASPHALT CO.         24
  WI-411    1" COP WIDGET   THE ASPHALT CO.          6
  GA-101    8MM GASKET      THE ASPHALT CO.         12
  GA-003    3MM GASKET      AMERICAN TIRE CO.       18
  GA-411    30MM GASKET     AMERICAN TIRE CO.       24
  CP-121    1" COUPLER      AMERICAN TIRE CO.        1
  CP-117    3/4" COUPLER    AMERICAN TIRE CO.        8
  WI-242    1/4" COP WIDGET AMERICAN TIRE CO.      100
  WI-316    1/2" COP WIDGET AMERICAN TIRE CO.       12
  GA-111    12MM GASKET     AMERICAN TIRE CO.       10
  GA-118    18MM GASKET     AMERICAN TIRE CO.       12
  CP-121    1" COUPLER      AMERICAN TIRE CO.       24
  HF-103    1/4" HF VALVE   AMERICAN TIRE CO.        5
  HF-227    1/2" HF VALVE   WALNUT CREEK STEEL       3
  HF-289    3/4" HF VALVE   WALNUT CREEK STEEL      12
  WI-002    1/4" RUB WIDGET WALNUT CREEK STEEL      22
  WI-367    3/4" COP WIDGET WALNUT CREEK STEEL      18
  WI-182    1" RUB WIDGET   WALNUT CREEK STEEL      75
Press any key to continue...
```

See the following trap.

■ *5.26 Trap:* *You cannot use the SET RELATION command to estab-*
lish a relation with a file that is not indexed on the key
expression.

If you try to SET RELATION into a file that is not indexed on the key expression, dBASE will respond "Database is not indexed". Whenever you use SET RELATION, the related file must be indexed on the key expression specified in the SET RELATION command.

For example, if you want to use

```
SET RELATION TO PART_CODE INTO IN_PARTS
```

IN — PARTS must be indexed on the PART — CODE field.

5.27 Tip: *You can establish up to ten relations, one per workspace, and you can link one file to several others in a chain of relations.*

dBASE allows you to establish a different relation in each workspace. The relations can be linked as in a chain, so that moving the record pointer in one file will move pointers in more than one linked file.

In the example given in Tip 5.25, IN __ VEND is linked to IN __ PARTS, which is linked to IN __ ORDER. Moving the record pointer to a particular entry in IN __ ORDER causes the pointer in IN __ PARTS to move to the entry with a matching PART __ CODE. This in turn causes the pointer in IN __ VEND to move to the record with a VEND __ CODE that matches the code in the record in IN __ PARTS.

Be sure to read the following two traps.

5.28 Trap: *You cannot establish more than one relation from a particular workspace.*

dBASE is limited to one relation per workspace. When you use SET RELATION to establish a link between files, dBASE automatically closes any existing relation in the workspace.

A chain of linked files (see the preceding tip) must therefore be carefully planned; each file can control the record pointer in one other file only. For instance, in the example given in Tip 5.25, IN __ VEND is linked to IN __ PARTS, which is in turn linked to IN __ ORDER. When you choose a record in IN __ ORDER, dBASE moves to the corresponding records in IN __ PARTS and IN __ VEND.

It is not possible to arrange a similar chain with IN __ PARTS in the current workspace. You can link IN __ PARTS to either IN __ ORDER or IN __ VEND, but not to both at the same time.

5.29 Trap: *You cannot establish a cyclic relation.*

Here is an example of a simple cyclic relation involving two files:

```
SELECT 1

USE CUSTOMER INDEX CU_CODE

SELECT 2

USE ORDERS INDEX ORD_NUM

SELECT 1

SET RELATION TO CUST_CODE INTO ORDERS RANDOM

SELECT 2

SET RELATION TO ORDER_NUM INTO CUSTOMER RANDOM
```

dBASE makes it impossible to maintain these two relations, because if it were possible, the following would happen: If you moved to a certain record in CUS-TOMER, the first relation would move the record pointer in ORDERS to a matching record; then the second relation would move the record pointer in CUSTOMER to another record, forcing movement in ORDERS, and so on.

Any number of files could be involved in such an impossible cycle. Conse-quently, anytime a chain of relations would involve a particular file more than once, dBASE responds "Cyclic relation" and refuses to establish the relation that would link a file to another already involved in the chain.

5.30 Trap: *If the key expression is not unique in a related file, dBASE will locate only the first record with a matching key expression.*

Suppose you are processing customer orders. Two of the files in your system are

- SUMMARY, which includes records for order number, date, and total price for each order.

- ORDER, which includes records for order number, quantity, and part code for each item ordered.

For each item in each order in the SUMMARY file, you'd like to display a listing that shows the date, order number, part code, and quantity. Here is the result if you try to do so by establishing a relation with SUMMARY as the selected file:

```
. SELECT 1
.
. SET RELATION TO ORDER_NUM INTO ORDER
.
. LIST OFF DATE, ORDER_NUM, B->PART_CODE, B->QUANTITY
  DATE       ORDER_NUM B->PART_CODE B->QUANTITY
  02/11/85 01345      WI-242              18
  02/11/85 01362      GA-411              81
  02/12/85 01379      WI-316              15
  02/12/85 01396      CP-121              64
  02/12/85 01413      WI-002              34
  02/14/85 01447      GA-028              12
  02/14/85 01464      HF-226              18
  02/14/85 01481      WI-101              50
.
```

Each record in SUMMARY is displayed only once, with the first record in ORDER that has a matching order number. No other items in each order are displayed.

This problem will occur with any dBASE command that uses this relation; only the first matching record in ORDER will be processed.

See the following tip.

5.31 Tip: *If one of your files has more than one record with the same key expression, establish the relation so that the files are linked many-to-one rather than one-to-many.*

When one file has exactly one record for each key expression and a second file has several records for each expression, you need to establish the relation between them carefully if you want all records to be processed.

The preceding trap gives an example of a one-to-many relationship. Each customer order results in one record in SUMMARY and several records in ORDER; if you SET RELATION from SUMMARY into ORDER, only the first of the matching records will be processed.

To access all records in the ORDER file, set the relation *from* the file that has many records for each transaction *into* the file that has only one record for each transaction:

Working With More Than One Database File

```
. SELECT 2
.
. SET RELATION TO ORDER_NUM INTO SUMMARY
.
. LIST OFF A->DATE, ORDER_NUM, PART_CODE, QUANTITY
  A->DATE   ORDER_NUM PART_CODE QUANTITY
  02/11/85 01345     WI-242        18
  02/11/85 01345     WI-012        24
  02/11/85 01345     WI-411       100
  02/11/85 01345     GA-101       144
  02/11/85 01345     GA-003        64
  02/11/85 01362     GA-411        81
  02/11/85 01362     CP-121        28
  02/11/85 01362     CP-117         4
*** INTERRUPTED ***
.
```

This many-to-one relation allows every record in ORDER to be processed, with its associated record in SUMMARY available as needed.

5.32 Trap: *LOCATE and CONTINUE will work much more slowly in a file that has a relation established.*

The LOCATE command works by starting at the beginning of the file and checking each record in order against the LOCATE condition. CONTINUE extends this sequential access to find subsequent matching records (see Chapter 4 for a discussion of LOCATE and CONTINUE).

If a file has a relation established, then each time the record pointer is moved in the first file, dBASE repositions the pointer in the related file. Since LOCATE and CONTINUE move the record pointer through the file, execution takes longer.

See the following tip.

5.33 Tip: *In your dBASE programs, first use the LOCATE command to find the record to be processed, and then use SET RELATION to link your file to other files as needed.*

The preceding trap explains why LOCATE and CONTINUE are slowed down by a link to a related file. If your program will use these commands to process groups of related records, it will execute more quickly if you LOCATE records without the relation.

Here is an example of a program segment that uses this approach. The IN __ PARTS file is open in the current workspace, and IN __ VEND is open in workspace 2:

```
LOCATE FOR ON_HAND < RE_ORDER

DO WHILE .NOT. EOF()

    SET RELATION TO VEND_CODE INTO IN_VEND

    ? PART_CODE, DESCRIPT, ORDER_AMT, B->VEND_NAME

    SET RELATION TO

    CONTINUE

ENDDO
```

The program will find the first record in which ON __ HAND is less than RE __ ORDER. Then the relation is set into IN __ VEND and the part code, description, quantity to be ordered, and vendor name are displayed.

The command

```
SET RELATION TO
```

disconnects the relation that was established. As a result, while CONTINUE searches the file for a subsequent record that meets the LOCATE condition, it no longer is moving the record pointer in a second file.

✊ *5.34 Trap: If your dBASE program uses related files, don't forget that a matching record may not be found in the related file.*

When one file is linked to another by SET RELATION, dBASE moves the record pointer in the related file to a record that matches the current record in the active file. Each time your program moves to a new record, dBASE executes the SEEK command on the related file, searching for a matching key expression (see Chapter 4 for a discussion of SEEK).

If a matching record is found, your program can read data from it while processing the current record in the active file. If the SEEK procedure is unsuccessful (that is, no matching key expression is found), dBASE positions the record pointer in the related file to EOF( ). If your program tries to read the contents of a field when the record pointer is at EOF( ), program execution is interrupted and the error message "Variable not found" is displayed.

For example, suppose you are processing a customer order. Each item ordered has been entered into the file ORDER. A relation has been set into the file PARTS, and as each part code is entered your program displays the part description and unit price.

If an inaccurate part code is entered, dBASE searches PARTS, does not find a matching code, and places the record pointer at EOF( ). When the program tells dBASE to display the part data, execution will be interrupted with an error message.

See the following tip.

5.35 Tip: *Use EOF( ) to test for the existence of a related record in programs that process related files.*

Let's continue with the example used in the preceding trap. Your program asks the user to enter a part code and places the entry in the field PART_CODE of the ORDER file. dBASE then automatically searches PARTS for a record with a matching entry in the PART_CODE field. If there is a match, the data can be displayed. If there is no match, you want the program to display a message and ask the user to enter a valid part code. Here is a program segment that does this:

```
SELECT 1

USE ORDER

SELECT 2

USE PARTS INDEX PA_CODE

SELECT 1

APPEND BLANK

SET RELATION TO PART_CODE INTO PARTS

STORE .F. TO VALID

DO WHILE .NOT. VALID

    @7,0

    @9,0

    @3,5 SAY "Enter Part Code:" GET PART_CODE
```

```
SELECT PARTS
IF .NOT. EOF()
    STORE .T. TO VALID
ELSE
    @7,5 SAY "*** INVALID PART CODE ***"
    @9,0
    WAIT "*** Press RETURN to re-enter Part Code ***"
ENDIF ** .NOT. EOF()
SELECT ORDER
ENDDO ** WHILE .NOT. VALID
```

Since a relation causes dBASE to execute SEEK each time the record pointer is moved, this program has the same basic structure as programs that execute SEEK. (This program structure is described in detail in Chapter 4.)

First the relation is established, and a logical memory variable, VALID, is initialized. VALID becomes true when a valid part code is entered. The DO WHILE loop continues asking for part codes until a valid code is entered. The loop begins by clearing the lines where error messages will be displayed so that a message from an incorrect entry will not remain on the screen when the next entry is being made. The part code is then entered into ORDER; dBASE automatically moves to the corresponding part code in PARTS, since the relation has linked the two files.

Now the program selects the PARTS file and checks to see if the record pointer is at EOF( ). If it is not, a matching part code has been found and VALID becomes true; the loop will not repeat and the program can go on to process the record. If EOF( ) is true in the related file, no matching part code was found. The error message is displayed, and WAIT gives the user time to read and understand the message. When RETURN is pressed, the loop executes again, and the user is asked for another part code.

6

Customizing
The Screen Display

People communicate with dBASE III through the keyboard and the screen display. Whether you are working from the dot prompt or are writing a program for yourself or others to use, dBASE gives you many options for customizing the display:

- You can make data entry faster and easier

- You can provide assistance for an inexperienced dBASE user

- You can put limits or controls on the kind of data that is accepted.

When you are writing dBASE programs, you can control many aspects of data input and display. Well-designed screens will make your programs easier to use (especially if they are to be used for hours on end) and will help minimize user errors. This chapter focuses on the many dBASE tools you can use to manage data entry and screen displays.

Displaying Data on the Screen

6.01 Tip: *Use the ? and ?? commands to display text on the screen and to ask dBASE about data that is not visible on the screen.*

The ? and ?? commands display the value of dBASE expressions. Typing a single question mark moves the cursor to the beginning of the next line before the expression is displayed; typing two question marks begins the display at the current cursor position.

Both ? and ?? can be followed by any valid dBASE expression. Here are some examples:

? "Program now loading"	Displays the text between the quotes.
? L_NAME	Displays the current contents of the field L_NAME.
? AMOUNT > 0	Displays .T. if the contents of the field AMOUNT are greater than 0 and displays .F. otherwise.
?? 5*7+(64/3)	Displays the results of the calculation.

Typing ? with no expression following it displays a blank line.

The ? command is very useful from the dot prompt, since you can use it to ask dBASE questions about data that is not visible on the screen. By typing ? at the beginning of each line, you can write a simple program that uses only one screen display. However, to keep displayed elements from scrolling off the screen, most programming applications require more precise placement of output than ? and ?? provide; see the following tip.

6.02 Tip: *To position output precisely on the screen, use @.*

The @ command (read as "at") tells dBASE exactly where to position an expression on the screen. @ is always followed by two numeric expressions that identify a row and a column on the screen. On a 24-row, 80-column monitor, the rows are numbered from 0 to 23 and the columns from 0 to 79. Thus, the command

@1,20

tells dBASE to position the next expression in the second row from the top of the screen, beginning in the twenty-first column from the left edge.

When you use the @ command to move the cursor to a specified position on the screen, the command you follow it with depends on what you want to do: follow it with SAY (see the following tip) if you just want to display an expression; follow it with GET (see Tip 6.18) if you want to edit the expression.

6.03 Tip: *Use the SAY command to display any valid dBASE expression at a position defined by the @ command.*

SAY tells dBASE to display an expression on the screen. You can use SAY with any valid dBASE expression — a string, the contents of a field or memory variable, the results of a calculation — except a memo field. Here are some examples:

@23,5 SAY "Press RETURN to Continue"	Displays exactly what appears between the quotes.
@14,3 SAY L_NAME	Displays the current contents of the field L_NAME.
@12,3 SAY "Name:" + M_NAME	Displays the text between the quotes followed by the contents of the memory variable M_NAME.
@5,20 SAY COST*1.15	Displays the result of multiplying the contents of COST by 1.15.

SAY cannot be used on its own; it must immediately follow (on the same program line) a screen location defined by the @ command.

6.04 Tip: *You can format the data displayed with SAY in a variety of ways.*

You can use a PICTURE clause to format the output displayed by SAY. The PICTURE clause follows the expression being displayed by SAY, on the same command line, and includes a PICTURE function, a PICTURE template, or both.

A PICTURE *function* tells dBASE to display the entire expression in a certain form. It is enclosed in quotes, and the specific function is preceded by the @

symbol. For example:

```
@2,5 SAY L_NAME PICTURE "@!"
```

tells dBASE to display the current contents of L—NAME in uppercase letters, regardless of how the data has been entered.

PICTURE functions can be useful in financial applications in the following manner:

PICTURE "@("	Encloses negative numbers in parentheses.
PICTURE "@C"	Displays CR after a positive number.
PICTURE "@X"	Displays DB after a negative number.

You can also combine two PICTURE functions: PICTURE "@CX" displays CR after numeric data if it is positive and DB if it is negative.

PICTURE can also be followed by a *template,* which specifies the format for each character of the display. A template includes a single symbol for each character of the output, and it is enclosed in quotes. For example,

```
@12,15 SAY BALANCE PICTURE "###,###.##"
```

tells dBASE to display the current contents of BALANCE and to insert a comma in the correct position if there are numbers to the left of that position.

You can combine a PICTURE function with a template by placing the function first, followed by a space and then the template. For instance,

```
@15,25 SAY AMOUNT PICTURE "@( ##,###.##"
```

displays the contents of AMOUNT inside parentheses if it is negative, and inserts a comma if the number has more than three digits to the left of the decimal point.

Pages 4 through 18 in the dBASE manual contain a complete list of PICTURE functions and template symbols.

6.05 Tip: Use the R function to insert symbols into an expression that is being displayed.

One useful PICTURE function (see the preceding tip) is @R; when followed by a template, it allows you to insert any character into the data being displayed.

The template is formed by using the letter **X** (which must be uppercase) to represent a character from the data being displayed, and placing the symbols to be inserted in the desired positions. For example, suppose the field **PHONE** stores telephone numbers as strings of ten digits without punctuation. If the current contents of **PHONE** is 6179613486, then the line

```
a3,5 SAY PHONE PICTURE "aR (XXX)XXX-XXXX"
```

will display the data with the symbols inserted:

```
(617)961-3486
```

6.06 **Tip:** *TEXT...ENDTEXT displays many lines of text without your having to write a separate @...SAY for each line.*

Say you want to display several instructions to the user who is exiting your application system, reminding the user to back up the disks correctly. You can tell dBASE to display an entire block of text by using

```
TEXT
    The lines of instructions, typed in exactly as you
    would like them to appear on the screen.
ENDTEXT
```

The text will be output exactly as it was entered in your program.

6.07 **Trap:** *A macro embedded within TEXT...ENDTEXT will not be expanded.*

dBASE sends the characters between **TEXT** and **ENDTEXT** to the screen directly, without interpreting the content. If you include a macro (discussed in Chapter 9), it will simply be displayed as &. Use **TEXT...ENDTEXT** only with data that you want displayed exactly as it is entered in the program.

✋ *6.08 Trap: TEXT...ENDTEXT displays data wherever the cursor was left by the most recent positioning command.*

TEXT...ENDTEXT does not reposition the cursor before it begins displaying data; your text could begin in the middle of a screen line.

Always precede TEXT...ENDTEXT with @*row, column,* as explained in Tip 6.02, to position the cursor precisely where you want the text display to begin.

Designing Effective Screen Displays

✋ *6.09 Trap: If you display text on line 0, your display may be partially blanked out or overwritten by dBASE messages.*

dBASE uses line 0 to display status messages, such as "Invalid date—press space bar". If you try to position text on this line with the @ command, that text may be overwritten by a message. In addition, certain dBASE operations like **APPEND** and **READ** automatically clear portions of line 0 as they are executed. If you have positioned text on this line, parts of your display will be blanked out.

Some books suggest you can make this line available for your own messages by using **SET STATUS OFF**, which prevents dBASE from displaying status messages on line 0. But parts of your text may still be blanked out by a dBASE operation. You should always consider line 1 to be the top of the available dBASE screen.

💡 *6.10 Tip: You can center an expression on the screen or display text ending at the right edge of the screen, even when the length of the expression will vary.*

Suppose your program uses the memory variable M _TASK to store the name of the particular program task currently being executed. The length of the task name varies according to the part of your program being used.

TRIM( ) is used to remove any trailing blanks from the contents of the memory variable. To center the expression, use

```
@2,(80-LEN(TRIM(M_TASK)))/2 SAY M_TASK
```

To display the task name on the far right of the screen, use

`@2,78-LEN(TRIM(M_TASK)) SAY M_TASK`

✋ *6.11 Trap:* *If your program does not clear the screen before begin-*
ning a new display, portions of your old screen may show
in the blank areas of your new screen.

Be sure to use the **CLEAR** command to erase the screen each time your program begins to display a new screen.

💡 *6.12 Tip:* *You can erase selected portions of the screen.*

dBASE allows you to clear selected parts of the screen, so you can change user prompts, erase messages that are no longer needed, or give new instructions without having to repeat the entire screen display. Here are examples:

@22,0	Clears all of line 22.
@22,12	Clears line 22 from row 12 to the right edge of the screen.
@17,0 CLEAR	Clears all of the screen below row 16.
@20,30 CLEAR	Clears a rectangle in the lower-right corner of the screen, columns 30-79 in all rows below row 19.

💡 *6.13 Tip:* *Whenever you can in your applications, display messages*
to the user in the same location on the screens.

If various messages from the program—prompts, error messages, instructions, and the like—appear in different places on your screens, the person using your programs will have to scan the entire screen after each entry and will therefore find your programs more difficult than they need be.

It's very helpful to consistently display such messages in the same screen location. You can use selective erasing (as explained in the preceding tip) to remove messages from the screen location when they are no longer needed, without having to clear the entire screen.

6.14 Tip: *Display a heading on each screen to indicate its function.*

It is wise to have each screen indicate its unique function within your application, so an inexperienced user will not try to enter the wrong type of data.

You can use @...SAY to display such a heading. The screen shown in Figure 6-1 has the heading

```
*** EDITING MAILING LIST ***
```

The person using the screen shown in Figure 6-1 knows what kind of data your application is prepared to accept: changes in a record in the mailing list. If an inexperienced user tried to print out mailing labels, the heading would clearly indicate that dBASE was not set up to do so at that time.

6.15 Tip: *Display important instructions on a screen that is to be used by someone who is not expert with dBASE.*

Note the instruction line at the bottom of the screen in Figure 6-1:

```
*** Enter ^END When Finished Editing ***
```

Without such instructions an inexpert user, not knowing the correct way to exit EDIT or APPEND mode, might return to the dot prompt by pressing ESC, thus losing data. By including key instructions on your custom screens, you help the people who will use the screen.

6.16 Tip: *Define a memory variable LINE to draw a double line across the screen.*

A double line is useful for separating distinct portions of the screen display. If you define a memory variable with these program lines:

```
               *** EDITING MAILING LIST ***


   Title (Mr., Ms., etc.): [      ]
   First Name: [                  ]    Last Name: [                  ]

   Company: [                ]

   Street Address: [                  ]
      City: [                ]           State: [   ]    Zip: [      ]

   Phone: [ (   )   -     ]             Use first name? (y/n) [?]


          *** Enter ^END When Finished Editing. ***
```

Figure 6-1.   Screen display with informative heading

```
LINE = CHR(205)
DO WHILE LEN(LINE) < 78
   STORE LINE + LINE TO LINE
ENDDO
LINE = SUBSTR(LINE,1,78)
```

then whenever you would like a double line across the screen, you can tell dBASE to

```
@ row,column SAY LINE
```

*6.17 Tip: Include a procedure in your procedure file that will create
             a heading for each screen in the application system.*

In an application system that uses many screen displays, you can use a procedure to generate a heading with a title you select for each screen. Each program within the system can call the procedure as needed to generate a heading for each new screen display, as shown here:

```
PROCEDURE HEADING

   PARAMETER HEADTEXT

   a2,2 SAY SYS_NAME

   a2,(80-LEN(HEADTEXT))/2 SAY HEADTEXT

   a2,70 SAY DATE()

   a3,1 SAY LINE

RETURN
```

This procedure, HEADING, is called after the screen has been cleared within a program:

```
DO HEADING WITH "DESIRED HEADING"
```

It places the application program name on the left, centers the heading specified by the program, displays the date on the right, and draws a double line across the screen under the heading, as explained in the preceding tip.

Handling Input

6.18 Tip: *To allow data to be entered into a field or a memory variable, or to allow the contents of the field or memory variable to be changed, use GET.*

The GET command, followed by the name of a field or memory variable, displays the current contents of that field or memory variable and allows the user to make changes.

When dBASE is in APPEND mode, the record pointer is positioned at a blank record at the end of the file. Each field of the blank record is empty; GET *field name* displays a blank space that is the same width as the field and allows the user to write data into the field. Once a memory variable has been initialized (see Chapter 3), use GET to display its contents and to allow the user to write data into it. When dBASE is in EDIT mode, GET displays the current contents of a field or memory variable and allows the user to overwrite the entry.

GET cannot be used on its own; it must appear on a program line following an @ location definition. You can use

```
@2,5 GET L_NAME
```

to display the current contents of L—NAME at the indicated position. You can also use GET immediately after SAY:

```
@2,5 SAY "Enter last name:" GET L_NAME
```

dBASE will position the contents of L—NAME, with a blank space preceding them, after "Enter last name:".

6.19 Tip: *The field or memory variable named after each GET determines the length of the data-entry area and the type of input that will be accepted.*

If you tell dBASE

```
@3,3 SAY "Name:" GET NAME
```

and the field called NAME is 15 characters long, the data-entry area after the GET will be limited to 15 characters.

A date field or memory variable accepts only valid dates, and presents a date screen display:

```
@5,5 SAY "Enter today's date:" GET DATE
```

displays

```
Enter today's date: [  /  /  ]
```

in APPEND mode, and the cursor jumps over the slash marks as data is entered. If an invalid date like 5/45/84 is entered, dBASE beeps, displays a status line message, and refuses the entry.

If the field or memory variable that follows GET is numeric, the screen will display a decimal point if you have given your field or memory variable decimal places. The command

```
ə5,14 SAY "Price:" GET PRICE
```

will result in

```
Price: [   .   ]
```

when PRICE has been defined as a numeric field with two decimal places. Only numeric data will be accepted.

If the field or memory variable in the GET statement is of the logical type, dBASE will accept only logical data (T/t, F/f, Y/y, or N/n) and will display a question mark (?) in the data-entry area.

✋ **6.20 Trap:** *You cannot GET input into a memory variable that has not been initialized or into a record that has not been appended to your file.*

When dBASE encounters GET *field name* or GET *memvar*, it assumes the field or memory variable named has already been accessed. The field must be available in the current record; a memory variable must already exist and must contain an initial value.

See Chapter 3 for a detailed discussion of initializing memory variables and appending records to a file.

6.21 Tip: *Use a PICTURE clause to avoid repetitive typing.*

Any symbols that you enter into a template following a PICTURE clause are displayed in the data-entry area and are included in the field contents.

For example, if you use the command line

```
ə4,5 SAY "Phone number:" GET PHONE PICTURE"(XXX)XXX-XXXX"
```

the screen display will look like this:

```
Phone number: [(   )   -    ]
```

The area code's parentheses and the hyphen are already in place, saving the user typing time. As you enter data, dBASE jumps over each symbol to the next blank space, and includes the symbols in the telephone number that is entered into the **PHONE** field.

6.22 **Tip:** *Use a PICTURE clause to limit the type of data that can be accepted into a field or memory variable.*

Template symbols can be used to tell dBASE to accept only certain types of data. For example, if the part code for each item in your inventory is in the form of two letters, followed by a hyphen and three numbers, you can use a template that tells dBASE to accept only entries of this form:

```
@15,2 SAY "Enter Part Code:" GET PART_CODE PICTURE "AA-999"
```

The screen display will then show only the hyphen:

```
Enter Part Code: [  -   ]
```

The AA tells dBASE to accept only letters into the first two spaces, and the 999 allows only digits 0 through 9. If the user tries to enter any other symbols, dBASE will beep and refuse the data.

6.23 **Tip:** *You don't need to use a PICTURE clause with logical data.*

If a field or memory variable is defined as logical data, no PICTURE clause is needed to limit input into the field or memory variable, since dBASE accepts only logical data (T/t, F/f, Y/y, or N/n) in a logical variable or field.

6.24 **Tip:** *Use a PICTURE clause to convert keyboard entries to uppercase.*

The exclamation point (!) tells dBASE to convert a letter to uppercase before displaying the data and entering it into the field. If you use

```
@25,15 GET STATE PICTURE "!!"
```

the two exclamation points are not displayed on the screen; instead, whatever letters are typed in will be converted to uppercase.

If you want a long string converted to uppercase, use the @! function as follows:

```
@20,3 GET CO_NAME PICTURE "@!"
```

The function converts the entire entry to uppercase, whatever its length.

6.25 Trap: *If a PICTURE clause containing a decimal point is used with a numeric field, it is harder to enter numbers of varying lengths.*

A decimal point contained in a PICTURE clause will be fixed in position in the data-entry area. For example,

```
@5,5 SAY "Enter List Price:" GET PRICE PICTURE "###.##"
```

will produce this display with a fixed decimal point:

```
Enter List Price: [   .   ]
```

To enter 3.49, you would have to press the space bar twice before typing the number 3; dBASE will not accept a decimal point at any other position in the entry.

There is no need to use a PICTURE clause at all in this situation: since PRICE is defined to be a numeric field with two decimal places, dBASE will automatically produce the display just shown. Omitting the PICTURE clause and allowing the decimal point to come from the field makes data entry easier. dBASE accepts the decimal point within a numeric entry and positions the data to fit the definition of the field.

6.26 Tip: *Use RANGE to specify upper and lower bounds for accept-able entries into fields or memory variables of the numeric or date type.*

You can tell dBASE to accept only a certain range of entries in a numeric or a date field or in a memory variable by using RANGE after the GET statement. For example, if you keep financial data for each quarter in separate files, you can tell dBASE to accept only dates in the first quarter of 1985 by using

```
@4,2 SAY "Enter date:" GET DATE RANGE 01/01/85,04/30/85
```

dBASE will limit entries into the field **ON___HAND** to the numbers 0 through 100 if you say

```
@15,4 GET ON_HAND RANGE 0,100
```

To limit entries into the field called **PRICE** to positive numbers, use a lower bound only:

```
@2,7 GET PRICE RANGE 0
```

If you attempt to enter a number or date outside of the specified range, dBASE will beep, refuse to accept the entry, and display a message on line 0. The message specifies the acceptable range and tells the user to press the space bar to continue.

6.27 Trap: *If you use a memo field with GET, the contents of the field will not be displayed.*

As explained in Chapter 3, a memo field can only be accessed in **EDIT**, **APPEND**, or **CHANGE** mode. You cannot write in a memo field from within an application program.

If you are using a format file to define the screen in one of these modes, and you include the line

```
a3,3 SAY "Memo:" GET MEMO_FIELD
```

the display will look like this:

```
Memo: [memo]
```

The cursor will be placed on the word "memo".
    See the following trap and tip.

6.28 Trap: *If you try to write directly into a memo field from a cus-tom screen without first pressing CTRL-PGDN, dBASE will beep and refuse to accept your entry.*

If you place the cursor on the "[memo]" that is displayed on your custom screen (see the preceding trap) and start typing, the data will not be entered into the memo field. The only way to access a memo field is to press CTRL-PGDN with the cursor in this position.
    See the following tip.

6.29 Tip: *Include instructions if your custom screen will be used to enter or update data in a memo field.*

Here is an example of an effective way to handle a memo field in a custom screen:

```
              *** ENTERING JOURNAL REFERENCES ***

     Title: [                      ]
     Author (Last name, first name): [                      ]
     Name of Periodical: [                  ]
     Date of Periodical: [ / / ]      Starting page number: [     ]
     Topics covered: [                  ]

     Press ^PgDn to enter ABSTRACT: [memo]
```

```
*** PRESS PgDn TO ENTER NEXT REFERENCE ***
```

```
*** PRESS Ctrl-End WHEN ALL REFERENCES HAVE BEEN ENTERED ***
```

dBASE automatically places the cursor on "[memo]" when it reaches that line of the display, so pressing CTRL-PGDN will access the memo field.

6.30 **Tip:** *You can change the appearance of the data-entry areas on your custom screen by using the SET DELIMITER and SET INTENSITY commands.*

dBASE uses reverse video to highlight the data displayed by a GET statement. You can change this display in a variety of ways:

- To turn the reverse video off, enter

```
SET INTENSITY OFF
```

- To display a colon (:) at each end of the data-entry area, tell dBASE to

```
SET DELIMITER ON
```

The colon is the default delimiter.

- To surround each data-entry area with [and], as shown in the examples in this chapter, enter

```
SET DELIMITER TO "[]"
```

```
SET DELIMITER ON
```

You can use any symbols you like for the delimiters. If you want to use the same symbol, such as ¦, at both ends, enter

```
SET DELIMITER TO "¦"
```

If you want to use double quotes (") for your delimiter, just enclose the symbol in single quotes in the SET command:

```
SET DELIMITER TO '"'
```

6.31 Trap: *If you forget to include READ in your program, the GET lines will not accept input.*

When you use the GET command in a dBASE program, the current contents of a field or a memory variable are displayed on the screen. dBASE will not position the cursor to accept changes in the data until the READ command is encountered. This allows your program to display a number of GET statements at once, before the data is entered into each field or memory variable. Be sure to use READ when your program has established the data-entry screen and is ready to accept user input.

6.32 Tip: *You can display the fields in your file in any order and in any location on a data-entry screen.*

dBASE can accept data into the fields of a record in any order and in any location; since each GET statement specifies the field it will access, the order of placement on the screen is up to you.

See the following tip and trap.

6.33 Tip: *To make it easier to edit data, place the fields that are most likely to need changing at the top of your custom screen.*

Here is the structure of the file IN_PRICE, which is used in a purchasing/inventory system to hold the current price of each item in the inventory:

```
. DISPLAY STRUCTURE
Structure for database : B:IN_PRICE.dbf
Number of data records :      72
Date of last update    : 01/01/80
Field  Field name  Type        Width    Dec
    1  PART_CODE   Character      6
    2  VEND_CODE   Character      4
    3  PRICE       Numeric        6       2
** Total **                     17
.
```

Here is dBASE's default EDIT screen:

```
            Record No.      72
            PART_CODE    [AJ-211]
            VEND_CODE    [AJAX]
            PRICE        [  0.78]
```

Notice that the fields are displayed in the order in which they are listed by DIS-PLAY STRUCTURE; that is, in the sequence used when the database was created. The most common changes to the IN_PRICE file will be the prices, and PART_CODE or VEND_CODE will rarely need editing. With the dBASE default screen, a person entering data must move past these two code fields before PRICE can be changed.

You can write a format file that will display every record with the cursor in the desired field to make editing IN_PRICE faster and easier:

```
*PRICE_ED.FMT
*
*8/17/85
*
a2,20 SAY "***UPDATING PRICE LIST***
*
a6,5 SAY "Current Price: $" GET PRICE
a10,5 SAY "Part Code:" GET PART_CODE
a14,5 SAY "Vendor Code:" GET VEND_CODE
*
a19,12 SAY "*** PRESS PgDn TO MOVE TO NEXT RECORD***"
*
a22,5 SAY "*** PRESS Ctrl-End WHEN ALL UPDATES HAVE BEEN ENTERED***"
*
*EOF PRICE_ED.FMT
```

Here is the EDIT screen that results:

```
              *** UPDATING PRICE LIST ***


        Current Price: $ [  0.78]


        Part Code: [AJ-211]


        Vendor Code: [AJAX]



          *** PRESS PgDn TO MOVE TO NEXT RECORD. ***

      *** PRESS Ctrl-End WHEN ALL UPDATES HAVE BEEN ENTERED. ***
```

Each record appears on the screen with the cursor in the **PRICE** field, and the instructions at the bottom of the screen explain how to move to the next record from any field on the screen.

Be sure to read the following trap.

✋ *6.34 Trap:* *If the initial position of the cursor is not in the top field of the screen display, the person entering data will find it difficult to access the fields above the starting position.*

Consider the situation described in the preceding tip, where a person entering data must move past two code fields before **PRICE** can be changed. Here is an attempt to solve that problem:

```
*VERSION WITH TRAP
*
*PRICE_ED.FMT
*
@2,20 SAY "***UPDATING PRICE LIST***"
*
@14,5 SAY "Current Price: $" GET PRICE
@6,5 SAY "Part Code:" GET PART_CODE
@10,5 SAY "Vendor Code:" GET VEND_CODE
*
@19,12 SAY "***PRESS PgDn TO MOVE TO NEXT RECORD***"
*
@22,5 SAY "***PRESS Ctrl-End WHEN ALL UPDATES HAVE BEEN ENTERED***"
*
*EOF WITH TRAP
```

The result of this format file is shown here:

```
                     *** UPDATING PRICE LIST ***



      Part Code: [AJ-211]


      Vendor Code: [AJAX]
      ˜

      Current Price: $ [   0.78]



             *** PRESS PgDn TO MOVE TO NEXT RECORD. ***

      *** PRESS Ctrl-End WHEN ALL UPDATES HAVE BEEN ENTERED. ***
```

The field **PRICE**, the one most likely to need updating, is placed in the lowest position on the display, but dBASE is told to **GET** that field first.

However, with the cursor positioned in the **PRICE** field, it's very hard to access the two code fields on this screen. While they do not change as often as **PRICE**, these fields may occasionally need editing. With this screen, the user must press the down arrow key to access these fields, even though they are above the cursor location. Pressing the up arrow key, which would seem to be the logical method of moving up on the screen, moves the user to another record. Because of this you should avoid having your custom screen displayed with the cursor positioned below the top input field; it makes field access very confusing for the users.

6.35 Tip: *dBASE provides three commands that allow you to simultaneously create a memory variable and input its contents.*

The following three dBASE commands create a memory variable and accept data into it in one program line:

Command	Type of Variable Created	Length
WAIT	character	1
ACCEPT	character	Long enough to hold the keyboard entry, up to 254 characters.
INPUT	numeric	Same length and number of decimal places as the data entered at the keyboard.

Each of these commands can display a message to the user, and each must be followed by the name of the memory variable to be created. For example,

```
ACCEPT "Enter your name:" TO NAME
```

displays the message "Enter your name:" and accepts up to 254 characters of input.

These commands cannot be used on the same program line with the **@** command; to position them precisely on the screen, you must move the cursor to the desired position with **@** and then use **WAIT**, **INPUT**, or **ACCEPT** on the next program line. Here is an example:

```
ə20,0
INPUT "Quantity ordered:" TO ORD_AMT
```

✋ *6.36 Trap:* *If your program asks for input with WAIT, ACCEPT, or INPUT, you cannot assume that a memory variable was created.*

If you respond to a WAIT, ACCEPT, or INPUT message by just pressing RETURN, the data you hoped to have stored in a memory variable will not be present. Your program will run into problems if it tries to use that data.

See the following tip.

💡 *6.37 Tip:* *If your program will use the results of WAIT, ACCEPT, or INPUT, be sure to test the memory variable.*

If the person using your program responds to WAIT, ACCEPT, or INPUT by pressing RETURN,

- ACCEPT and WAIT will create a *null variable* (an empty memory variable)
- INPUT will not create a memory variable at all.

To test for a null variable after ACCEPT or WAIT, enter

```
IF LEN(MEMVAR) = 0
    <procedure for null entry>
ELSE
    <procedure for a memvar with data entered>
ENDIF
```

To test for the existence of a memory variable after INPUT, enter

```
IF TYPE("MEMVAR") = "U"

   <procedure for no data entered>

ELSE

   <procedure for a memvar with data entered>

ENDIF
```

Format Files

dBASE III provides you with a number of options for entering and updating the records in your database files. You can use the built-in dBASE modes; you can use those modes with a custom screen of your own design; or you can write an application program to test the data as it is entered.

In Chapter 3 each of these options is discussed in detail. See the tips and traps in that chapter when you are trying to decide how to handle data entry and updating for your files.

Custom screens can be defined within dBASE application programs or in special files called *format files*. The tips and traps in this section discuss specific considerations for these special files.

6.38 Tip: *Use a format file to define a custom screen in data-entry and update modes.*

Whenever you enter a dBASE full-screen mode — EDIT, APPEND, INSERT, or CHANGE — dBASE displays the contents of the fields in the current record. The default dBASE screen lists the fields in the order in which they were created and labels each field with the field name used in your file.

When a format file is open, dBASE will use a screen you have designed in these full-screen modes. There are many advantages to using a custom screen to enter and update data; see Chapter 3 for a detailed discussion of these screens and their usefulness.

A format file contains only the commands @, SAY, and GET. (These are discussed in the first two sections of the chapter.) The * symbol identifies programmer's comments. The file is given the file extension .FMT. Here is an example of a format file:

```
*MAIL_IN.FMT
*
*9/27/85
*
a1,20 SAY "*** EDITING MAILING LIST ***"
*
a4,1 SAY "Title (Mr.,Ms.,etc.):" GET TITLE PICTURE "a!"
a6,1 SAY "First Name:" GET F_NAME PICTURE "a!"
a6,40 SAY "Last Name:" GET L_NAME PICTURE "a!"
a10,1 SAY "Company:" GET CO_NAME PICTURE "a!"
a13,1 SAY "Street Address:" GET STREET PICTURE "a!"
a15,3 SAY "City:" GET CITY PICTURE "a!"
a15,40 SAY "State:" GET STATE PICTURE "!!"
a15,57 SAY "Zip:" GET ZIP PICTURE "99999"
a19,1 SAY "Phone:" GET PHONE PICTURE "(999)999-9999"
a19,40 SAY "Use first name? (y/n)" GET USE_FIRST
*
a22,12 SAY "*** Enter ^END When Finished Editing ***"
*
*EOF MAIL_IN.FMT
```

Here is the custom screen it defines, as displayed in APPEND mode:

```
                   *** EDITING MAILING LIST ***


        Title (Mr., Ms., etc.): [      ]

        First Name: [                ]    Last Name: [                 ]


        Company: [              ]

        Street Address: [          ]

          City: [           ]         State: [ ]    Zip: [      ]

        Phone: [(   )   -   ]          Use first name? (y/n) [?]


            *** Enter ^END When Finished Editing. ***
```

The comment lines (beginning with *) are ignored when dBASE lays out the screen. They are included in the format file to make it easier for a programmer to read and modify. The title of the file, the date it was last revised, and the end-of-file line are part of good program documentation.

6.39 Tip: *To activate a format file, enter SET FORMAT TO.*

If you begin working with the **CHECKS** file by telling dBASE to

```
SET FORMAT TO CHECK_IN
```

then every time you enter **APPEND, EDIT, INSERT**, or **CHANGE** mode, dBASE will use the custom screen defined by **CHECK _ IN.FMT**.

If you have more than one database file open simultaneously (as described in Chapter 5), you may have a different format file open in each workspace.

6.40 Tip: *To close a format file, enter SET FORMAT TO without entering a filename.*

If you want to work with your file without the custom screen, or if you want to use **MODIFY COMMAND** to make changes in the format file, enter

```
SET FORMAT TO
```

with no filename to close the format file in the currently selected workspace.

6.41 Tip: *dBASE will close a format file for you when you open another file with the USE command.*

You don't have to worry about closing your format file when you change the database you are working with; **USE** will close the open format file along with the database file.

6.42 Tip: *To write a format file, use the SED utility and MODIFY COMMAND.*

If you tell dBASE to

```
MODIFY COMMAND FORMAT.FMT
```

you will enter MODIFY COMMAND mode and can write or edit the file FOR-MAT.FMT exactly the same way command files are accessed in this mode. See Chapter 9 for tips and traps on working in MODIFY COMMAND mode.

MODIFY COMMAND is the best tool for making changes in a format file that already exists, but if you choose MODIFY COMMAND to write a new format file, you will have to enter each @...SAY...GET line of the file. Getting the cursor positions exactly where you want them can be quite time-consuming; SED offers an efficient alternative. The SED utility (on the Sample Programs and Utilities disk provided with dBASE III) allows you to generate a custom screen by simply keying onto the monitor what you would like the screen to look like. SED takes your template and generates the @...SAY and @...GET commands to produce the screen.

For example, the following illustration shows a template that was typed on the SED screen:

```
        B:MLIST_IN        INSERTING      AltH for help
                 *** MAILING LIST ***

   TITLE (Mr., Ms., etc.): < TITLE

   FIRST NAME:<F_NAME                      LAST NAME:<L_NAME


   COMPANY:<CO_NAME

   STREET ADDRESS:<STREET

     CITY:<CITY                    STATE:<STATE!"!!"    ZIP:<ZIP


   PHONE:< PHONE

   Use first name in letters? (y/n)<USE_FIRST
```

For each data-entry area, the prompt to be displayed is typed in the position desired, followed by the < symbol and the name of the field to be accessed. For instance, the line

TITLE (Mr.,Ms.,etc.):<TITLE

tells SED that you want "TITLE (Mr.,Ms.,etc.):" (everything before the < symbol) to be displayed on the screen in this position. The < symbol tells SED to access the field named TITLE after this prompt.

With SED, instead of writing out @ *row, column,* you can just position each prompt where you want it. Whatever you want to SAY can be typed out directly, and < indicates the field you want to GET.

The STATE field name is followed by a PICTURE clause in the preceding illustration; ! is the symbol for PICTURE on the SED screen.

After you finish composing your screen, enter ESC-D, and SED will save the template to disk. Then select option G from the main SED menu, and a dBASE file will be generated.

Here is the file generated by SED from the preceding template:

```
* MLIST_IN.PRG
@ 0,16 SAY "*** MAILING LIST ***"
@ 3,1 SAY "TITLE (Mr., Ms., etc.):"
@ 3,23 GET TITLE
@ 5,1 SAY "FIRST NAME:"
@ 5,13 GET F_NAME
@ 5,39 SAY "LAST NAME:"
@ 5,50 GET L_NAME
@ 9,1 SAY "COMPANY:"
@ 9,10 GET CO_NAME
@ 12,1 SAY "STREET ADDRESS:"
@ 12,17 GET STREET
@ 14,3 SAY "CITY:"
@ 14,9 GET CITY
@ 14,37 SAY "STATE:"
@ 14,44 GET STATE PICTURE "!!"
@ 14,57 SAY "ZIP:"
@ 14,62 GET ZIP
@ 18,1 SAY "PHONE:"
@ 18,8 GET PHONE
@ 21,1 SAY "Use first name in letters? (y/n)"
@ 21,34 GET USE_FIRST
```

SED has used the row and column of each entry to determine an @...SAY for each prompt and an @...GET for each field name. Look back at Figure 6-1 to see this custom screen as used in EDIT mode.

Be sure to read the following trap.

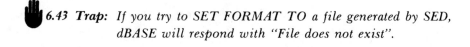

6.43 Trap: *If you try to SET FORMAT TO a file generated by SED, dBASE will respond with "File does not exist".*

SED always gives the file extension .PRG to the dBASE files it creates. When you tell dBASE to SET FORMAT TO *filename,* dBASE searches the default drive for the specified filename with the extension .FMT (format). If your filename has any other extension, dBASE will not consider it for a potential format file.

When you use SED to generate a format file, you must enter

```
RENAME SED_FILE.PRG TO SED_FILE.FMT
```

before you can use the file as a format file. You should also add some comment lines (the date, EOF, and any other pertinent notes) to a file generated by SED, as discussed in Chapter 9. To make these changes, tell dBASE to

```
MODIFY COMMAND SED_FILE.FMT
```

and use the dBASE Word Processor to add the comment lines.

6.44 Tip: *Print out the summary pages from the SED on-line manual.*

The SED manual is on the same disk as the SED program, and you can refer to the manual while you are working in SED. It's helpful to print out the following summary pages from that manual; just locate the page and press P:

Page Number	Summary Topic
21	SED functions and work flow
41	Commands needed for .FMT files
43	PICTURE formats
61	Cursor-control commands
63	Saving and exiting commands

6.45 Tip: *With SED you can easily enclose areas of your screen by generating boxes.*

To emphasize part of a custom screen, use the SED block commands to draw a box around it. Simply mark the upper-left and lower-right corners of your block and enter a control code to draw the border.

The block commands are on page 55 of the SED on-line manual; print out this page for reference if you're interested in using boxes on your SED-generated screens.

🔆 *6.46 Tip:* *You can use PICTURE clauses with SED, and you can save time by defining a PICTURE format that will be used repeatedly.*

The following SED screen creates a custom input screen for a file that includes four telephone numbers in each record:

```
        B:MEMB_IN      INSERTING     AltH for help
            *** OFFICERS LIST, REGION II ***

CHAPTER NAME:<CHAPTER

LOCATION:<CITY

     PRESIDENT:<PRES_NAME

       PHONE:<PRES_PH !a

     VICE-PRESIDENT:<VP_NAME

       PHONE:<VP_PH !a

     SECRETARY:<SEC_NAME

       PHONE:<SEC_PH !a

     TREASURER:<TR_NAME

       PHONE:<TR_PH !a

!a (999)999-9999
```

Notice that each field that needs the telephone PICTURE is followed by "!a". This tells SED to use the format defined as PICTURE "a".

At the bottom of the screen, format "a" is defined. Note that the ! symbol (for PICTURE) appears in the first space of that line, in column 0. This tells SED that what follows is a PICTURE definition. You can place these definitions anywhere on the SED screen, before or after you use them in your screen composition, as long as you begin the line with the ! symbol.

Notice also that the PICTURE definition is not delimited with quotes.

Page 43 of the SED on-line manual summarizes the defining of PICTURE formats.

✋ *6.47 Trap:* *If you do not specify the file extension .FMT for your format file, dBASE will not be able to find the file when you enter SET FORMAT TO filename.*

When dBASE receives the command

```
SET FORMAT TO CHECK_IN
```

it searches the default drive for a file named CHECK—IN with the extension .FMT. If there is no file CHECK—IN.FMT on the disk, dBASE responds "File does not exist".

If you use MODIFY COMMAND to write your format file, you must specify the .FMT extension, or dBASE will assign your file the default extension .PRG. To write a format file named CHECK—IN, tell dBASE to

```
MODIFY COMMAND CHECK_IN.FMT
```

This file will be available to dBASE as a format file.

If you forget to specify this extension when you create the file, you can always do this:

```
RENAME CHECK_IN.PRG TO CHECK_IN.FMT
```

If you use SED to generate your screen layout, you must rename the file created by SED (see Trap 6.43).

6.48 Tip: *Use macros to make writing, testing, and revising your format files easier.*

The sequence for writing or modifying a format file with **MODIFY COMMAND** is usually the following:

1. MODIFY COMMAND CUST—SC.FMT
You write the first draft of your format file.

2. SET FORMAT TO CUST—SC
APPEND
You take a look at the screen that results from your first attempt at the format file. It helps to use SHIFT-PRTSC to generate a printout of the screen, which you can keep as a reference during your revisions.

3. SET FORMAT TO

dBASE cannot modify an open file, so you have to close CUST__SC.FMT before you can revise it.

4. Repeat step 1 for revisions and improvements.

This sequence usually has to be repeated several times before the format file will work correctly and generate an acceptable screen. You can make the whole process faster by using macros (described in Chapter 9), as shown here:

```
STORE "MODIFY COMMAND CUST_SC.FMT" TO MOD
STORE "SET FORMAT TO CUST_SC" TO ON
STORE "APPEND" TO A
STORE "SET FORMAT TO" TO OFF
```

Now the sequence above is reduced to the following:

Macro	Purpose
&MOD	To write in the file
&ON	To activate the file
&A	To enter APPEND mode and see the screen
&OFF	To close the file

6.49 Trap: *dBASE ignores all commands except @...SAY...GET or the ∗ comment in a format file.*

dBASE uses a format file to set up the screen in data-entry and updating modes. Format files are limited to the screen layout commands only. If your .FMT file contains a command other than @...SAY...GET or a comment, dBASE will ignore the command line that contains it.

If you want to control more than the layout of the screen, you can include a screen format in a program (.PRG) file.

6.50 Tip: *You can use a format file to define the screen that is used by your dBASE program.*

If you use the line

```
SET FORMAT TO NAME_IN
```

within a dBASE program, the screen display defined by NAME — IN.FMT will be activated whenever the **READ** command is executed.

It's often helpful to define the screen in a separate format file. This keeps your main program shorter and keeps it focused on its own processing tasks.

7

The **REPORT FORM** Command

The **REPORT FORM** command can format output from dBASE III database files in three different ways: for the screen, for the printer, and for an ASCII file. It can also direct the output to each of these places.

You know, of course, that you can generate reports in dBASE III by using the LIST and DISPLAY commands both by themselves and in conjunction with the SET ALTERNATE command. Reports generated with these commands can also be directed to the screen, to the printer, or to an ASCII file.

However, the **REPORT FORM** command is much more useful for custom formatting your data and for providing totals and subtotals of numeric information. Although the use of LIST or DISPLAY with SET ALTERNATE allows you to list unformatted records to the printer (and sometimes that's all you need), these commands can't compete with **REPORT FORM** when it comes to producing high-quality formatted output from dBASE III.

If you ever used REPORT FORM in dBASE II, you might have found it cumbersome. However, in dBASE III, REPORT is much improved—it is both easy and flexible. Because of this, you will not need very many tips and traps; this brief chapter should provide all the extra help you need.

Creating and Modifying Report Forms

7.01 Tip: *CREATE REPORT and MODIFY REPORT are identical commands. They can be used interchangeably with exactly the same results.*

Once you create a report, you often want to modify it (for example, to add a field). dBASE allows you to do both with the same command, which has two different names: **CREATE REPORT** and **MODIFY REPORT**. You can create a report with **MODIFY REPORT**, and you can modify a report with **CREATE REPORT**: there is no difference between the two commands.

7.02 Tip: *To create a report form that is similar to an existing one, use the COPY FILE command to replicate it and then use MODIFY REPORT to make the desired changes.*

Suppose you want to create a report that's identical to an existing one in all but one (or a few) respects. You could use the **CREATE REPORT** command and build the report from scratch, but it would be much faster to use the **COPY FILE** command to make a copy of the existing report form and then make the necessary modifications to the copy with **MODIFY REPORT**.

An important detail to remember in using **COPY FILE** is that the copy must also have the .FRM file extension.

7.03 Trap: *In setting the value for the right margin of a report form, do not enter the number of characters you want to have between the left and right margins. Instead, enter the number of characters you want to have between the right edge of the page and the right margin.*

For example, in the following illustration, the page width is 55 characters, the left margin is 8, and the right margin is 5.

```
                 Left Margin - 8 characters   Right Margin - 5 characters
   Page Width |------->|--------------------------------------|<----|
   55 characters
```

If you wanted the distance between the two margins to be 42 characters, and you therefore entered 42 instead of 5 as the right margin, you would get nonsense characters when you tried to run the report.

7.04 Trap: *If the numerical difference between the page width and the left margin in a report form is exactly 256, you will get nonsense characters when you try to run the report.*

Occasionally you want to create a very wide report. dBASE can do so, but beware of the unlucky number 256, which could cause dBASE to lock up. You may have to do a *warm boot* (by pressing CTRL-ALT-DEL) to get out of it.

To avoid this trap, you must decrease the page width of the report or increase the left margin so that the difference is 255 or less. Increasing the difference to greater than 256 will get rid of the nonsense characters, but the report title may not display properly.

7.05 Tip: *Before creating any reports, be sure you understand the distinction between a field in a dBASE record and a field in a dBASE report.*

Think of a field in a dBASE report as a column. The content of each column in a dBASE report is defined in the "Field contents" area of the input screen.

A column, or field, in a dBASE report can contain a single field from a dBASE record. However, it can also contain several fields, a combination of fields and character strings, a mathematical expression, a function, or simply a string of characters. A report field can even contain fields from related database files. The possibilities are endless.

7.06 Tip: *When you create or modify reports, logical fields and date fields must always be given widths of at least 3 and 8, respectively.*

dBASE III will allow you to enter a width that is less than 3 in a logical field and that is less than 8 in a date field. However, these smaller values will be ignored when the report is run, and the values will be replaced automatically by the defaults of 3 and 8, respectively.

Keep in mind that when **REPORT FORM** is used, logical fields will always be output in the format .T. or .F. — 3 characters. Date fields will always be output in the format MM/DD/YY (for example, 10/07/86) — 8 characters.

✋ *7.07* **Trap:** *If you don't set the width of a report field so that it is large enough to hold the combined total of a column, only asterisks will be printed for the total.*

```
Page No.        1
10/09/85
                                        DAILY SALES REPORT

                                                10/07/85


SALES PERSON                SALES -  SALES -     TOTAL
                            PRODUCT  PRODUCT     SALES
                            LINE A   LINE B


    Fred Beasley            54324.19 28379.25  82703.44
    Nancy Devine             3899.84 57888.38  61788.22
    Judith Kravitz          93832.90     0.00  93832.90
    Kevin O'Brady               0.00  7700.99   7700.99
    Joan Russell              235.35 85844.37  86079.72
    Naomi Tully             38992.98 40078.34  79071.32

*** Total ***               ******** ******** 411176.59
```

```
Structure for database : A:sales.dbf
Number of data records :      6
Date of last update    : 10/07/85
Field  Field name  Type        Width    Dec
    1  FIRST_NAME  Character      10
    2  LAST_NAME   Character      10
    3  REGION      Character       4
    4  SALES_A     Numeric         8      2
    5  SALES_B     Numeric         8      2
    6  SUPERVISOR  Character       3
    7  SALE_DATE   Date            8
** Total **                       52
```

Figure 7-1. Record structure of SALES file

As you can see, the totals for the first two report fields were not printed. Looking at Figure 7-1, you can see that fields SALES _ A and SALES _ B (the fields with the unprinted totals) do have a width of 8 in the source database. dBASE therefore set the default field width to 8 for the corresponding fields in the report.

However, if you add all the values in each field, the sum has a width of 9 characters. In creating the report, you must therefore modify the default width of 8 accordingly. A useful rule of thumb would be to specify the widths of fields to be totalled as two more than the widths of the corresponding source database fields.

Figure 7-2 shows the same report after the field width has been changed to 9 for both report fields.

7.08 Tip: In designing reports, you can break the contents of a report field into several lines in a printout by entering the ; symbol to force a new line.

Figure 7-3 shows the input screen for report field 1 of the report shown in Figure 7-2. Notice that the report field is comprised of two concatenated character fields, FIRST_ NAME and LAST_ NAME. (The TRIM function has been used to remove trailing blanks from the FIRST_ NAME field. However, if you aren't familiar with TRIM, don't worry — it isn't essential for understanding this tip.)

```
                              DAILY SALES REPORT

                                   10/07/85

    SALES PERSON           SALES -    SALES -      TOTAL
                           PRODUCT    PRODUCT      SALES
                           LINE A     LINE B

    Fred Beasley           54324.19   28379.25   82703.44
    Nancy Devine            3899.84   57888.38   61788.22
    Judith Kravitz         93832.90       0.00   93832.90
    Kevin O'Brady              0.00    7700.99    7700.99
    Joan Russell             235.35   85844.37   86079.72
    Naomi Tully            38992.98   40078.34   79071.32

    *** Total ***         191285.26 219891.33 411176.59
```

Figure 7-2. SALES report with field width of 9

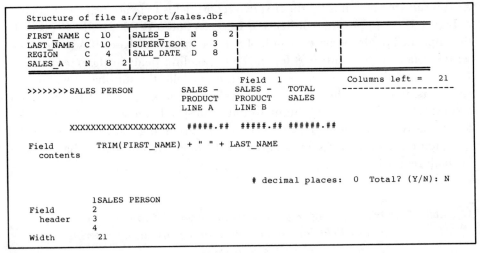

```
Structure of file a:/report/sales.dbf

FIRST_NAME  C  10   |SALES_B    N    8  2|
LAST_NAME   C  10   |SUPERVISOR C    3   |
REGION      C   4   |SALE_DATE  D    8   |
SALES_A     N   8  2|

                                Field 1            Columns left =    21
>>>>>>>>SALES PERSON         SALES -   SALES -   TOTAL    --------------------
                             PRODUCT   PRODUCT   SALES
                             LINE A    LINE B

         XXXXXXXXXXXXXXXXXXXX  #####.##  #####.##  ######.##

Field          TRIM(FIRST_NAME) + " " + LAST_NAME
  contents


                                              # decimal places:  0  Total? (Y/N): N


               1SALES PERSON
Field          2
  header       3
               4
Width           21
```

Figure 7-3. Input screen for report field 1

You can use the ; symbol so that the two character fields will be printed on separate lines within the same report field, as they appear in Figure 7-4.

Figure 7-5 shows the modified custom input screen in which the ; symbol

```
                                      DAILY SALES REPORT

                                        10/07/85

       SALES PERSON           SALES -   SALES -     TOTAL
                              PRODUCT   PRODUCT     SALES
                              LINE A    LINE B


       Fred
       Beasley               54324.19  28379.25   82703.44
       Nancy
       Devine                3899/84   57888.38   61788.22
       Judith
       Kravitz               93832.90      0.00   93832.90
       Kevin
       O'Brady                   0.00   7700.99    7700.99
       Joan
       Russell                 235.35  85844.37   86079.72
       Naomi
       Tully                 38992.98  40078.34   79071.32

 *** Total ***             191285.26 219891.33  411176.59
```

Figure 7-4. Sales report with multiple lines

```
Structure of file a:/report/sales.dbf
FIRST_NAME C  10   |SALES_B     N   8  2|
LAST_NAME  C  10   |SUPERVISOR  C   3    |
REGION     C   4   |SALE_DATE   D   8    |
SALES_A    N   8  2|
                                 Field  1              Columns left =   21
>>>>>>>>SALES PERSON          SALES -   SALES -   TOTAL   --------------------
                              PRODUCT   PRODUCT   SALES
                              LINE A    LINE B

              XXXXXXXXXXXXXXXXXXXX  #####.##  #####.## ######.##
Field              TRIM(FIRST_NAME) + ";" + LAST_NAME
   contents


                                      # decimal places:  0  Total? (Y/N): N

                   1SALES PERSON
Field              2
   header          3
                   4
Width              21
```

Figure 7-5. Report field 1 using the ; symbol

forces a new line between the two fields. Note that you need to enter ; as if it were a character string concatenated with the two fields.

Adding an additional separator line in the report specification, as in Figure 7-6, will produce an even more visually appealing report, as shown in Figure 7-7.

```
Structure of file a:/report/sales.dbf
FIRST_NAME C  10   |SALES_B     N   8  2|
LAST_NAME  C  10   |SUPERVISOR  C   3    |
REGION     C   4   |SALE_DATE   D   8    |
SALES_A    N   8  2|
                                 Field  1              Columns left =   21
>>>>>>>>SALES PERSON          SALES -   SALES -   TOTAL   --------------------
                              PRODUCT   PRODUCT   SALES
                              LINE A    LINE B

              XXXXXXXXXXXXXXXXXXXX  #####.##  #####.## ######.##
Field              TRIM(FIRST_NAME) + ";" + LAST_NAME + ";" + "----------"
   contents


                                      # decimal places:  0  Total? (Y/N): N

                   1SALES PERSON
Field              2
   header          3
                   4
Width              21
```

Figure 7-6. Report field 1 using additional character string

SALES PERSON	DAILY SALES REPORT		
		10/07/85	
	SALES - PRODUCT LINE A	SALES - PRODUCT LINE B	TOTAL SALES
Fred Beasley ----------	54324.19	28379.25	82703.44
Nancy Devine ----------	3899.84	57888.38	61788.22
Judith Kravitz ----------	93832.90	0.00	93832.90
Kevin O'Brady ----------	0.00	7700.99	7700.99
Joan Russell ----------	235.35	85844.37	86079.72
Naomi Tully ----------	38992.98	40078.34	79071.32
*** Total ***	191285.26	219891.33	411176.59

Figure 7-7. Sales report with separator line

7.09 Trap: *When you use the CREATE REPORT and MODIFY REPORT commands, dBASE sometimes automatically resets the values for the number of decimal places and for the width of a given report field to the default values when a change is made to any aspect of that field.*

Look at Figure 7-5 again. As you can see, the width of the report field has been set to 21. When the modifications shown in Figure 7-6 were made to Figure 7-5's screen, the width automatically jumped to the default value of 32 (the total number of characters defined in "Field contents"). Therefore, the desired width of 21 had to be reentered.

Numeric fields are particularly tricky, because both "# decimal places:" and "Width" automatically revert to default values, no matter what part of the screen you are working in.

Even if you don't actually make a change on a given input screen, dBASE temporarily resets the values to their defaults as you move the cursor through the various portions of the screen. However, those default values are *not* saved unless you make some change to the information on the screen.

There is one exception to this trap: if the width of a report field has already been set to a value greater than the default value, dBASE will not reset the width to the default when you are editing that screen.

7.10 Tip: *Use the CTRL-HOME key to speed movement from screen to screen when you are creating or modifying a report.*

When you use CTRL-HOME, dBASE takes you to a menu containing these options: Title, Grouping, First, Middle, Last, Append, Save, and Quit.

Selecting the Title, Grouping, First, or Last option immediately takes you to that particular input screen (First and Last are the first and last report fields). Choosing Middle takes you to another menu that shows the field contents for each report field except for the first report field and the last. From this menu you can select the report field in which you want to work.

Selecting the Append, Save, or Quit option executes the APPEND, SAVE, or QUIT command, respectively.

7.11 Trap: *If you are creating a report with subtotals and want a summary report, be aware that summary reports are not printed exactly as specified in the dBASE III user manual.*

Figure 7-8 shows a completed summary report (created from the same database as that in Figures 7-1 through 7-7) that has two subtotals, one for REGION and one for SUPERVISOR. Figure 7-9 shows the second input screen for the report form; this is the input screen in which the names of the fields you want sub-totalled are entered—in this case, REGION and SUPERVISOR.

There are four report fields in this report. The first report field (with the heading SALES PERSON) is the only non-numeric field. Figure 7-10 shows the input screen for that field. According to the user manual, the contents of the SALES PERSON field should have printed out for the first record in each group. As you can see from the report in Figure 7-8, none of the salespeople's names were printed.

dBASE III Tips and Traps

SALES PERSON	SALES – PRODUCT LINE A	SALES – PRODUCT LINE B	TOTAL SALES
** REGION: East * SUPERVISOR - CLD * Subsubtotal *	235.35	85844.37	86079.72
* SUPERVISOR - MGD * Subsubtotal *	132825.88	40078.34	172904.22
** Subtotal **	133061.23	125922.71	258983.94
** REGION: West			
* SUPERVISOR - BEW * Subsubtotal *	58224.03	86267.63	144491.66
* SUPERVISOR - MDD * Subsubtotal *	0.00	7700.99	7700.99
** Subtotal **	58224.03	93968.62	152192.65
*** Total ***	191285.26	219891.33	411176.59

DAILY SALES REPORT

10/07/85

Figure 7-8. Summary report with subtotals and subsubtotals

```
Structure of file a:/report/sales.dbf

FIRST_NAME  C   10    SALES_B     N   8   2
LAST_NAME   C   10    SUPERVISOR  C   3
REGION      C   4     SALE_DATE   D   8
SALES_A     N   8   2

Group/subtotal on:              REGION


Summary report only? (Y/N): Y      Eject after each group/subtotal? (Y/N): N

Group/subtotal heading:         REGION:


Subgroup/sub-subtotal on:       SUPERVISOR



Subgroup/subsubtotal heading: SUPERVISOR -
```

Figure 7-9. Input screen for subtotals

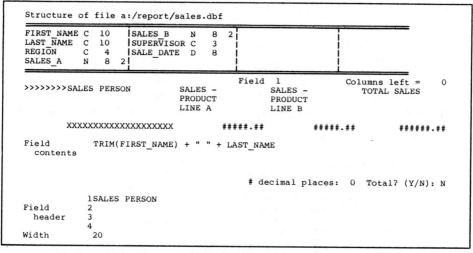

```
Structure of file a:/report/sales.dbf

FIRST_NAME  C  10    │SALES_B      N   8  2│
LAST_NAME   C  10    │SUPERVISOR   C   3   │
REGION      C   4    │SALE_DATE    D   8   │
SALES_A     N   8  2 │                     │

                                  Field  1           Columns left =    0
>>>>>>>>SALES PERSON       SALES -            SALES -          TOTAL SALES
                           PRODUCT            PRODUCT
                           LINE A             LINE B

           XXXXXXXXXXXXXXXXXXXXX       #####.##         #####.##        ######.##
Field                 TRIM(FIRST_NAME) + " " + LAST_NAME
   contents


                                   # decimal places:  0   Total? (Y/N): N

                      1SALES PERSON
Field                 2
   header             3
                      4
Width                20
```

Figure 7-10.   Report field 1 from summary report

✋ **7.12 Trap:** *If you enter more than 1440 characters of data while using CREATE or MODIFY REPORT, you will get the error message "Internal error—bucket overfilled".*

Report forms accept a maximum of 1440 characters of input data. If you enter more characters than that and get the error message just quoted, do not panic and hit the ESC key—if you do, you will lose the entire report if you have not yet saved it to disk. Instead, if you see the error message, press PGUP or RETURN. Once the error message has gone away, save the report immediately by pressing CTRL-END or CTRL-W.

After the report has been saved, you can go back and edit it with CREATE or MODIFY REPORT. The report should be intact except for the screen that you were working on when you got the error message, and only part of that screen will have been saved.

Included in the total character count are the report heading, subtotal headings, subtotal expressions, field headings, field expressions, one extra character for each line of a heading, and another extra character for each expression. To decrease the total count, look for ways to cut down on any or all of the above.

7.13 Tip: The SET RELATION command allows you to create reports that contain information from more than one database file.

Say you want to create a report that includes information about an individual from two different files. The first file is a simple name and address file, as shown here:

```
Structure for database : A:address.dbf
Number of data records :        6
Date of last update     : 11/07/85
Field   Field name   Type        Width     Dec
    1   FIRST_NAME   Character       10
    2   LAST_NAME    Character       10
    3   ADDRESS      Character       20
    4   CITY         Character       20
    5   STATE        Character        2
    6   ZIP          Character        5
 ** Total **                         68
```

```
NAME - ADDRESS                  REGION SUPERVISOR DAILY SALES TOTAL

Fred Beasley                    West   BEW        $ 82703.44
2459 Oak Grove Rd.
Walnut Creek, CA  94598

Nancy Devine                    West   BEW        $ 61788.22
24 Tower Court
San Francisco, CA  94111

Judith Kravitz                  East   MGD        $ 93832.90
2351 Putty Hill Rd.
Towson, MD  21204

Kevin O'Brady                   West   MDD        $  7700.99
873 Tenth St.
San Jose, CA  95112

Joan Russell                    East   CLD        $ 86079.72
1535 Boylston St.
Cambridge, MA  02138

Naomi Tully                     East   MGD        $ 79071.32
10R Boston St.
Somerville, MA  02143
```

Figure 7-11. Report with data from two files

The second file is the SALES file shown in Figure 7-1. You want dBASE to be able to treat these two files as if they were one file. The SET RELATION command allows you to do just that by linking the files together via a common field — in this case, the LAST_NAME field. Use the following commands to link the two files together:

```
SELECT 1
USE Sales
SELECT 2
USE Address INDEX Name
SELECT 1
SET RELATION TO Last_name INTO Address INDEX Name
```

The Name index referred to in the USE and SET statements is indexed on the LAST_NAME field. The linked file (in this case, ADDRESS.DBF) must be indexed on the linking field (LAST_NAME) for the SET RELATION command to work properly.

Figure 7-11 shows a report that includes information from both files. Figure 7-12 shows the report field used to pull the address information from the linked ADDRESS file. Note that the prefix B--> was used to identify fields from the linked file in workspace 2 (workspace B). (Chapter 5 presents additional information about this prefix convention.)

```
    Structure of file a:/report/ADDRESS.dbf

    FIRST_NAME C  10      STATE    C  2
    LAST_NAME  C  10      ZIP      C  5
    ADDRESS    C  20
    CITY       C  20

                                  Field  1         Columns left =   5
    >>>>>>>> NAME - ADDRESS        REGION SUPERVISOR DAILY SALES TOTAL -----


            XXXXXXXXXXXXXXXXXXXXXXXXXXXXXX ?       ?          ?

    Field       TRIM(FIRST_NAME) + " " + LAST_NAME + ";" + TRIM(B->ADDRESS) + ";" +
      contents  TRIM(B->CITY) + ", " + B->STATE + "   " + B->ZIP + ";" + ";"


                                  # decimal places:  0  Total? (Y/N): N

              1NAME - ADDRESS
    Field     2
      header  3
              4
    Width        76
```

Figure 7-12. Report field with data from two files

Using Report Forms

7.14 Tip: *You can use the TO FILE option with the REPORT FORM command to save a report for future printing or for editing with a word processor.*

The **REPORT FORM...TO FILE** command can be particularly useful if you want to run a report but don't want to tie up your printer at that particular time. This command also allows you to take a report file you have on disk and print it from another computer/printer environment that has a faster or higher-quality printer. Since the report is stored on the disk as a standard ASCII text file, it can be printed out in any DOS environment by using DOS commands. dBASE III is not required.

Reports created with the TO FILE option can be further customized, or incorporated into a larger document, by using a word processing program that reads a standard ASCII text file. With this feature you can make the report look exactly as you want it to, even if dBASE can't format it as you want.

In any use of the TO FILE option, the file created will have a .TXT extension unless otherwise specified. You must remember this for later editing or printing.

7.15 Trap: *If you use the REPORT FORM command with the TO PRINT option and your printer isn't hooked up and ready to go, you will lock up your system.*

If this occurs, you may be able to unlock your system if you put your printer on-line. Otherwise, reboot to continue.

7.16 Trap: *If your file is not indexed or sorted on the fields being subtotalled, the subtotals won't come out right.*

If your report has both subtotals and subsubtotals, as shown in Figure 7-13, you must index or sort on both fields. The multiple index for the report in Figure

7-13 was created with the following commands (refer to Figure 7-1 for the file's record structure):

```
.USE Sales
.INDEX ON Region + Supervisor TO Regsup
```

Figure 7-14 shows the results of printing the same report by using the file without the index; both subtotals and subsubtotals are wrong.

SALES PERSON	SALES – PRODUCT LINE A	SALES – PRODUCT LINE B	TOTAL SALES
DAILY SALES REPORT			
10/07/85			
** REGION: East			
* SUPERVISOR – CLD			
Joan Russell	235.35	85844.37	86079.72
* Subsubtotal *	235.35	85844.37	86079.72
* SUPERVISOR – MGD			
Naomi Tully	38992.98	40078.34	79071.32
Judith Kravitz	93832.90	0.00	93832.90
* Subsubtotal *	132825.88	40078.34	172904.22
** Subtotal **	133061.23	125922.71	258983.94
** REGION: West			
* SUPERVISOR – BEW			
Fred Beasley	54324.19	28379.25	82703.44
Nancy Devine	3899.84	57888.38	61788.22
* Subsubtotal *	58224.03	86267.63	144491.66
* SUPERVISOR – MDD			
Kevin O'Brady	0.00	7700.99	7700.99
* Subsubtotal *	0.00	7700.99	7700.99
** Subtotal **	58224.03	93968.62	152192.65
*** Total ***	191285.26	219891.33	411176.59

Figure 7-13. SALES report with subtotals and subsubtotals

7.17 Tip: *You can use the same report form with different databases, as long as the database being used contains the fields defined in the report form.*

Say your company maintains one database for your suppliers and another database for your customers, each with its own record structure. It is possible to use

	DAILY SALES REPORT		
	10/07/85		
SALES PERSON	SALES - PRODUCT LINE A	SALES - PRODUCT LINE B	TOTAL SALES
** REGION: West			
* SUPERVISOR - BEW			
* Subsubtotal *	54324.19	28379.25	82703.44
** Subtotal **	54324.19	28379.25	82703.44
** REGION: East			
* SUPERVISOR - MGD			
* Subsubtotal *	93832.90	0.00	93832.90
* SUPERVISOR - CLD			
* Subsubtotal *	235.35	85844.37	86079.72
** Subtotal **	94068.25	85844.37	179912.62
** REGION: West			
* SUPERVISOR - MDD			
* Subsubtotal *	0.00	7700.99	7700.99
* SUPERVISOR - BEW			
* Subsubtotal *	3899.84	57888.38	61788.22
** Subtotal **	3899.84	65589.37	69489.21
** REGION: East			
* SUPERVISOR - MGD			
* Subsubtotal *	38992.98	40078.34	79071.32
** Subtotal **	38992.98	40078.34	79071.32
*** Total ***	191285.26	219891.33	411176.59

Figure 7-14. Report with subtotals and subsubtotals made from an unindexed file

the same report form to produce a standard address list from each database, assuming that the fields for company name and address information have the same names in both databases. Remember, field names in both reports must match *exactly*.

7.18 Tip: *Using a single report form with different indexes on the same file will give you reports sorted in different orders.*

Figure 7-15 shows a report generated with the same report form as that in Figure 7-2. The new report uses the same file, but it is now indexed on the SALES __ A field rather than on the LAST __ NAME field as in Figure 7-2. Another report could easily be printed by using SALES __ B as the indexed field.

7.19 Trap: *When you use the Heading option of the REPORT FORM command, the heading will wrap (begin a new line) at 40 characters.*

If you want one-line headings and you use the Heading option, be sure your headings are fewer than 40 characters in length.

```
                          DAILY SALES REPORT

                              10/07/85

    SALES PERSON        SALES -    SALES -     TOTAL
                        PRODUCT    PRODUCT     SALES
                        LINE A     LINE B


    Kevin O'Brady          0.00    7700.99    7700.99
    Joan Russell         235.35   85844.37   86079.72
    Nancy Devine        3899.84   57888.38   61788.22
    Naomi Tully        38992.98   40078.34   79071.32
    Fred Beasley       54324.19   28379.25   82703.44
    Judith Kravitz     93832.90       0.00   93832.90
    *** Total ***

                     191285.26 219891.33 411176.59
```

Figure 7-15. Report from a file indexed on different field

✋ *7.20 Trap:* *When reports that contain memo fields are being printed, any memo field that is long enough to require more than one line in the report may print continuously across a page break.*

This situation depends on the format of the individual report you are using. One way around the problem is to increase the column width of the report field that contains the memo field. In some cases, you may have to alter the contents of the memo field itself.

✋ *7.21 Trap:* *If you use the Plain option with the command REPORT FORM...TO PRINT, the report will print through to the end without any page breaks.*

Because the Plain option ignores page breaks, it is ideal for viewing reports directed only to the screen and not to the printer. But before you print a report, be sure the Plain option has been deactivated.

✋ *7.22 Trap:* *If you use the Plain option and the Heading option of the REPORT FORM command at the same time, the Heading option will be cancelled out.*

If you really want headings, be sure to turn off Plain.

8

Data Sharing
And Conversion

dBASE III users often want to copy data out of their dBASE III files so that they can use the data with other software — with Lotus 1-2-3, MicroPro's MailMerge, or WordStar, for example. dBASE III users also often want to take data from other software environments and manipulate it with dBASE III. But different software programs store information in files that have very different internal characteristics. Consequently, it is seldom possible for another program to use a file in unaltered form.

However, there are ways to convert data files into a standard format so that they can be used by different programs. dBASE III data files can be used by other programs, and vice versa. The tips and traps in this chapter will help you with the ins and outs of data sharing between dBASE III and other software.

Importing Data Into dBASE III

Before you begin converting data, find out if there is a utility program that converts data files from your external software environment into a dBASE III format.

An important utility program of this type is DCONVERT, which comes with dBASE III. DCONVERT translates dBASE II files into dBASE III format. The use of this utility is well documented in Adam Greene's booklet entitled "dBASE Bridge," which comes in the dBASE III package.

Certain software programs like Lotus 1-2-3 Version 2.0 have built-in utilities that perform the conversion to a dBASE III format. (The Lotus utility is called TRANS.) Symphony and 1-2-3 files can both be converted into the proper format using a product called dB III Translate, developed by Syscomp. Another way is to convert 1-2-3 and Symphony files to dBASE II format using their built-in translation utility. Once this has been accomplished, you can use the dBASE DCONVERT program to complete the conversion to dBASE III format.

8.01 Tip: *When no direct conversion utility exists, you can use the dBASE APPEND FROM command to copy text or data files produced by other software into dBASE III if the other software's files can be put into either an SDF or DELIMITED format.*

SDF (System Data Format) and DELIMITED are the specific terms used by Ashton-Tate to refer to two standard formats for ASCII text files. (The data in ASCII files is character coded rather than binary coded.)

To be usable in dBASE III, ASCII text data must not contain the control characters commonly inserted by word processing programs. In order to produce an ASCII file from WordStar, for example, you must use non-document mode, in which no control characters are inserted.

Files in SDF format are ASCII files with fixed-length fields that are placed end-to-end with nothing separating them. Blank spaces are not removed and records are separated from one another by a carriage return and a line feed. Here is a file in SDF format:

```
Fred      Beasley   2000.0019530524T
Judith    Kravitz   1500.0019620329F
Joan      Russell   2500.0019511222T
Kevin     O'Brady   2500.0019430814T
Nancy     Devine    2100.0019480930F
Naomi     Tully     2200.0019510429T
```

The records in this file have five fields, containing a first name, last name, monthly salary, birth date, and marital status. Blank spaces appear in the first and last name fields because these fields allow for ten characters. All of the fields follow one after the other with no separation. The last field, MARRIED, is a logical field containing either a T for true (married) or an F for false (not married).

The same file is shown below in DELIMITED format:

```
"Fred","Beasley",2000.00,19530524,T
"Judith","Kravitz",1500.00,19620329,F
"Joan","Russell",2500.00,19511222,T
"Kevin","O'Brady",2500.00,19430814,T
"Nancy","Devine",2100.00,19480930,F
"Naomi","Tully",2200.00,19510429,T
```

This is a standard format used by BASIC and many other software programs. Notice that the characters fields are surrounded by quotation marks and that blank spaces have been eliminated. All fields are separated by commas. As with the SDF format, individual records are separated with a carriage return/line feed combination.

APPEND FROM *filename* SDF is the proper command for importing a file in SDF format into a dBASE database. APPEND FROM *filename* DELIMITED is the proper command for importing a file in the DELIMITED format.

✊ *8.02 Trap: If your character fields include quotation marks as part of the data, your file will not be properly imported into dBASE when you use the DELIMITED option of APPEND FROM.*

If your character fields contain quotation marks when you use the DELIMITED option, dBASE gets confused about where fields begin and end in the imported data. To correct such a situation, dBASE III allows you to specify an alternate character other than quotation marks to surround character fields. Any character can be used for this purpose, but you must be sure that the character you choose does not occur in any of your character fields.

Unfortunately, most other software environments with the ability to create DELIMITED files do not offer such a choice; character fields are usually surrounded by quotation marks. In such a case, SDF format would be preferable if it is possible. If it is not possible, you can use the search and replace function of your word processor to replace the unwanted quotation mark delimiters in your DELIMITED file with another character.

For example, you could decide to use the * character to surround character fields. In this case a file in DELIMITED format would look like this sample file:

```
*Fred*,*Beasley*,2000.00,19530524,T
*Judith*,*Kravitz*,1500.00,19620329,F
*Joan*,*Russell*,2500.00,19511222,T
*Kevin*,*O'Brady*,2500.00,19430814,T
*Nancy*,*Devine*,2100.00,19480930,F
*Naomi*,*Tully*,2200.00,19510429,T
```

To append such a file, the proper command is

```
APPEND FROM names DELIMITED WITH *
```

8.03 Tip: *DELIMITED WITH BLANK is the easiest format to work with when no field has embedded blanks.*

This format differs from the other DELIMITED formats in that fields are separated by a blank space rather than by a comma, and also in that character fields are not surrounded by any special delimiter character. Here is a file of names in **DELIMITED WITH BLANK** format:

```
Fred Beasley 2000.00 19530524 T
Judith Kravitz 1500.00 19620329 F
Joan Russell 2500.00 19511222 T
Kevin O'Brady 2500.00 19430814 T
Nancy Devine 2100.00 19480930 F
Naomi Tully 2200.00 19510429 T
```

A restriction with this format is that it does not allow embedded blanks between characters in any character field. More than one blank between fields in a record results in data following the multiple blanks not being appended for that particular record.

8.04 Tip: *If date information in an ASCII file in SDF or DELIMITED format is to be appended into a DATE field in dBASE, it must be in YYYYMMDD format.*

For example, September 30, 1985, should be formatted as 19850930.

```
    Structure for database : A:parts.dbf
    Number of data records :        5
    Date of last update      : 11/18/85
    Field   Field name   Type        Width   Dec
        1   PART_NUM     Numeric         5
        2   DESCRIPT     Character      10
        3   LIST_PRICE   Numeric         6     2
        4   OUR_PRICE    Numeric         6     2
        5   OUR_COST     Numeric         6     2
        6   COMMENT      Memo           10
        7   LAST_UPDAT   Date            8
    ** Total **                         52
```

Figure 8-1. Structure of PARTS file

 8.05 Trap: *APPEND FROM will not copy data into a memo field.*

If you try to use APPEND FROM...DELIMITED, nothing terrible happens, but the data intended for the memo field does not get copied properly. If you try to use APPEND FROM...SDF, not only will the memo field's data not be transferred, but any fields following the memo field will not be accurately copied, because dBASE ignores the first ten characters of a memo field's data and treats the eleventh character as the beginning of the next field.

In fact, there is no easy way to get large amounts of textual information created by other software into dBASE III memo fields. But see the following tip.

8.06 Tip: *You can append text to memo fields in a dBASE file without rekeying all of the data.*

Figure 8-1 shows the record structure of a dBASE file used to control pricing and gross margins for a company's product line. Figure 8-2 shows a listing of records from that file.

```
    Record#  PART_NUM  DESCRIPT  LIST_PRICE  OUR_PRICE  OUR_COST  COMMENT  LAST_UPDAT
        1    10001     Part 1        25.00      19.95     15.00   Memo     09/13/85
        2    10002     Part 2        20.00      17.95     12.00   Memo     09/13/85
        3    10003     Part 3        15.00      12.95      9.00   Memo     09/13/85
        4    10004     Part 4        12.00       9.95      7.20   Memo     09/13/85
        5    10005     Part 5        10.00       7.95      6.00   Memo     09/13/85
```

Figure 8-2. Listing of PARTS file

Say you have a report, created by a word processing program, from which you want to copy comments into the COMMENT field of your dBASE file. Some of the comments are lengthy, and you don't want someone to have to rekey all of that data.

There is an alternative. First convert the report file, which was created with your word processor, to an ASCII format. (Many word processors have this capability.) The resulting ASCII file should then be divided into smaller files, each of these smaller files representing the comments for one of your products. You should end up with one ASCII text file for every record in your dBASE file. You'll be attaching one memo to each record.

Once the files are set up, enter dBASE and use the EDIT command on the first record in PARTS.DBF. Move the cursor to the COMMENT field and press CTRL-PGDN to get into the dBASE Word Processor. Once in the Word Processor, you can read in the appropriate ASCII file for that COMMENT field by pressing CTRL-KR. CTRL-W or CTRL-END saves that data in the COMMENT field and returns you to the EDIT screen. CTRL-C moves you to the next record in the file, and the process is repeated with the appropriate ASCII file for that record's COMMENT field. Repeat this process for every record in the dBASE file until all ASCII text files have been copied into dBASE.

This method requires that you work on every record individually. You will therefore use it only when rekeying the text directly into a dBASE memo field is particularly burdensome.

8.07 Trap: *If you APPEND FROM another file into a dBASE file containing memo fields that are not the last fields in the record, your records will not be copied correctly unless you create a dummy field in the ASCII file wherever a memo field occurs.*

Say an ASCII file produced in a DELIMITED format by a spreadsheet program contains data that you want to copy to an existing dBASE file. Figure 8-1 shows the structure of the dBASE file; Figure 8-2 shows a listing of its records.

The DELIMITED file has the following structure:

```
10006,"Part 6",35.00,27.95,20.00,19850925
10007,"Part 7",59.00,47.95,40.00,19850925
```

The only field missing from the records in the DELIMITED file is the COM-MENT field, which is a memo field. Since you know from Trap 8.05 that the APPEND command will not append data into memo fields, we've skipped the memo field in the data to be imported.

The following illustration shows a listing of all the records from the dBASE price file after the attempted APPEND:

```
Record#  PART_NUM DESCRIPT    LIST_PRICE OUR_PRICE OUR_COST COMMENT LAST_UPDAT
      1     10001 Part 1         25.00     19.95    15.00 Memo    09/13/85
      2     10002 Part 2         20.00     17.95    12.00 Memo    09/13/85
      3     10003 Part 3         15.00     12.95     9.00 Memo    09/13/85
      4     10004 Part 4         12.00      9.95     7.20 Memo    09/13/85
      5     10005 Part 5         10.00      7.95     6.00 Memo    09/13/85
      6     10006 Part 6         35.00     27.95    20.00 Memo     /  /
      7     10007 Part 7         59.00     47.95    40.00 Memo     /  /
```

Notice that the LAST__UPDAT field was not copied into the dBASE file for the appended records. To correct this problem, you can simply add a dummy blank field to the DELIMITED file by inserting a comma before the LAST__UPDAT field:

```
10006,"Part 6",35.00,27.95,20.00,,19850925
10007,"Part 7",59.00,47.95,40.00,,19850925
```

Here are all the records from the dBASE PARTS file after the APPEND FROM command was used with the modified DELIMITED file as the source file. As you can see, everything copied properly:

```
Record#  PART_NUM DESCRIPT    LIST_PRICE OUR_PRICE OUR_COST COMMENT LAST_UPDAT
      1     10001 Part 1         25.00     19.95    15.00 Memo    09/13/85
      2     10002 Part 2         20.00     17.95    12.00 Memo    09/13/85
      3     10003 Part 3         15.00     12.95     9.00 Memo    09/13/85
      4     10004 Part 4         12.00      9.95     7.20 Memo    09/13/85
      5     10005 Part 5         10.00      7.95     6.00 Memo    09/13/85
      6     10006 Part 6         35.00     27.95    20.00 Memo    09/25/85
      7     10007 Part 7         59.00     47.95    40.00 Memo    09/25/85
```

If you experiment with this feature of dBASE III, two rules will emerge:

- When you APPEND FROM a DELIMITED file, the dummy field can be of any length. A blank dummy field is usually easiest.

- When you APPEND FROM an SDF file, the dummy field must be exactly ten characters in length. The content of the dummy field is irrelevant; any characters will work.

```
Structure for database : A:name.dbf
Number of data records :      6
Date of last update    : 09/29/85
Field  Field name  Type        Width    Dec
    1  FIRST_NAME  Character      10
    2  LAST_NAME   Character      10
    3  BIRTHDAY    Date            8
    4  MARRIED     Logical         1
** Total **                       30
```

Figure 8-3. Structure of NAME file

8.08 Trap: *If you are trying to APPEND FROM an SDF file, records will not be properly copied into dBASE unless the field lengths in the SDF file are exactly correct.*

An example is the structure of the dBASE file shown in Figure 8-3. Figure 8-4 provides a listing of records from the file. Suppose you want to append to the file the following records in SDF format:

```
Judy      Warburton      19600310y
George    Ogilvie        19380707y
```

Figure 8-5 shows a listing of records after using APPEND FROM...SDF has been used. Obviously, something went wrong. If you examine the SDF file you will find that there was one character too many (11) in the FIRST__NAME field. For a way to detect errors such as this, see the following tip.

```
Record#  FIRST_NAME  LAST_NAME  BIRTHDAY  MARRIED
      1  Fred        Beasley    05/24/53  .T.
      2  Judith      Kravitz    03/29/62  .F.
      3  Joan        Russell    12/22/51  .T.
      4  Kevin       O'Brady    08/14/43  .T.
      5  Nancy       Devine     09/30/48  .F.
      6  Naomi       Tully      04/29/51  .T.
```

Figure 8-4. Listing of NAME file

8.09 Tip: *If you APPEND FROM another file into dBASE and get*
unexpected results, trace the error by using the COPY TO
command on the target dBASE file with exactly the same
syntax as you used in your APPEND FROM command.

If the format of the ASCII file produced by the **COPY TO** command differs in any way from the file you are trying to **APPEND FROM** (the source file), make whatever modifications are necessary to correct the problem. You may need to change either the structure of the dBASE file you're appending to (the target file) or the format of the source file.

Let's look at an example. Figure 8-5 shows the results of an unsuccessful **APPEND FROM...SDF** command—records 7 and 8 have no data in the **BIRTHDAY** field, and the **LAST__NAME** field has an extraneous space before the first character of the actual last name. To find out what's wrong here, first execute this command:

```
COPY TO TEST SDF FOR RECNO()=1
```

Then list both this **TEST** file and the first record of the source file, so you can compare them by eyeball. You should see something like this:

```
Judy        Warburton      19600310y
Judy        Warburton      19530524y
```

The first record shown above is from the source SDF file. The second record is from the target database file. It's obvious from comparing the two records that the

```
Record#  FIRST_NAME  LAST_NAME  BIRTHDAY  MARRIED
    1     Fred        Beasley    05/24/53  .T.
    2     Judith      Kravitz    03/29/62  .F.
    3     Joan        Russell    12/22/51  .T.
    4     Kevin       O'Brady    08/14/43  .T.
    5     Nancy       Devine     09/30/48  .F.
    6     Naomi       Tully      04/29/51  .T.
    7     Judy         Warburton   /  /    .F.
    8     George      Ogilvie     /  /     .F.
```

Figure 8-5. Listing of NAME file after APPEND...SDF

first field in the source file contains one more character than the first field in the target.

To correct the problem, you could either modify the structure of the target database to accommodate an extra character in the first field, or edit out that extra character from the source file. If you do the latter and reexecute the APPEND FROM, you get the result you originally wanted.

```
Record#  FIRST_NAME  LAST_NAME  BIRTHDAY MARRIED
      1  Fred        Beasley    05/24/53 .T.
      2  Judith      Kravitz    03/29/62 .F.
      3  Joan        Russell    12/22/51 .T.
      4  Kevin       O'Brady    08/14/43 .T.
      5  Nancy       Devine     09/30/48 .F.
      6  Naomi       Tully      04/29/51 .T.
      7  Judy        Warburton  03/10/60 .T.
      8  George      Ogilvie    07/07/38 .T.
```

(You should be aware that dBASE files with memo fields have strange idiosyncrasies when they are being copied or appended to. If you are having trouble with the COPY TO or APPEND FROM command and memo fields are involved, review the preceding tips and traps about memo fields.)

Exporting Data From dBASE III

8.10 Tip: *Use the DCONVERT utility program to convert dBASE III database files into dBASE II format so that other software can use the files.*

DCONVERT, which comes with dBASE III, can convert dBASE III database files into dBASE II format if the dBASE III files do not exceed the limitations of dBASE II files — for example, the fields-per-record limit. (Refer to the dBASE II and dBASE III manuals for lists of the respective limits of the two programs.) You can convert dBASE III files to Lotus 1-2-3 and Symphony formats by using their built-in translation utility after first converting to dBASE II format. You can also convert dBASE III files into 1-2-3 or Symphony format by using Syscomp's dB III Translate.

Some programs, like Framework, will directly read dBASE III data files in their original format. However, it is more typical for a particular piece of software to only be able to read foreign files as ASCII files. If this is the case, you can create ASCII files from dBASE III data files by using the COPY TO command or LIST and DISPLAY with the SET ALTERNATE command.

The following tips and traps provide details.

8.11 Tip: *To create ASCII files from dBASE III, use the COPY TO command with either the SDF or DELIMITED options.*

dBASE III database files can be converted to ASCII files with either SDF or DELIMITED format. (See Tip 8.01 for information on SDF and DELIMITED.)

Here is an example of an ASCII file created from dBASE using the command COPY TO...SDF:

```
Fred       Beasley    19530524T
Judith     Kravitz    19620329F
Joan       Russell    19511222T
Kevin      O'Brady    19430814T
Nancy      Devine     19480930F
Naomi      Tully      19510429T
```

The structure of the dBASE file copied is shown in Figure 8-3. A listing of records from that file can be found in Figure 8-4. Here is the same file copied by using the DELIMITED option:

```
"Fred","Beasley",19530524,T
"Judith","Kravitz",19620329,F
"Joan","Russell",19511222,T
"Kevin","O'Brady",19430814,T
"Nancy","Devine",19480930,F
"Naomi","Tully",19510429,T
```

When using the COPY TO command with the DELIMITED option, specify the character to be used to surround character fields. The default is the double quotation mark, as just shown, but any character can be used. This variation is necessary when character fields contain embedded quotation marks.

The following illustration shows the same file again, this time copied using the DELIMITED WITH * option:

```
*Fred*,*Beasley*,19530524,T
*Judith*,*Kravitz*,19620329,F
*Joan*,*Russell*,19511222,T
*Kevin*,*O'Brady*,19430814,T
*Nancy*,*Devine*,19480930,F
*Naomi*,*Tully*,19510429,T
```

A special DELIMITED option, DELIMITED WITH BLANK, differs from the other DELIMITED formats in two ways: first, fields are separated by a blank space rather than a comma; second, character fields are not surrounded by any special character. It looks like this:

```
Fred Beasley 19530524 T
Judith Kravitz 19620329 F
Joan Russell 19511222 T
Kevin O'Brady 19430814 T
Nancy Devine 19480930 F
Naomi Tully 19510429 T
```

8.12 Tip: *If you want to create an ASCII file from a dBASE III data-base and you can't create the proper format by using the COPY TO command with SDF or DELIMITED, you may be able to use LIST or DISPLAY with the SET ALTER-NATE command to achieve your desired results.*

By using the SET ALTERNATE command, you can create an ASCII file that is a recording of whatever appears on the screen as you work in dBASE III. LIST, DISPLAY, and other commands can be used while SET ALTERNATE is ON to produce ASCII files of various formats. (Be sure to execute SET ALTERNATE TO *filename* before SET ALTERNATE ON.)

The following is an ASCII file that was produced with SET ALTERNATE ON and LIST:

```
Record#   FIRST_NAME  LAST_NAME   BIRTHDAY  MARRIED
      1   Fred        Beasley     05/24/53  .T.
      2   Judith      Kravitz     03/29/62  .F.
      3   Joan        Russell     12/22/51  .T.
      4   Kevin       O'Brady     08/14/43  .T.
      5   Nancy       Devine      09/30/48  .F.
      6   Naomi       Tully       04/29/51  .T.
```

A limitation in using SET ALTERNATE is that screens displayed while you are using any of the full-screen functions like APPEND, BROWSE, CHANGE, CREATE, EDIT, INSERT, and MODIFY cannot be recorded.

8.13 Tip: *If you want to use a dBASE III report as the basis of a document to be created on your word processor, use REPORT FORM__TO FILE.*

REPORT FORM *filename* TO FILE *filename* creates an ASCII file with exactly the same structure and content as a hard-copy printout of the report. You can then use your external word processor to go into the file and edit the report.

8.14 Trap: *The COPY TO command cannot be used with the SDF or DELIMITED option to copy the contents of a memo field.*

Figures 8-1 and 8-2 show the structure of a dBASE file and a listing of records. Here is a DELIMITED file created from that dBASE file by using the COPY TO command:

```
10001,"Part 1",25.00,19.95,15.00,19850913
10002,"Part 2",20.00,17.95,12.00,19850913
10003,"Part 3",15.00,12.95,9.00,19850913
10004,"Part 4",12.00,9.95,7.20,19850913
10005,"Part 5",10.00,7.95,6.00,19850913
```

Note that there is no trace whatsoever of the COMMENT field in the DELIMITED file. Using the SDF option instead of DELIMITED will not work, either.

Refer to the following tip for other methods of copying a memo field's data out of dBASE III.

8.15 Tip: *Create ASCII files containing a memo field by using LIST or DISPLAY with SET ALTERNATE or REPORT FORM...TO FILE.*

If you want to list the contents of a memo field, specify the field name for the memo field in the LIST command. If the field name for the memo field is not specified explicitly, the contents of the memo field will not display.

Figure 8-1 shows the structure of a dBASE file. Figure 8-2 shows the ASCII file created by using SET ALTERNATE ON and then LIST. Note that the contents of the memo field COMMENT do not display. In order to get the contents of the memo field, you must specify that field explicitly, as in the following command:

```
LIST PART_NUM,DESCRIPT,COMMENT
```

Here is a listing of the ASCII file created by that command with SET ALTER-NATE ON:

```
Record#   PART_NUM DESCRIPT   COMMENT
      1     10001 Part 1      This is a note about Part 1.

      2     10002 Part 2      This is a note about Part 2.

      3     10003 Part 3      This is a note about Part 3.

      4     10004 Part 4      This is a note about Part 4.

      5     10005 Part 5      This is a note about Part 5.
```

The contents of a memo field can also be displayed in a dBASE III report. An ASCII file can be produced by sending the report to a file rather than to the printer.

Here is an example of an ASCII file produced from a simple report used with the same dBASE file. Note that the contents of the memo field COMMENT appear on the report.

```
Page No.    1
11/18/85
                                       MEMO TEST

PART NUMBER COMMENT

     10001 This is a note about Part 1.

     10002 This is a note about Part 2.

     10003 This is a note about Part 3.

     10004 This is a note about Part 4.

     10005 This is a note about Part 5.
```

✋ *8.16 Trap: If you a try to create an ASCII file by using the COPY TO command with the SDF option, your ASCII file will contain nonsense characters if the dBASE file includes a memo field that is not the last field in the record.*

Here is the SDF file created from the file shown in Figures 8-1 and 8-2:

```
10001Part 1     25.00 19.95 15.00\memo.fr
10002Part 2     20.00 17.95 12.00\memo.fr
10003Part 3     15.00 12.95  9.00\memo.fr
10004Part 4     12.00  9.95  7.20\memo.fr
10005Part 5     10.00  7.95  6.00\memo.fr
```

Note that the last field reliably copied is OUR__COST. The remainder of each record in the SDF file is nonsense characters.

It is possible to get around this problem if you specify the fields that you want copied. When you specify fields as in the command

```
COPY TO <file name> FIELDS
    PART_NUM,DESCRIPT,LIST_PRICE,OUR_PRICE,OUR_COST,LAST_UPDAT SDF
```

this SDF file will result:

```
10001Part 1     25.00 19.95 15.0019850913
10002Part 2     20.00 17.95 12.0019850913
10003Part 3     15.00 12.95  9.0019850913
10004Part 4     12.00  9.95  7.2019850913
10005Part 5     10.00  7.95  6.0019850913
```

Using the COPY TO command with the DELIMITED option will give correct results even if you do not use the FIELDS option.

💡 *8.17 Tip: Place memo fields at the end of your records if at all possible.*

Memo fields frequently require special care when you are transferring data in or out of dBASE III (see Traps 8.07 and 8.16 for details). Placing these fields at the end of your records will minimize the difficulties.

8.18 Tip: *You can convert dates to other formats before copying data out of dBASE.*

dBASE stores dates in the format YYYYMMDD; for example, September 30, 1972, is stored as 19720930. To transfer date information from dBASE to other software, you must convert the data if the target software requires a different format.

Suppose you want to copy the records from the NAME.DBF file (Figures 8-3 and 8-4) to a file in DELIMITED format. Suppose also that you need to format the date information as MM/DD/YY in order for the target software to accept it. You can do so with the following steps:

1. Copy the structure of NAME.DBF to a temporary file, TEMP.DBF.

2. Use MODIFY STRUCTURE on TEMP.DBF to insert a new field in —BIRTHDAY2, which is a character field six characters wide. This is where you will put the converted data from the original date field. When you complete the MODIFY STRUCTURE, then LIST TEMP to make sure you successfully inserted the new field:

```
Record#  FIRST_NAME  LAST_NAME  BIRTHDAY  BIRTHDAY2  MARRIED
      1  Fred        Beasley    05/24/53             .T.
      2  Judith      Kravitz    03/29/62             .F.
      3  Joan        Russell    12/22/51             .T.
      4  Kevin       O'Brady    08/14/43             .T.
      5  Nancy       Devine     09/30/48             .F.
      6  Naomi       Tully      04/29/51             .T.
```

3. Use the REPLACE command to build the new converted date data in BIRTHDAY2:

```
REPLACE ALL Birthday2 with SUBSTR(DTOC(Birthday),1,2)+
SUBSTR(DTOC(Birthday),4,2)+SUBSTR(DTOC(Birthday),7,2)
```

The results follow:

```
Record#  FIRST_NAME  LAST_NAME  BIRTHDAY  BIRTHDAY2  MARRIED
      1  Fred        Beasley    05/24/53  052453     .F.
      2  Judith      Kravitz    03/29/62  032962     .T.
      3  Joan        Russell    12/22/51  122251     .T.
      4  Kevin       O'Brady    08/14/43  081443     .T.
      5  Nancy       Devine     09/30/48  093048     .F.
      6  Naomi       Tully      04/29/51  042951     .T.
```

4. Use the COPY TO command to produce the desired DELIMITED file:

```
COPY TO name.txt FIELDS First_name,Last_name,Birthday2,Married DELIMITED
```

Here is the resulting DELIMITED file, with the date information in the appropriate format:

```
"Fred","Beasley","052453",T
"Judith","Kravitz","032962",F
"Joan","Russell","122251",T
"Kevin","O'Brady","081443",T
"Nancy","Devine","093048",F
"Naomi","Tully","042951",T
```

9
Programming
In dBASE III

One of the most exciting features of dBASE III is its programming capability. With it, you can write your own programs, thereby extending the dBASE language to suit your own needs. You can define a whole series of operations that will take place whenever you tell dBASE to run your program.

The chapter begins with planning and designing your dBASE programs, perhaps the most crucial phase of writing effective programs. The second section discusses the use of memory variables to store and manipulate essential data that is not part of a database file. The chapter closes with a discussion of various dBASE programming tools.

Planning and Designing dBASE Programs

9.01 Tip: *Before starting to write a dBASE program, draw up a clear, detailed plan of your program.*

When you need to write a dBASE program, it's tempting to sit down at the computer and begin writing command lines. This almost always leads to problems, especially with longer and more complex dBASE programs. There are so many details of dBASE code and options to keep track of that it's easy to forget an essential component of the program.

Always precede actual programming by writing a plan of the program, or system of related programs, as a whole. Identify the tasks the program or programs will accomplish, and determine the correct order of those tasks. For example, suppose you are writing a program that will be used by a person taking sales orders over the telephone. The first step in creating such a program is to outline the plan:

Establish working environment

Open database files

Ask for customer name

Find customer record; if new customer, add to file

Take in order data

Look up prices

Calculate item costs and total costs

Display costs

Print out order form

9.02 Tip: *Use pseudocode to translate your plan into an outline.*

Once you have your overall plan, you are ready to write a more detailed outline of the program steps. Figure out what tasks you want performed, rather than worrying about the details of the dBASE commands that will be used.

An effective tool for this stage of your planning is *pseudocode,* a combination of ordinary language and dBASE commands describing the function of each part of the program. A line of pseudocode describes the task that will be performed by a line or two of dBASE code. Using pseudocode, you write a step-by-step outline of the program that identifies the purpose of each of the dBASE commands.

Here is the pseudocode for a program to process customers' telephone orders:

```
Establish working environment

Open database files

SET RELATIONs to link files
```

```
REPEAT for all orders

    GET customer name

    FIND customer

        IF customer not found

            APPEND new record

            GET new customer data

        ENDIF customer not found

    REPEAT for each item of order

        REPEAT until valid partcode

            GET partcode

            FIND partcode

                IF partcode not found

                    SAY "Invalid part code"

                ENDIF partcode not found

        END repeat until valid partcode

        GET quantity

        Calculate item cost

    END repeat for each item of order

    SAY total cost

    PRINT order form

END repeat for all orders

Close files
```

This list can be used to write the dBASE code for each step of the program.

It is a good idea to save the pseudocode for your important programs. The outline can be very useful when you need to modify the program, since it describes the function of each step within the overall program task.

9.03 Tip: *Choose the correct programming process to accomplish each task addressed by your application program.*

Each task carried out by your dBASE program will require one of three basic programming structures:

- *The one-time process.* Some portions of your program code will be processed exactly once each time the program is run (for example, initializing the contents of the memory variables). Once the memory variables have been established, the program moves beyond this portion of the code.

- *The reiterative process.* Many parts of dBASE programs repeat, or reiterate, the same sequence of steps, over and over, until all of the relevant data has been processed or until a certain condition has been met. For example, if a program is processing all of the records in a file, it repeats the same steps for each record until every record has been processed.

  If a program is processing a certain group of records, the repetition will continue until a condition is met. For instance, with a file indexed on ZIP code, a program would locate the first record with a particular ZIP code and then process each record until the ZIP code changed.

- *The branching process.* Often your programs will have to *branch:* to select from two or more possible actions according to the particular data being processed. For example, when an order-processing program encounters an order from a new customer, it will need to ask for such data as name and address; but it will omit those steps for an order from an established customer, one already in the database file.

Plan your program in terms of these three structures, and indicate clearly in your plan when the program will repeat a certain portion of the code or when a decision will be made. For example, in the outline developed in the preceding tip, each block of steps that will be repeated begins with **REPEAT** and is indented to show which steps will be repeated. Each branch is indicated by **IF**, followed by the condition for taking the following steps, which are again indented.

Memory Variables and Macros

dBASE III reserves a section of your computer's memory to hold up to 256 memory variables. When you create a memory variable, you assign it a name and place a particular piece of data in that memory location. For instance, if you tell dBASE to

```
STORE 234.15 TO M_AMOUNT
```

a portion of memory will be set aside with the name M —AMOUNT, and 234.15 will be stored in that memory location. Whenever you refer to M —AMOUNT, dBASE will return to this memory location and access the data stored there.

A memory variable can contain numeric, date, logical, or character data, depending on the type of data you enter when you create the variable (See Tip 9.06). Character memory variables can be used with & (the *macro* function) to tell dBASE to use the contents of the memory variable within a string or a command. If you enter

```
STORE "CUSTOMER" TO FILE
```

and then tell dBASE to

```
USE &FILE
```

dBASE will replace &FILE with the contents of the memory variable FILE and then execute the command USE CUSTOMER. See the tips and traps beginning with 9.19 for a discussion of working with macros.

9.04 Tip: *Use memory variable names that clearly indicate the data stored in each memory variable.*

The name of a memory variable can be as many as ten characters long. Like a field name, it must begin with a letter and can contain only letters, numbers, or the underscore character. dBASE reserved words cannot be used as memory variable names, since dBASE interprets these words as dBASE commands.

To make your programs easier to read and revise, always select names for memory variables that describe the contents of the memory variables. For instance, M_LNAME and M_FNAME are better variable names than N1 and N2. The letter M indicates that the name is for a memory variable, and the part following the underscore indicates exactly which kind of data (first name or last name) is contained in the memory variable.

Say you are writing a dBASE program that asks the user for the name of a particular customer and then locates all records in your ORDERS file for that customer. Within the ORDERS file, the field CUSTOMER contains the name of the customer placing each order. There are several advantages to naming the memory variable that will contain the customer name with M_CUSTOMER:

- Whenever the name appears in your dBASE code, it will clearly refer to the memory variable.

- You avoid any confusion with the field name (see the following trap) when dBASE executes your program.

- The purpose of the memory variable is clearly indicated; the program line

```
IF M_CUSTOMER = CUSTOMER
```

is easy to understand: dBASE will check to see if the customer name in the current record matches the name stored in the memory variable.

✊ **9.05 Trap:** *If a memory variable and a field in the active database file have the same name, dBASE gives preference to the field name.*

Suppose you have written a dBASE program that locates all records in your ORDERS file placed by the same customer. If the ORDERS file includes a field named CUSTOMER, whenever the ORDERS file is open, dBASE will interpret the word CUSTOMER as a reference to the contents of this field in the current record.

If your dBASE program uses a memory variable that is also named CUSTOMER, all commands in the program that use this memory variable will be executed on the field CUSTOMER instead of on the memory variable. The solution is to consistently begin all memory variable names with the letter M and an underscore, as described in the preceding tip.

💡 **9.06 Tip:** *Initialize each memory variable to be of the type that handles the kind of data you want it to store.*

A dBASE memory variable can be one of four data types: character, numeric, logical, or date. Many data-handling processes compare the contents of a memory variable to the contents of a field or replace the contents of a field with the contents of a memory variable, so they require data of matching types.

You determine the data type of each memory variable when you create it. The line

```
STORE 0.00 TO M_NUM
```

creates a numeric memory variable, M—NUM, which can be used in calculations, compared to other numeric data, or placed into a numeric field. The line

```
STORE "Smith" TO M_LNAME
```

creates a character variable, M—LNAME, which can be concatenated with other character strings, compared to other character data, placed into a character-type field, or expanded by use of the macro function. The line

```
STORE .F. TO IS_TRUE
```

creates a logical memory variable, IS—TRUE, which can be used with IF or DO WHILE to control processing within a program.

 9.07 Trap: You cannot store more than 254 characters to a character-type memory variable.

A character-type memory variable can hold long strings, but it is limited to 254 characters. If you try to store more than this, dBASE will create a logical memory variable instead of a character memory variable and store .F. in this memory location. Be sure to check the length of a long character string before you store it to a memory variable.

 9.08 Trap: You cannot create a date-type memory variable directly.

If you enter

```
STORE "10/09/86" TO M_DATE
```

dBASE will create a character-type variable containing the given string. If you need a date memory variable in order to compare to other dates or to enter into a date field, you must create it indirectly. Use the CTOD function:

```
STORE CTOD("10/09/86") TO M_DATE
```

9.09 Tip: *Use the SPACE( ) function to initialize character memory variables to a particular length.*

If you enter

```
STORE SPACE(18) TO M_CITY

STORE SPACE(2) TO M_STATE
```

dBASE will create two memory variables: M—CITY, which contains a string of 18 blanks, and M—STATE, containing a string of 2 blanks.

The SPACE( ) function is particularly useful when you need a memory variable of a specific length to use with @...GET for data entry and editing. (See the tips and traps in Chapter 3 on using memory variables with data entry.)

9.10 Trap: *A numeric memory variable will not accept numbers of more than ten digits unless it has been initialized to do so.*

When you create a numeric memory variable with, for example,

```
STORE 0.00 TO M_AMOUNT
```

dBASE establishes a default length of 10 for the memory variable. If your program tries to store a larger number in this memory variable, it will be truncated, dBASE will issue an error message, or both will happen.

If a memory variable will be involved in calculations that could result in a number longer than ten places, including the decimal point, be sure to STORE a longer number to the memory variable when it is created. For example, if M— TOTAL may need to store numbers larger than 9,999,999.99, initialize it with

```
STORE 10000000.00 TO M_TOTAL
```

9.11 Trap: *If a calculation that uses memory variables produces a result with more decimal places than the memory variables will accommodate, you will get an incorrect result.*

When dBASE performs calculations on memory variables, it uses the number of decimal places present in the memory variables to determine the number of decimal places in the answer. Unless you have planned ahead, you can get some strange results:

```
STORE 3 TO NUM_ONE
STORE 4 TO NUM_TWO
? NUM_ONE/NUM_TWO
   0
```

See the following tip.

9.12 Tip: *If you will be using your memory variables in calculations, give at least one of them decimal places when you create them.*

When memory variables are used in calculations, dBASE uses the memory variable with the most decimal places to determine the number of decimal places in the result. If you don't plan for this, you can get some strange results, as illustrated in the preceding trap.

Give at least one memory variable enough decimal places to accommodate the result of a calculation. For example, to solve the problem illustrated in the preceding trap, use

```
STORE 3.00 TO NUM_ONE
STORE 4 TO NUM_TWO
? NUM_ONE/NUM_TWO
   .75
```

9.13 Tip: *Use DISPLAY MEMORY to see the current contents of all memory variables.*

DISPLAY MEMORY will give you a list of all the memory variables that are defined, along with the current contents of each of them:

```
. DISPLAY MEMORY
M_TOTAL      pub   N       213   (        213.00000000)
LIMIT        pub   N       144   (        144.00000000)
M_CUST       pub   C     "AMERICAN TIRE CO."
IS_VALID     pub   L     .T.
FOUND        pub   L     .F.
M_TAX        pub   N       6.5   (          6.50000000)
      6 variables defined,        50 bytes used
    250 variables available,    5950 bytes available
.
```

DISPLAY MEMORY can be useful when you need to name a new memory variable, since you can quickly check which names are already in use. It can also be helpful in debugging programs, since you can see the contents of each memory variable at a particular point in the execution of your program.

9.14 Tip: *You can save the current contents of memory variables to a disk file and recall them later as needed.*

Whenever you work with a database file, dBASE saves the data to disk for you when you close the file with USE or QUIT. Data stored in memory variables is not written to a disk file automatically; when you QUIT dBASE, the contents of the memory variables will be lost unless you first tell dBASE to save them.

If you will want to access data stored in memory variables (such as a useful set of macros — see Tip 9.19 and those following it) in another work session, you can save them in a special disk file.

To save the contents of all defined memory variables to disk, tell dBASE to

SAVE TO B:MEMVARS

You can also save selected memory variables. To save all memory variables whose names begin with M — C, use

SAVE ALL LIKE M_C* TO B:MEM_COSTS

To save all current memory variables except those with names beginning with M — C, use

SAVE ALL EXCEPT M_C* TO B:MEM_PR

See Tip 9.16 for a discussion of selecting memory variable names so that it is easy to save them in related groups.

To recall memory variables from a disk file, use **RESTORE**:

```
RESTORE FROM B:MEM_SALES
```

But before you use **RESTORE**, be sure to read the following trap.

 9.15 Trap: *RESTORE will erase all current memory variables and leave only those from the disk file.*

If you want to recall memory variables from a disk file without losing the memory variables currently in memory, use

```
RESTORE FROM B:MEM_SALES ADDITIVE
```

9.16 Tip: *If you give all related memory variables names that have a common identifier, you can manipulate them as a group.*

If your program uses several memory variables related to, say, a particular sale, you can name each memory variable with a leading S, like this:

M—SDATE	To hold the date of sale
M—SORD—NO	To hold the order number
M—STOTAL	To hold the total price

This arrangement allows you to save or recall all of these related variables with one command for each operation:

```
SAVE ALL LIKE M_S* TO B:MEM_SALES
```

or

```
RESTORE ALL LIKE M_S* FROM B:MEM_SALES
```

dBASE will save or restore only the specified memory variables, ignoring any others in memory or in the disk file.

9.17 Trap: *Memory variables created within a dBASE program are not available after the program has finished executing.*

If a memory variable is created within a dBASE application program, dBASE will automatically release it from memory when the program finishes executing, even if you have saved the memory variable to disk.

See the following tip.

9.18 Tip: *To keep the contents of memory variables available after a dBASE program has finished executing, use the PUBLIC command.*

When you are writing and debugging a program, it can be important to examine the contents of the memory variables after the program has finished executing, but dBASE automatically releases the memory variables once program execution is finished. You can make the memory variables remain available by declaring them PUBLIC. You do so by including the line

```
PUBLIC M_SDATE, M_SORD_NO, M_STOTAL
```

in your dBASE program before these memory variables are initialized.

9.19 Tip: *Use macro expansion when you want dBASE to act as if you entered the contents of a memory variable.*

The macro expansion function, &, tells dBASE to replace the name of the memory variable with its contents before executing a particular command. For example, if you enter

```
STORE "SET DEFAULT TO B:" TO COMM

&COMM
```

dBASE will replace &COMM with the contents of COMM, "SET DEFAULT TO B:", and will execute this command.

Macros are particularly useful when the response of the user determines which action a program takes. For example, a program may ask the user for the name of the file to be processed and then USE the file specified:

```
READ @5,5, SAY "Enter name of file to be processed:" GET M_FILE
USE &M_FILE
```

9.20 Tip: *Use macro expansion to replace command lines that appear many times in your program.*

If a command will be used frequently in your program, using a macro for the command line will make the program easier to read and understand, and save typing time as well. For example, if you have to process a particular number of records, you can use

```
STORE 1 TO COUNT
STORE "Store COUNT + 1 to COUNT" TO ADD_ONE
DO WHILE COUNT < 25
   <process a record>
   &ADD_ONE
   SKIP
ENDDO **WHILE COUNT < 25
```

The command &ADD_ONE is easy to read and understand, and it can be used throughout the program to increment a counter.

9.21 Tip: *Use macro expansion to replace conditional statements.*

You can make the conditional statements that appear in your programs easy to read and understand if you use macros. Here is an example:

```
STORE "NUMBER > 50" TO TOO_BIG
   <processing where NUMBER is changed>
IF &TOO_BIG
```

```
<processing for NUMBER > 50>
ENDIF
```

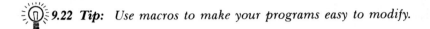 **9.22 Tip:**   *Use macros to make your programs easy to modify.*

If a program will need to be modified to accommodate different conditions in the future, use macros to write the key steps that will need changing. Then when the time comes, you can modify the entire program simply by changing the definitions of the macros.

For example, suppose the maximum order size for parts stored in your inventory is currently 144, but that number may change in the future. If you write a program that checks for this specific upper limit, you will need to replace the number 144 in each program line where it occurs when the limit is raised. If you enter

```
STORE "144" TO LIMIT
```

and use &LIMIT to check the order size, the entire program can be modified by changing the contents of LIMIT in this one line. If your maximum order size increases to 288, changing this line to

```
STORE "288" TO LIMIT
```

will update the entire program.

9.23 Trap: *Macro expansion works only with a memory variable of the character type.*

If you try to use macro expansion (&) with a memory variable that is not a character string, dBASE will respond "MACRO IS NOT A CHARACTER STRING" and will stop executing your program. But see the following tip.

9.24 Tip: *To use macro expansion with a numeric memory variable, use the STR( ) function to obtain a character memory variable with the same contents.*

Say you have a numeric memory variable named VALUE of length 5. The line

```
STORE STR(VALUE,1,5) TO C_VAL
```

will create a character memory variable, C—VAL, with the data stored as a string. C—VAL can now be expanded with the macro function.

Writing dBASE Code

9.25 Tip: *Use indentation to make your programs easy to read and modify.*

When you write your dBASE programs, make them as clear and easy to read as possible. When you are debugging the program, and especially if you must return to it in the future to make changes, you'll find it helpful to indent the lines between DO WHILE and ENDDO, IF and ENDIF, and DO CASE and END-CASE, so that each distinct program segment is grouped together. All of the examples in this book follow this convention.

Be sure to read the following tip.

9.26 Tip: *Use comments to clarify the structure and the functions of your programs.*

Comment lines begin with an asterisk (*) and are ignored by dBASE when your program is running. They are included to make the code easier to read and understand. Here are a few suggestions on when to use comment lines:

- Begin each program with the date it was last modified; this will be helpful if you find several versions of a program.

- Include the name of the person who did the modifications if more than one person has been involved in writing a program.

- End each program with an end-of-file comment; this ensures that you or someone else reviewing part of a program listing will not think that it is the entire program.

- Precede major subgroups of a long program with a brief description of their purpose.

- Include comments to explain program lines whose function is not clear or that make assumptions about the data being processed.

- When you use nested **DO WHILE** loops or **IF** structures, follow each **ENDDO** or **ENDIF** with a comment that specifies which program structure is being ended. These can be included on the same program line with the **ENDDO** or **ENDIF**.

In general, include any comments that will help you understand the code if you need to return to it in the future.

9.27 Trap: *You cannot place comments on the same line as execut-able commands other than ENDDO, ENDIF, ELSE, or ENDCASE.*

All dBASE comments, except those that follow **ENDDO**, **ENDIF**, **ELSE**, or **END-CASE**, must begin on a separate program line.

9.28 Trap: *If you are writing your program with the dBASE MOD-IFY COMMAND, an inserted line will not be saved unless it ends with a RETURN indicator.*

The dBASE MODIFY COMMAND mode allows you to insert a new line into a program by pressing CTRL-N. This key combination opens up a blank line on the screen. After you type a command into this new line, be sure to press RETURN at the end of the line. When you press RETURN the < symbol will appear on the line, at the far right side of the screen. Only lines with this symbol are saved when you exit MODIFY COMMAND.

9.29 Tip: *To print out a listing of a program file, use TYPE.*

You can print out the contents of a program file, which ends in the file extension .PRG, from within dBASE III. Be sure the file is closed and that you are at the dot prompt. Tell dBASE to

```
TYPE filename.PRG TO PRINT
```

You must include the file extension, and if the file is not on the default disk drive, you need to specify the proper drive designator (such as B:) before the filename.

9.30 Tip: *Use a semicolon to continue a command line on another screen line.*

dBASE III accepts command lines of up to 254 characters in length (each space, such as between words, is counted as a character). On an 80-column monitor, a command line 254 characters long would occupy a little more than three screen lines.

Whenever a command will continue beyond the end of a screen line, tell dBASE that the command line has not ended by typing a semicolon (;). Place the semicolon immediately after the end of a word; it's not necessary to continue a command line to column 80.

Be sure to read the following trap.

9.31 Trap: *If you put a space after the semicolon, dBASE will not read a multi-line command correctly.*

dBASE requires that a semicolon be the very last symbol on the screen line if a command is continued onto the following screen line. If you enter a space before you press RETURN, only the first screen line of the command will execute and you will get a "Syntax Error" message when dBASE encounters the second line.

9.32 Trap: *If you use the dBASE manual to guide your construction of commands and you enter square or angled brackets ([ ] or <>) in the command line, your program will not work.*

In the dBASE manual, square brackets indicate optional parts of a command syntax—parts that can be used if needed but are not required by the command (such as a FOR/WHILE condition). Angled brackets indicate parts of a command line that are chosen by the user: for example, the name of a particular field. In the manual these symbols are there only to help you distinguish the different options you have in structuring dBASE commands; do not include these brackets in your command lines.

9.33 Tip: *Use the SET TALK OFF command to keep routine dBASE messages off the screen.*

In the default dBASE mode, SET TALK is ON, and dBASE issues a screen response to almost every command that is executed. When your program is running, these comments clutter up the screen and can confuse the person using the program. Your program should control what appears on the screen, displaying only responses that are appropriate for the user.

SET TALK OFF is generally one of the first lines in a dBASE program.

9.34 Tip: *Have your program verify that the user has inserted the correct data disk before it searches for a particular file.*

If your dBASE program requires the user to insert a certain data disk into a floppy drive, you can have the program check to be sure the user has done so before it attempts to access the disk. The program lines

```
STORE .F. TO DISK_IN
DO WHILE .NOT. DISK_IN
    @15,3
    @17,3
    IF FILE('B:CUSTOMER.DBF')
        STORE .T. TO DISK_IN
    ELSE
        @15,3 SAY "Insert CUSTOMER data disk into drive B:"
        @17,3
        WAIT "Press RETURN when disk is inserted."
    ENDIF
ENDDO
```

will check for the file CUSTOMER on drive B and remind the user to insert the correct data disk before the program attempts to USE B:CUSTOMER.

 9.35 Trap: *If the memory variable in a DO WHILE condition does not exist when the DO WHILE line is executed, dBASE will issue an error message and stop executing your program.*

Consider this portion of a dBASE program:

```
SET TALK OFF
USE CUSTOMER
DO WHILE .NOT. VALID
    <processing>
ENDDO
```

The logical variable VALID does not exist in memory when the DO WHILE line is reached. dBASE will respond with a "Variable not found" message and stop executing the program. Always initialize the variable or variables used to control a DO WHILE loop before you enter the loop.

 9.36 Trap: *If the condition clause of a DO WHILE loop is not true when your program reaches the DO WHILE line, the loop will never be executed.*

A DO WHILE loop will continue to execute program lines until the condition clause becomes false — but in order to begin execution, dBASE must be able to enter the loop.

Consider this portion of a program:

```
USE CUSTOMER
COUNT FOR BALANCE > 199.99
DO WHILE .NOT. EOF()
    <processing>
ENDDO
```

Here the DO WHILE loop will never be entered. The COUNT command moves the record pointer to the end of the file, so the condition for entering the loop is not true when the DO WHILE line is encountered. This code needs the line

```
GO TOP
```

inserted before the DO WHILE line; then the condition will be true and all records in the database file will be processed.

9.37 Trap: *If a DO WHILE loop has no exit, it will continue loop-ing indefinitely.*

Every DO WHILE loop requires a way for dBASE to enter the loop (see the preceding trap) and a way to exit the loop. If a loop begins

```
DO WHILE .NOT. VALID
```

the commands within the loop must include a way for VALID to be changed to .T.; otherwise, dBASE will continue repeating the loop indefinitely. You will have to press ESC to interrupt the program, possibly losing your data.

9.38 Tip: *If a command will take some time to execute, display a message informing the program user.*

If your program takes much time to process data, display a message to that effect. Never leave a program user sitting in front of a screen for any length of time without some feedback from the program. The user is likely to become confused. If, as is also likely, the user thinks the program has "locked up" or failed and tries to reboot, data could be lost.

9.39 Tip: *Use IF (with an optional ELSE) when your program needs to choose one of two possible procedures.*

A program often needs to choose one of two possible activities, depending on the current data. When only one type of data requires processing, use IF; here is an example:

```
SEEK M_CUSTOMER
IF EOF()
   @15,3 SAY "New Customer: Press RETURN to enter data"
   WAIT
   DO ADD_CUST
ENDIF
```

When each of the two possible types of data requires processing, use IF with ELSE; for instance,

```
IF S_DATE < CTOD("1/1/85")
   DO S_LETTER
ELSE
   DO NS_LETTER
ENDIF
```

9.40 Tip: *Use DO CASE when your program needs to respond to one of several possibilities.*

DO CASE is a quick way to write what would otherwise be an extended list of IF statements. Whenever only one of several possible actions can be chosen, use **DO CASE**. The classic example is the use of a menu to allow a user to select from several options:

```
@5,3 SAY "1 - ADD NEW CUSTOMER"
@7,3 SAY "2 - EDIT EXISTING CUSTOMER DATA"
@9,3 SAY "3 - DELETE CUSTOMER"
@12,3
WAIT "Enter choice (1, 2, or 3)" TO CHOICE
DO CASE
   CASE CHOICE = 1
```

```
    DO ADD_CUST
  CASE CHOICE = 2
    DO EDIT_CUST
  CASE CHOICE = 3
    DO DEL_CUST
ENDCASE
```

 9.41 Trap: *DO CASE responds only to the first condition that is met by the data.*

DO CASE is intended for a situation in which only one of the available actions is needed. Once a CASE condition has been met and the following command lines have been executed, dBASE proceeds to the command line following ENDCASE. No other CASE conditions will be checked.

See the following tip.

9.42 Tip: *Use nested IF statements when each of several conditions must be checked.*

Suppose you are writing a dBASE program to mail different letters to the people in your MAIL_LST file. Which letter a person is sent depends on three conditions:

- Where the person lives

- Whether the person made a purchase from you in the last six months

- Whether the person has been approved for credit.

Your program will have to check several conditions for each record in the file. You will need to use nested IF statements to accomplish this:

```
IF REGION = "A"
   IF S_DATE > (M_DATE - 180)
      IF CREDIT
         DO CRED_LETA
```

```
      ELSE

          DO CASH_LETA

        ENDIF ** IF CREDIT

      ELSE

        DO OLD_LETA

      ENDIF ** IF S_DATE > (M_DATE - 180)

  ENDIF ** REGION = "A"
```

Nested IF statements allow you to check one condition only after another has been met; unlike DO CASE, each record will be tested against all of the conditions nested inside an IF statement whose condition is met.

9.43 Trap: *If you nest DO WHILE or IF statements improperly, your program will not execute at all, or if it does execute, the results will not be what you expect.*

If one **DO WHILE** loop appears inside another, or if one IF statement is within the command lines of another, it is imperative that the nested structure be completely contained within the outer structure. This means that the inner loop (or IF structure) must end inside the outer one. dBASE will interpret each ENDDO (or ENDIF) as referring to the most recent **DO WHILE** (or IF), so your program must be written this way as well.

A quick way to check for proper nesting is to take a printed copy of your program and draw lines to connect each **DO WHILE** to its ENDDO and each IF to its ENDIF. None of the lines should cross; each nested programming structure should be fully contained within the outer structure.

9.44 Tip: *Your programs will run more quickly if you use WHILE instead of FOR wherever possible to specify a scope.*

Many dBASE commands that operate on one record at a time (such as AVERAGE, COUNT, SUM, CHANGE, COPY TO, DELETE, DISPLAY, LIST, and RE-PLACE) allow you to specify a scope for their processing. You have two choices, FOR *condition* or WHILE *condition.*

The command line

```
DISPLAY ALL FOR CUSTOMER = "AMERICAN TIRE CO"
```

tells dBASE to begin at the top of the file, check each record to see if the entry in CUSTOMER is AMERICAN TIRE CO, and display only the records that pass this condition. Every record in the file will be checked.

If the file is indexed on CUSTOMER, these program lines will execute much more quickly:

```
SEEK "AMERICAN TIRE CO"

DISPLAY ALL WHILE CUSTOMER = "AMERICAN TIRE CO"
```

The SEEK command quickly moves the record pointer to the first record for this customer, and records are displayed until the entry in CUSTOMER changes. Only a small part of the entire file has to be processed.

Speed up your programs whenever possible by moving the record pointer with FIND or SEEK and then processing records while they meet a condition, rather than using FOR to process every record in the file. This will save a lot of time with large database files.

9.45 Tip: *Use dBASE debugging tools to help you locate and fix errors in your program code.*

dBASE provides several tools to help with debugging programs:

- SET ECHO ON displays each command line as it is executed.

- SET STEP ON halts a program, executing it one step at a time and only after you have pressed a key to execute the next step. You can see the result of each line of code and stop the program at any point to check memory variables or make corrections. STEP should be used with ECHO so that you can see the program lines as they are executed.

- SET DEBUG ON sends each command line, and the results of its execution, to the printer.

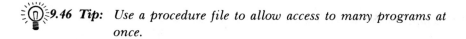 ***9.46 Tip:*** *Use a procedure file to allow access to many programs at once.*

A procedure file can contain as many as 32 procedures, each a separate dBASE program. There are two main advantages to using procedure files:

- Short program tasks that need to be done many times within a longer program or that need to be done by different programs can be kept in the file and called on as needed, saving typing time and disk space.

- You can execute more than one program much more quickly if programs are in a procedure file together. Whenever you open a .PRG file with the DO command, dBASE must read the file from the disk, and this can result in many delays. A procedure file is read in its entirety when it is opened; all of the procedures are quickly available to your main program.

A procedure file is structured like this:

```
PROCEDURE Proc_Name_1

    <command lines>

RETURN
PROCEDURE Proc_Name_2

    <command lines>

RETURN
```

and so on, up to 32 separate procedures.

To open a procedure file, include this line in your dBASE program:

```
SET PROCEDURE TO <procfile>
```

Now the program can call on any of the procedures in the file with the command

```
DO PROC_B
```

dBASE will execute the command lines in the procedure until it reaches RETURN. It will then go back to the program that called the procedure, returning to the program line immediately after the DO command.

✋ **9.47 Trap:** *Only one procedure file can be open at a time.*

Whenever you open a procedure file, any other procedure file that was open will be closed. You cannot have access to the procedures in two different files at the same time.

✋ **9.48 Trap:** *If a procedure in an open procedure file has the same name as a command file, dBASE will interpret the name as a reference to the procedure.*

If one of the procedures in an open procedure file is called **ADD — CUST**, you will not be able to call on the command file named **ADD — CUST.PRG** that is on your disk. To avoid this problem, name procedures with **P —**; if the procedure is named **P — ADD — CUST**, you can have this file open and still access the command file **ADD — CUST**.

Trademarks

dBASE III®	Ashton-Tate
dBASE II®	Ashton-Tate
WordStar®	MicroPro International Corporation
MailMerge®	MicroPro International Corporation
MicroPro®	MicroPro International Corporation
Lotus®	Lotus Development Corporation
1-2-3®	Lotus Development Corporation
Symphony®	Lotus Development Corporation

Index